The Changing Landscape of South Etruria

T. W. Potter

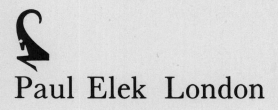

Paul Elek London

First published 1979 by
Paul Elek Limited
54–58 Caledonian Road, London N1 9RN

ISBN 0 236 40147 5

Printed in Great Britain by Unwin Brothers Ltd,
The Gresham Press,
Old Woking, Surrey

For
John Ward Perkins

Contents

Plates

Figures

Preface

Early in the 1950's the British School at Rome began an archaeological survey of the part of the Etrurian uplands that lie immediately to the north of Rome. Initially the research concentrated upon the identification of elements of the Etruscan and Roman road network, together with associated sites and monuments; but before long the survey had been extended so as to become a systematic field survey of all parts of this historically crucial region. As it turned out, such work could not have been more timely. The land reforms of 1950 had brought large areas of woodland and pasture into cultivation for the first time since the Classical period; as the Director of the British School, John Ward Perkins, wrote in 1955: 'whole regions are accessible today as they have never been before, and within them the bulldozer and the mechanical plough are busy destroying whatever lies in their path'. There was, in other words, a rescue situation of enormous proportions, whose scale was further increased by the density and wealth of the hundreds of sites that were coming to light.

The result was one of the largest field surveys ever carried out. Over a period of some twenty years, John Ward Perkins and numerous members of the British School systematically examined nearly 1000 square kilometres of the area north of Rome. During this time more than 2000 sites were recorded and, in addition, much was learnt about the successive road systems and other monuments of the Etruscan, Roman and medieval periods. Parallel to this, there was a programme of limited excavation, designed largely to build up a dated sequence of local pottery types and to answer specific questions about certain types of site or monument. Consequently we are now in a position to say a good deal about this landscape and the way in which the settlement patterns changed.

Although my own involvement with the south Etruria project has been for a period of more than a dozen years, this book does not pretend to be in any sense a formal report of this research. This can be found in recent volumes of the School's *Papers*. Instead, I have tried to provide a general account of the work that has been done, together with some basic interpretation of the ways in which the landscape changed—particularly the settlement patterns. I have taken the opportunity to republish drawings and photographs that have so far appeared only in specialist journals, and have also included a fair amount of new material (largely from my own work). I have been fortunate to have available the archives of the British School, in which most of the South Etruria Survey records are stored: consequently the distribution maps are now the most up-to-date yet published. Inevitably, however, I have had to compress the data a great deal, especially since I have also tried to convey some of the wider archaeological background. I hope therefore that colleagues who find their careful arguments too briefly and schematically summarized will pardon the lacunae, and that those who wish to read more about the Survey will turn to the full reports in the School's *Papers*.

Acknowledgements

This book draws upon material laboriously compiled by a great many people over a period of some twenty-five years. A full list of acknowledgements is therefore out of the question and, in default of this, I would like to pay a very warm general tribute to all those who have contributed by fieldwork, discussion and advice to the work presented in this book. I would, however, like to mention the many present and former staff and student members of the British School at Rome, under whose aegis most of the research described here has been carried out. In particular, my greatest debt is to John Ward Perkins, who both directed the work in south Etruria between 1950 and 1974 and initiated most of the projects; just as his is an unrivalled knowledge of the area, so have many of the fundamental conclusions been first advanced by him. I should also like to thank the present Director, David Whitehouse, for a great deal of encouragement and help over the last three years, and also Luciana Valentini, the librarian, Anna Fazzari, the former secretary of the School, and Molly Cotton, all of whom have done an enormous amount for the south Etruria project. It is also a pleasure to acknowledge the support and help given by many members of the Italian Superintendency of Antiquities, especially Dr Mario Moretti; and of numerous colleagues in Italian universities. Many of the projects described here have been collaborative efforts of the most rewarding and fruitful kind.

In the U.K. I should like particularly to thank Professor Donald Bullough, who encouraged me to write this book, and my colleagues at Lancaster who helped and advised with its production, especially Hugo Blake, David Shotter and Ruth Whitehouse. My department gave me every facility, including a sabbatical term in Rome, whilst the final typescript was produced through the patient efforts of Janet Atkins, Pat Kitchen and Barbara Douglas, greatly helped at publication stage by Ann Douglas and Chriss Ambrose. To all of these I offer my warmest thanks.

1
Survey and excavation
in south Etruria

Etruria—and particularly its southern region—has attracted the attention
of many great topographers, amongst them the celebrated cartographer,
Eufrosino della Volpaia (1547), the English scholar, Sir William Gell
(1834–46) and his contemporary and friend, A. Nibby (1837). But it was
not until 1848, when George Dennis's *Cities and Cemeteries of Etruria* was
published, that the region received its first topographical study along modern
lines. Dennis, who spent most of his life in the British consular service and
was not a trained scholar, nevertheless possessed both an acute eye for detail
and the ability to interpret his observations in lively and absorbing prose.
Cities and Cemeteries of Etruria proved to be a literary and an archaeological
masterpiece which popularized Etruscan studies in his own lifetime and
continues to form a valuable record down to the present day. His fieldwork
took the form of a series of extended tours, between 1842 and 1846, several
in the company of the artist Samuel Ainsley. During this time he visited
most of the major and many of the minor sites of Etruria, producing minute
descriptions of the visible standing features and the tombs, and placing these
in their topographical context. The resulting two volumes coincided with
a marked acceleration in the excavation of some of the Etruscan city sites
described by Dennis. The Regolini-Galassi tomb at Cerveteri had been
explored in 1836, for example, and this dramatic discovery was followed
by numerous studies of other sites, like Vulci and Tarquinia, although
largely of their cemeteries. Dennis was not always impressed, as later
editions of his book attest, with the standard of the work: 'it is lamentable
that excavations should be carried on in such a spirit; with the sole view of
gain, with no regard to the advancement of science', he remarks, after seeing
all but the best finds from tombs at Vulci being 'dashed to the ground' since
they were 'cheaper than seaweed'. But, at the same time, the foundations
of Etruscology were being laid, both in the form of great museum collections
and in terms of site information and analysis.

By the end of the century systematic classification along modern lines of
the material finds had been put in hand and this was being complemented
in the field by excavation and record of a high standard. It is perhaps
misplaced to choose Narce as an example, for the excavations that took
place on the cemeteries of this small Faliscan town between 1889 and 1892
became the subject of a public enquiry: but the publication of the results
in *Monumenti Antichi* for 1894 was a superbly illustrated catalogue which,

1

if unreliable in detail, nevertheless set high standards of draughtsmanship. Its principal authors were A. Pasqui and A. Cozza (1894) and it is interesting to note that they attempted to set the excavations at Narce in context by mapping other major and minor Iron Age centres within the Faliscan region, and providing brief descriptions of them. This emphasis upon topographical research was, for Etruria as a whole, taken up by other scholars like Nissen (1883–1902) and Solari (1915–20); and for Rome and its immediate environs by Rodolfo Lanciani (1909). But for south Etruria it found two principal exponents—one an English classicist, Thomas Ashby, and the other an Italian historian, Guiseppe Tomassetti.

Ashby came to know Italy at the end of the nineteenth century. He took up a scholarship at the newly founded British School at Rome in 1901 and in 1906 became Director, remaining in that post for nineteen years. During that time he carried out intensive fieldwork in the countryside round Rome, publishing a series of major articles upon the Roman roads and the sites that lined them. This work culminated in 1927 with the publication of his general synthesis, *The Roman Campagna in Classical Times*. There is little doubt that Ashby was a brilliant topographer and a scholar with interests that went far outside the Classical period. He was in many ways a worthy successor to Dennis, who had died in 1898. Moreover, he was in Rome at the right time, a period when the Campagna 'remains almost unspoilt . . . At an hour's distance on foot from almost any of [Rome's] gates one may plunge into a solitude surprisingly profound . . . The greater part of the Campagna is pasture land . . . so that the population at any time of year is extremely small in proportion to the area.' (Ashby, 1927, 20). Elsewhere he notes that the coastline along the western periphery of the Campagna is 'low and monotonous and very sparsely populated', a description that is astonishing to those who have driven today along the combination of lido and housing estate that dominates the shores of the Tyrrhenian Sea between Anzio and Civitavecchia. Yet, even by 1927, there were signs of change—new farmhouses 'rising everywhere', more land coming under cultivation and 'inexcusable and unnecessary vandalism' of many of the standing monuments. Ashby's meticulous and exhaustive study of these monuments and the often vestigial traces of the roads that linked them thus takes on special importance as a record that is in many respects irreplaceable.

Equally, just as Ashby laid the foundations for the study of the Campagna in the Classical period, so did his friend, Guiseppe Tomassetti, furnish the basis of medieval studies in the area of Rome. Tomassetti's approach was essentially that of a historian: the meticulous culling of documentary sources in the archives of Rome and elsewhere; but he was also intimately acquainted with the towns, villages and deserted sites of the Campagna and his descriptions show him to have been a precise and perceptive observer. His major work was a detailed topographical survey of the environs of Rome, entitled *La Campagna Romana, antica, medioevale e moderna*, which appeared in five volumes between 1910 and 1926. Even though parts of Tomassetti's work have been subsequently updated (e.g. Silvestrelli, 1970) it is true to say that his study of the region has remained indispensable, the more so since the topographical detail is usually excellent, and many of the sites he discusses have now undergone a significant degree of reconstruction. Equally important is the fact that Tomassetti made readily available much of the documentary record for both existing and deserted medieval settlements, a service which has done much to encourage medieval archaeology in the area.

By the 1920s therefore topographical studies had achieved a firm footing in Etruria and the basis of a proper 'sites and monuments' record had been laid. By this time, also, Guiseppe Lugli had begun to gather material for his *Carta Archeologica del Territorio di Roma* (finally published in 1962), and a number of surveys of individual sites such as Tarquinia (Pallottino, 1937) were in preparation. But as yet there had been no attempt to produce an integrated survey of the settlement patterns of a region of Etruria, where the main theme was the way in which the landscape had changed from prehistoric to medieval times. That there had been major fluctuations in the form of settlement was abundantly clear and, equally, it was apparent that the successive landscapes were well documented by the surviving remains. The impetus towards such a study did not come in fact until after the Second World War and was stimulated mainly by the extensive land reform schemes introduced in 1950. These measures were designed to increase the scale of agricultural production to a much higher level and, as a result, enormous areas of long-standing pasture were broken up by the plough for the first time in many centuries. This in itself was sufficient to cause a massive change in the appearance of the Roman Campagna; but at the same time there began an expansion of existing towns, the laying out of new suburbs (particularly around Rome), and a programme of modification and improvement to the road network. The effects were, literally, devastating. A region with a population of not much more than a half-million in 1920 now saw a steep rise in the number of inhabitants towards its present-day total of about three million. Equally, the introduction of mechanical ploughs and other plant meant that the ground was turned over with a degree of efficiency that had never before been possible. Woodland was rooted out, quarries for blocks of volcanic *tufo* became increasingly common and, in all but the most inaccessible regions, grazing land gave way to arable fields. Not surprisingly, an enormous amount of archaeological evidence, almost all of it from sites that had been previously unrecorded, also began to emerge and it gradually became clear that a major and urgent programme of 'rescue archaeology' was required.

Inevitably, the scale of the response was muted by the size of the problem. Much of the rescue work had to be restricted to checking the vandalism of standing monuments, whilst aerial photography (which became increasingly important in Britain after the war) was still employed only sparsely. Most of the photographs consisted in fact of high level verticals which, though useful (Bradford, 1947; 1957), rarely provided the detail of obliques taken specifically for archaeological purposes. In south Etruria there were, how-

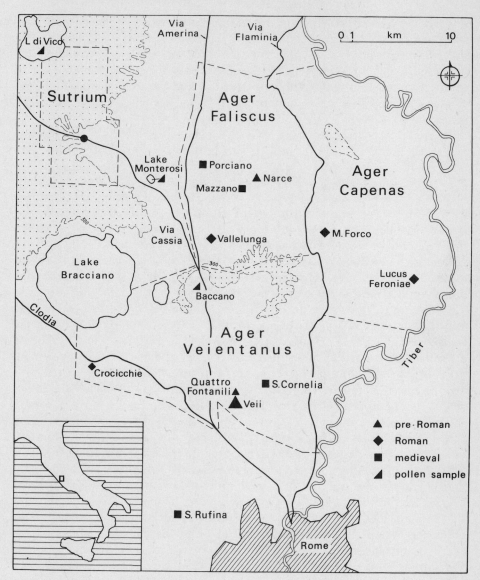

1 The survey area of south Etruria, and some of the principal excavated sites.

ever, two rescue responses of major importance. The first was implemented by the Topographic Institute of the University of Rome, under whose auspices a number of major surveys were initiated, including one of sites along the Via Aurelia between Cerveteri and Pyrgi (Guiliani and Quilici, 1964) and, later, surveys of other critical regions such as the area round Tuscania (Quilici, 1970) and the Via Gabina (Quilici, 1974). These handsome and well documented volumes provide an invaluable record of sites that have in many instances now been completely erased. The second rescue response began early in the 1950s when the British School at Rome commenced a programme of survey in the upland region immediately to the north of Rome, focusing in the area bordered to the east by the River Tiber and to the west by the prominent chain of mountains known as the Monti Sabatini (Fig. 1). The instigator of the survey—which, over the period of twenty years, was to extend over an area of nearly 1000 square kilo-metres—was the Director of the British School, John Ward Perkins. He appreciated very quickly that the project was of great urgency and in the first report, published in 1955, made this quite clear:

The romantic desolation of Southern Etruria is being transformed from one day to the next under the impact of a scheme of land-reform comparable in scale to the great reforms of classical antiquity, and vast estates . . . are being broken up and brought into cultivation with all the devastating thoroughness that modern mechan-ical equipment entails . . . Much of the damage to ancient sites is unavoidable . . . If this material is to be recorded, the record must be made at once. (Ward Perkins, 1955, 44)

This survey was concerned primarily with the road that left the Via Cassia at Tomba di Nerone, just to the north of Rome, and headed towards the acropolis of Veii, at Piazza d'Armi; but there was also a study of the Via Clodia between La Storta (*Ad Nonas*) and Bracciano, with an important discussion of the road-station of *Careiae*. It is perhaps salutary to reflect that this programme of salvage work (for this is what it was) preceded the currency of the term 'rescue archaeology' by nearly twenty years.

Shortly afterwards, further survey work was initiated in the central and northern sectors of the Faliscan region. This centred partly upon the town of Civita Castellana (ancient Falerii) and partly upon the Via Amerina, along its route through Nepi, Falerii Novi and north of the Treia Valley. The report was concerned principally with the elucidation of the major and minor road network 'within an area that is rapidly undergoing radical and, archaeologically speaking, often disastrous transformation' (Frederiksen and Ward Perkins, 1957, 70); but there were also descriptions of some of the nucleated and smaller sites and, significantly, a recognition of at least three major successive landscapes, a pre-Roman, a Roman and a medieval, all with quite different characteristics. The medieval landscape, for example, where the population was concentrated in small hill and promontory towns and villages, was clearly the product of very different social and economic circumstances from the dispersed settlement that characterized Roman south Etruria, and equally different was the Etruscan pattern, where the norm was apparently small nucleated centres with dependent farmsteads.

As a consequence, it became clear that systematic survey of substantial areas was now required, with the aim of providing documentation not only of roads and roadside sites but of the pattern of settlement over a whole region. Three territories were therefore chosen: the region to the north and south of Sutri, examined by Guy Duncan and published in 1958; the Ager

Capenas, which lay between the Via Flaminia and the River Tiber (Jones, 1962, 1963); and that part of the Ager Veientanus bounded by the Monti Sabatini to the north, the Via Flaminia to the east, the Via Cassia to the west and Veii itself to the south (Fig. 1; Ward Perkins, 1968). At the same time, the site of Veii was also thoroughly surveyed, an urgent task since most of the now deserted plateau where the Etruscan and Roman city grew up had been brought under cultivation in the late 1950s, with disastrous results: in November 1960, for example, 'the disc harrow [was] busy obliterating the visible traces of a Roman villa and of a large group of late Etruscan houses which were ploughed out recently in the Macchia Grande area' (Ward Perkins, 1961, 2). In the same period deep ploughing also brought to light a considerable number of burials on four of the Villanovan cemeteries, those of Grotta Gramiccia, Casale del Fosso, Vacchereccia and Quattro Fontanili (Ward Perkins, 1961, 90–114). Rescue excavation followed on two of these sites, those at Quattro Fontanili continuing up to the present day and proving of the utmost significance for Iron Age archaeology.

Until this time excavation had in fact played little part in the South Etruria Survey. Nevertheless there was a pressing need for stratified groups of dated pottery, so that the coarse wares picked up in the course of survey work could be approximately dated; and it was desirable too that some of the more mundane classes of site should be explored, so as to define their character more closely. A beginning was made in 1957–8, when an area beside the north-west gate of Veii was explored. This disclosed three superimposed Iron Age buildings, which had been destroyed to make way for the fifth-century defences of Veii (Ward Perkins, 1959a; Murray-Threipland, 1963). The associated levels yielded some useful groups of pre-Roman pottery which, when taken together with the finds from the Villanovan cemetery of Quattro Fontanili (where an annual programme of excavation was begun in 1960, in conjunction with Rome University's Institute of Etruscology), and the recovery of a massive dump of fifth-fourth-century domestic pottery at nearby Casale Pian Roseto (Murray-Threipland and Torelli, 1970), laid a sound basis for a pre-Roman type series for the Veii area. Meanwhile, in 1959, Guy Duncan excavated two small but important groups of Roman material in the Sutri area, one a refuse pit filled between c. 150 and 50 B.C. and the other a pottery kiln site dating to the first century A.D. (Duncan, 1964, 1965). These fixed points were extended three years later with the examination of a mausoleum at the Fosso della Crescenza (Pl. VIIb) built in A.D. 209 and associated with pottery of this period (Ward Perkins, 1964, 15). There were also earlier Roman buildings on the site which proved to have suffered at first intermittent and then continuous flooding, (Potter, 1976b). But the most important contribution to Roman pottery studies came not from the recovery of archaeological deposits but from the detailed study of African Red Slip-wares (terra sigillata chiara) made by John Hayes during the 1960s and published in 1972. North Africa provided much of the better class ceramic tableware used in central Italy between the late first century and c. A.D.

600, and these distinctive orange-slipped forms constitute a very common site find on mid to late Imperial sites. Hayes' contribution was twofold. In the first place he established a basic typology for the Red Slip-wares and attached to it a provisional chronology, where individual forms could often be dated to within a century or less. Secondly, he worked through very large quantities of the Red Slip-ware found in the South Etruria Survey and thus was able to provide a detailed picture of the later Roman history of many of the sites discovered in the course of the fieldwork. The extra historical dimension that this added becomes very apparent when we compare the results of, for example, the Sutri survey (Duncan, 1958) with those from the Ager Veientanus (Ward Perkins, 1968): ten years' work on the pottery contributed an enormous degree of refinement to the analysis of the evidence and may with justification be seen as a major breakthrough.

At the same time, the first steps were also made towards creating a medieval archaeology for the region. The study of the medieval period in Italy had hitherto been regarded primarily as the province of the historian and art historian and there had been little attempt either to excavate sites along modern archaeological lines or to define the types and chronology of more than the most exotic artifacts. Yet it was clear that the post-Roman settlement pattern (which generally had been relegated to a minor position in the earlier south Etruria surveys) could only be elucidated fully by a programme of excavation, combined with comprehensive study of the pottery and the documents. The first important step was the identification and subsequent exploration of the medieval site of Santa Cornelia, situated on open ground just to the north of Veii (Fig. 44). This extensive complex, which included the remains of a church and farm buildings, enclosed within a circuit wall, is likely to have been the administrative centre of the great Papal estate of Capracorum, founded c. A.D. 780. It was excavated between 1962 and 1964 by Charles Daniels (Ward Perkins, 1968, 178–9), and provided the first archaeological point of reference for the early medieval period in the Roman Campagna. At the same time, Hans Stiesdal of the Danish Academy at Rome carried out a brief investigation of three of the deserted sites in the Campagna—Torre Busson, Belmonte and Pietra Pertusa (Stiesdal, 1962)—and in 1965 Lady Wheeler began the excavation of an important early medieval church at Santa Rufina on the Via Clodia. Like Santa Cornelia this was a site positioned on open ground, without natural defences, and it proved to have both earlier Roman occupation, including traces of a villa and a mausoleum, as well as a small church with a mid-eighth-century mosaic and catacombs (Pl. Xb). Occupation apparently continued into the later medieval period, although on a reduced scale.

These excavations, supplemented in 1965–6 by the first detailed study of a deserted medieval village at Castel Porciano near Nepi (Mallett and Whitehouse, 1967), created a body of completely new data for the early Middle Ages in central Italy. The time was thus ripe for a considered appraisal of the medieval pottery from the region, extending existing studies of the rather exotic forms to the more local decorated and coarse wares.

David Whitehouse elected to undertake this study and between 1964 and 1967 produced the first thorough classification, published in a series of important articles (Whitehouse, 1965, 1967, 1969). Even though there appeared to be major lacunae in the ceramic sequence, for example between *c.* A.D. 600, the date of the latest African Red Slip-wares in central Italy, and *c.* A.D. 750, when the first medieval glazed wares were thought to have appeared, there nevertheless now existed a chronological framework within which the surface data could be fitted. At the same time O. Mazzucato was publishing important groups of medieval material from Rome which further helped to refine the life-spans of some of the major types (Mazzucato, 1968a, b; 1972).

The first tentative application of these dates to the surface finds from medieval sites within south Etruria did not come before the publication of the Ager Veientanus survey (Ward Perkins, 1968, 161–79). But there had already by this time been several attempts at a general synthesis of the results, most notably by Ward Perkins in two articles, one published in the *Geographical Journal* for 1962, and entitled 'Etruscan towns, Roman roads and medieval villages: the historical geography of southern Etruria', and the other being the J. L. Myres lecture for 1964, *Landscape and history in Central Italy*. Both papers sought to define the main characteristics of the successive phases of settlement and these were related to pollen analyses made in the Baccano and Monterosi craters (Bonatti, 1963; Hutchinson, 1970), along the western fringes of the survey zone (Fig. 1). Amongst the important conclusions, suggested by both the environmental and the archaeological evidence, was that the territory had remained largely forested until the foundation of the first Iron Age settlements like Veii, Capena and Falerii, a surprising conclusion in view of the concentration of prehistoric finds in nearby areas like the Fiora Valley (Vonwiller, 1967).

In 1966, however, the opportunity came to examine a prehistoric site in more detail. The site, known locally as Narce (Pl. Ib), lay on the east bank of the River Treia, in the heart of the Ager Faliscus. Above it was one of the three hills that formed the natural acropolis of a small Faliscan nucleated settlement, investigated by Pasqui and Cozza (1894). A flash flood had stripped away the undergrowth lining the banks of the river and revealed a deposit of stratified archaeological material, over five metres in depth. A preliminary search showed that the earliest layers had been laid down in the Bronze Age and above these were several metres of debris containing Iron Age pottery. Excavation of this rare historical sequence was evidently a matter of priority since the site was fast being eroded away, and in four subsequent seasons, between 1968 and 1971, the greater part of the river terrace was carefully examined. This work (Potter, 1976a) confirmed that this part of the valley was first settled in the Middle Bronze Age, *c.* 1400 B.C., and disclosed a series of superimposed houses, the latest of which dated to the seventh century B.C. Above these were late seventh- and sixth-century graves and these were in turn sealed by the buildings of an industrial complex, manufacturing tiles, of the fourth and third centuries B.C. The site seems finally to have been deserted *c.* 250 B.C., about the time of the Roman conquest of the area.

This large-scale excavation (one of the first in Italy to rely almost entirely on volunteer labour) provided an extremely valuable sequence of stratified domestic pottery and, consequently, a chronological framework for the region as a whole. At the same time, a useful sample of faunal and floral remains was recovered, providing a much closer insight into the economy of the Bronze and Iron Age settlements; and the opportunity was also taken to investigate the history of the river itself and to examine the consequences of fluvial patterns for human settlement (Cherkauer, 1976; Potter, 1976b). The results of the excavation were further integrated into the history of the region by a large-scale survey of some 200 square kilometres of the surrounding territory (Potter, 1975, 1978). This filled one of the major gaps in the South Etruria Survey and meant that a large part of the projected area had been covered. Meanwhile, Michael Craven was studying the wedge-shaped part of the Ager Veientanus between the Via Flaminia and the Tiber, Pamela Hemphill (1975) the hilly terrain to the south and east of Lake Bracciano, and Miranda Buchanan the countryside between Veii and Rome. By the early 1970s, the total area of south Etruria surveyed in detail amounted to over 850 square kilometres and there were in addition published studies of the Ager Eretanus (on the east side of the Tiber: Ogilvie, 1965) and the Via Gabina (Ward Perkins and Kahane, 1972), as well as numerous other site finds from elsewhere in south Etruria.

By then, however, priorities had begun to alter and the focus was already moving away from field survey. In part this was because the optimum period for this sort of work in south Etruria was now past: sites that had once been prolific of finds had either reverted to pasture or had been so damaged by deep ploughing that little of archaeological interest remained. But it was also the result of an increasing need for excavation of individual sites threatened by development and other damage. This was the case at the well known Etruscan, Roman and medieval site of Tuscania, where a violent earthquake in February 1971 was followed up with a programme of excavation, designed to examine the development of the town before rebuilding and restoration was commenced; or at Ponte di Nona, a rural Republican shrine on the Via Prenestina, where the small section of the site that survived massive quarrying in 1964 was being plundered for saleable finds. Undoubtedly the most appropriate archaeological response in south Etruria now lay with the excavation of selected sites, especially those at risk from development, where individual problems could be isolated and solved. To date, a good deal of useful work has been accomplished and some important conclusions have been reached.

Consequently, it is a good moment to examine the South Etruria Survey as a whole, assess its achievements and, so far as it is possible, evaluate the historical and archaeological implications of this twenty-five-year project.

The South Etruria Field Survey: the methodology

The study of landscape archaeology is a comparatively recent innovation. More often than not, individual sites have been viewed as single entities, regardless of their environmental setting or their relationship with other settlements and field systems. Yet the importance of integrating individual sites within their landscape setting had been demonstrated as early as 1923 by Sir Cyril Fox in his classic study of the region around Cambridge. This was a field survey which defined the evolution of settlement between the Neolithic and medieval periods and sought to explain many of the changes in terms of the surface geology. Shortly afterwards, O. G. S. Crawford (1924) showed how aerial photography could complement observations made at ground level and from that time the most effective contributions to landscape studies have taken advantage of both approaches. For example, in Britain, intensive block flying followed by systematic field walking combined to produce a remarkably clear picture of the layout and chronological development of Roman-period settlement in the Cambridgeshire and Lincolnshire Fens. Similarly, in Italy, the war-time aerial cover of the Tavoliere of Apulia which, like the English Fens, comprises a vast alluvial plain, disclosed in intricate detail the features of the three successive landscapes of Neolithic, Roman and medieval date (Bradford, 1957). It required only a modest programme of field survey and selective excavation to provide an outline chronology for these settlement types: and yet the archaeological and historical dividends were of far-reaching importance. It is of course true that both these areas have a surface geology that makes them particularly susceptible to high quality crop and soil marks. Moreover, both are under intensive cultivation and the yield of artifacts from ancient sites is consequently high. Nevertheless, both studies demonstrate in the clearest manner the value of an approach where sites are set in the wider context of their regional landscape and underline the dangers of generalization in areas where our knowledge is more restricted. That said, it has to be admitted that every region poses its own particular difficulties and requires an approach that is tailored accordingly. In the river valleys of north-west England, for example, the deserted farms, villages and field boundaries of earlier periods of settlement for the most part lie fossilized in long-established pasture, bordering the river-side meadows. The superimposition of walls and banks makes it quite clear that a number of phases are represented; but it will require a major programme of mapping, followed by careful selection of points for excavation, before the relative sequence can be worked out. Equally, the yield of surface finds is minimal and, as a consequence, there is no sure way of establishing an absolute chronology without very extensive sampling of individual sites. Thus, the prospect of reconstructing a landscape of, for example, the early Roman period in such areas is still far distant, despite the claims that are sometimes made.

It follows that the priorities should lie with the record of settlement landscapes where the yield of finds is generally high and, preferably, where aerial photography can document at low cost the subtler distinctions of land boundaries or building plans that are not normally visible to the field walker. The Roman landscape discovered by M. Agache (1970) in the Somme Valley of north France provides one excellent example. In Italy, work in the Biferno Valley of the Abruzzo (Barker, 1976b, 1977) and in the Bradano Valley of Apulia, has shown that these thinly developed regions still preserve abundant surface traces of many sites and, as Adamesteanu (1973a, 1973b) has shown in areas like Metaponto, it is likely that aerial photography will make a significant contribution.

In south Etruria, on the other hand, aerial survey has yet to be employed for anything more than the demonstration of the most obvious topographical features—although there are undoubtedly sites that will produce crop marks within the region. The available air cover is restricted mainly to verticals taken from a height of *c*. 10,000 feet which, whilst helping with the identification of ancient road cuttings, provide little specific information about the layout of individual sites (Pl. XIa). Twenty years of sustained ground survey have on the other hand yielded an enormous collection of artifacts and other information. Most of the medieval sites still preserve standing structures and a fairly complete plan of most of the major buildings can usually be made out. A number of Roman structures also survive, sometimes, as with the remarkable Le Mura di Santo Stefano, to several storeys (Ashby, 1907, 311–23; Ward Perkins, 1955, 66; Pl. IXb and Fig. 45); and in many cases it is possible to draw up something of a comprehensive plan, especially for the simpler buildings like mausolea. Details are also sometimes available for pre-Roman structures, although here the record is dominated by funerary monuments, especially rock-cut chamber tombs, rather than by domestic buildings. Even ploughed-out buildings do, for a short time, disclose a good deal of information. The larger Roman sites in particular are usually marked by dense concentrations of debris in which the location of individual buildings can sometimes be made out. More conspicuous are the heaps of dressed building stone, tile and, if the structure was of any importance, pieces of marble (much of it from outside Italy) and other wall and floor decoration, such as mosaic tesserae and painted wall plaster. Plaster-lined cisterns preserved either as large tanks or as a series of underground chambers are also durable features (Pl. IXa) and often provide a key to the location of the bath-house. In sum, therefore, a great deal of information about the layout and architecture of such sites, presumably the remains of rich suburban villas, can be gleaned solely from surface traces, at any rate for the more pretentious structure. Other sites seem to have been lower down the social scale and might be described as farms. Here the scatter of debris usually covers a far less extensive area and the architectural remains are normally confined to some masonry blocks, tile and occasionally a few tesserae of basalt and limestone, deriving from a simple geometric mosaic. The yields of pottery and other finds are also correspondingly thinner. These sites in turn rank above the smallest category where the archaeological traces consist solely of a scatter of pottery and tile, which rarely extends over an area of a few hundred square metres: here, we are perhaps dealing with the remains of a hut or other subsidiary farm building of a sort still common in the Roman Campagna today (Close-Brooks and Gibson, 1966) and often used by shepherds (Pl. IIIb).

This simple ranking scheme, the implications of which are explored in Chapter 5, is obviously subject to wide margins of error. A few years of deep ploughing can reduce the most prolific site to little more than a thin scatter of tile and pottery. The Roman road-station at Aquaviva on the Via Flaminia, south of Civita Castellana is a case in point. Discovered in 1968, it consisted of a number of separate concentrations of building material, representing a series of richly decorated buildings. There was also a large and well preserved inscription (Pl. Xa). By 1971, however, after several years of regular cultivation, the surface of the fields bore almost no trace of the settlement, apart from a thin and widely dispersed scatter of abraded pottery and tiles. This emphasizes all too clearly the importance of recording such sites before the visible evidence is broken up and buried in the wash deposits along the margins of the hills and ridges. Fortunately in south Etruria the survey work has coincided in most areas with the optimum period for field observation. Moreover, the total sample of sites is so large—over 2000—that the distortion of the total statistics caused by the poor preservation of individual sites is likely to be fairly small: providing that the figures are not pressed too far, we can probably gain a very fair idea of the relative proportions between villas, farms and huts in any one area.

There is, however, one major factor that needs taking into account: the variations in present-day land use. The Roman Campagna has come increasingly into the hands of developers in recent years and small clusters of residential villas are now a common feature of the landscape. At the same time there are still many areas of marginal land that are reserved as forest or scrub *macchia*—probably between 5 and 10 per cent of the survey region—and a rather larger proportion that serves as rough grazing. Survey work in terrain covered by pasture is not totally impracticable since the grass is usually sparse and there are sufficient erosion gullies to identify potsherds; but only the standing sites are visible in the thick *macchia* and the yield of sherds is normally minimal. Consequently the gaps in the distribution maps have to be interpreted in the light of present-day land use (even though such marginal areas are likely always to have been thinly settled). Yet another distortion in the distribution maps derives from the ever expanding overlay of modern suburbs and associated industry. Both Civita Castellana and Nepi, for example, have become important provincial towns and the roads between them are now lined with new houses and factories. Civita Castellana has also become the focus for the large-scale quarrying of *tufo* blocks (as, to a lesser extent, have many of the smaller villages (Pl. XIb)) and the environs of the town are now surrounded by huge excavations of this volcanic rock, covering many square kilometres.

We can only guess at the effect upon the distribution maps of these recent disturbances to the landscape: Civita Castellana, for example, was a major town in both medieval and pre-Roman times and is likely always to have been a focus of settlement. But a far more difficult problem is to assess the degree to which the pre-Roman landscape has been destroyed by Roman and medieval occupation. The scale of Roman settlement within the Campagna was closely analogous to that of today and was evidently a period of intensive agricultural development. Even though the ploughing was relatively superficial, the effect must still have been to accelerate the degree of erosion and, consequently, to obliterate something of the pre-Roman pattern of rural settlement. This explains why no realistic quantification of rank is possible for sites earlier than the first century A.D., with the exception of the larger villages and towns: too often, the smaller sites survive only as a thin spread of pottery, incorporated in secondary wash deposits, on the margins of the original nucleus. The implications for still older phases of settlement are thus even harder to assess. The surface evidence suggests that the first major period of colonization in south Etruria belongs to the late second millennium B.C. and that the rural population increased rapidly from that time. It has to be borne in mind, however, that part of the effect of later settlement will have been to disperse the nuclei of the early sites and it may be that the number of sites for these older periods is quite unrepresentative of the original total. If so, it has to be said that there is little support for this hypothesis either in the pollen cores (Bonatti, 1970; Frank, 1969) or in the artifact record; but it nevertheless remains a theoretical possibility. Certainly in high-erosion areas we should assume that the sample of sites will become increasingly unrepresentative with age and balance our interpretations accordingly.

The distribution maps are also affected by other geological features, most notably in the river valleys. The pattern of river behaviour seems to have fluctuated widely in recent times so that in some periods the valley floors were relatively dry and well suited to settlement, while at others they were marshy and subject to frequent flooding (Cherkauer, 1976, Potter, 1976b). The chronology of these fluctuations will be discussed in detail elsewhere but here it will suffice to note that the streams underwent a major phase of aggradation from late Roman times, resulting in the deposition of a thick and widespread layer of alluvium. Consequently most pre-medieval sites built on the floors of the valleys are deeply buried beneath a blanket of silt and are usually revealed only by chance river erosion (Pl. VIIb). Certainly we cannot expect to gain more than a very partial idea of the extent to which the valleys were settled or of the way that they were exploited, although the available evidence does suggest that they may have acted as the major routes of communication in the pre-Etruscan period (Ward Perkins, 1968, 14–17), and that there were attempts at drainage in the later first millennium B.C. (Judson and Kahane, 1963).

In sum, therefore, we must conclude that even for a well surveyed region like south Etruria there will be major gaps in the distribution maps of older phases of settlement. Contemporary activity and patterns of land use will account for some of the distortions while others are attributable both to older phases of agriculture and to geological factors. Thus our picture of human settlement within a landscape is usually biased towards the later periods and it is only the existence of a very large sample (such as we have for south Etruria) that can in any way compensate for such lacunae.

Types of site

The volcanic countryside of south Etruria favours two sorts of settlement. Numerically the more common is the 'open' site where the choice is for a position on a ridge or plateau, in relatively flat terrain. Such sites had the benefit of easy communications via ridgeway tracks and ready access to farmland; but they were on the other hand exposed and vulnerable to attack, and seem never to have been favoured situations in periods of political uncertainty, such as the Middle Ages. At such times the tendency was to retreat to the more isolated parts of the region and to settle in positions where there were strong natural defences. South Etruria is especially well provided with such sites, since one of the major effects of a continuing process of stream erosion has been to isolate promontories and pedestals of harder rock. These natural citadels stand high above the valley floors, protected on almost all sides by steep vertical cliffs (Pl. XV). A narrow causeway usually provides access to the plateau beyond and it requires little more than a ditch, perhaps backed up by a short stretch of wall, to turn the spur into a near-impregnable stronghold. The term 'defended site' is thus particularly appropriate to this class of settlement. Of course there could be wide variation in the topographic features of such sites. The lesser promontories met the requirements of the medieval settler especially well, for the population appears on the whole to have been quite small. In the pre-Roman period, on the other hand, when some of the defended settlements were much larger, it was a whole ridge, delineated by steep-sided canyons, that was often chosen: the sites of Veii or Civita Castellana (*Falerii Veteres*) both provide excellent examples. In either case, the common element is the emphasis upon natural defence and here the dissected terrain of south Etruria could offer almost any required permutation.

This distinction between 'open' and 'defended' sites based largely on topographical criteria can also be applied in another way. An analysis of the size of these settlements shows that all the defended sites were quite large—we should think of them as villages or, in some cases, towns—whereas the great majority of the ridge and plateau settlements consisted of farms or the centres of agricultural estates. The only major exceptions to this pattern outside recent times are the road-stations and a few rare examples of towns belonging to the Classical and post-medieval periods. An additional distinction can therefore be drawn between 'nucleated' and 'dispersed' settlement, where the majority of the larger settlements occupied a defensive position whilst the farms were almost always situated in open terrain. Later we shall see how the balance between nucleated and dispersed sites has fluctuated widely in the last three millennia, according to the current political, economic and social structure of the age.

Chronology

Most of the sites in south Etruria yield very large quantities of surface finds, particularly in the first few years after deep ploughing. It is not uncommon to find complete vessels, particularly objects like lamps, and all too often the search is supplemented by the results of clandestine looting where fragmentary but substantial pieces of pot have been discarded during the illicit excavations. There are occasionally objects of metalwork to be found (although coins are curiously rare) and other datable artifacts include brickstamps and even inscriptions. The recovery of a representative sample depends, naturally, upon the state of the ground and the quality of the search. But most deep-ploughed sites have been denuded of all their stratigraphy and some finds from the early layers have thus normally worked their way to the surface, even though they may be dispersed far from their original nucleus. Consequently, most periods of a site's history should be represented in the surface scatter.

The major source of bias in surface collections comes not from the nature of the surface scatter but much more from those collecting the finds. The temptation to pick out the brighter coloured fine wares such as the Arretine and Red Slip fabrics is particularly strong, and dull-coloured coarse wares may well be neglected in consequence. The effect of this for sites of the Roman period is probably marginal but with pre-Roman sites where drab wares predominate this natural selectivity becomes more critical. A second visit to a site has in quite a larger number of instances yielded sherds of a type not represented in the initial collection and the historical interpretation may be drastically changed as a result. That said, there is perhaps not too much need for pessimism. Just as good trowellers can sometimes reduce the need for sieves on excavations, so can the best 'sherders' achieve a high rate of objectivity in surface collections, something that can and has been tested by subsequent excavation. Moreover, in south Etruria many of the sites have been surveyed on more than one occasion and the collections of sherds are often very large. Yet, both points dwindle in importance when compared with the most telling statistic: the enormous size of the overall sample. Whereas it is easy to believe that the picture from an individual site may be misleading, it is extremely hard not to accept the cumulative significance of figures from over 2000 sites: provided the analysis is not unduly sophisticated, the broader pattern is likely to be sound.

Given the overall significance of the data from surface collections, the difficulty remains of expressing them in a meaningful way. In the early days of the South Etruria Survey little was known of the characteristics and development of local pottery and the conclusions about the history of settlement were correspondingly meagre. During the 1960s there was something of a data explosion in our knowledge of the pottery so that a

Period	Cultural Phase	Approximate Dates	Main Pottery Types
I	Apennine Bronze Age	15th–10th cents B.C.	Apennine decorated & coarse wares
II	'Proto-Villanovan' Villanovan	10th–8th cents B.C.	Characteristic decorated wares Handmade Red Slip-wares Various types of painted wares
III	Early Etruscan	7th–6th cents B.C.	Wheelmade Red Slip-wares Early bucchero Italo-Corinthian painted wares 6th-century painted wares Archaic tile
IV	Late Etruscan	5th–4th cents B.C.	Red Figure Grey bucchero Early almond rim Internal slip ware Archaic tile
V	Republican Roman	3rd–1st cents B.C.	Later black glaze wares Late almond rim
VI	Roman	Late 1st cent. B.C.- Late 1st cent. A.D.	*Terra sigillata* Fine beaker Some colour-coat wares Early flanged bowls
VII	Roman	2nd cent. A.D.	Red Slip-wares Late *terra sigillata*
VIII	Roman	3rd cent. A.D.	Red Slip-wares Rilled ware Late flanged bowls
IX	Roman	4th cent. A.D.	Red Slip-wares
X	Roman	5th–6th cents A.D.	Red Slip-wares
XI	Medieval	8th–9th cents A.D.	Combed cream ware Forum ware
XII	Medieval	9th–13th cents A.D.	Sparse glaze Early maiolica

Table 1

much clearer idea of the chronological phases began to emerge. The Ager Veientanus report (Ward Perkins, 1968) was the first to provide detailed quantification on a large scale and since then an attempt has been made to formalize the data into a period scheme (Potter, 1978). It is presented in modified form in Table 1.

The approximate life-spans of the pottery types are shown in Fig. 2 and the individual wares are discussed in the ensuing chapters. The division into periods is of course largely arbitrary and bears little or no relationship to historical phases. The only major exceptions are the divisions between periods IV and V (which coincides very approximately with the extension of Roman control over south Etruria) and between periods X and XI (the transition from Roman to medieval). A period chart of this sort does, however, have a number of uses. In the first place it enables some quanti- fication of the changing density of settlement during time, the critical

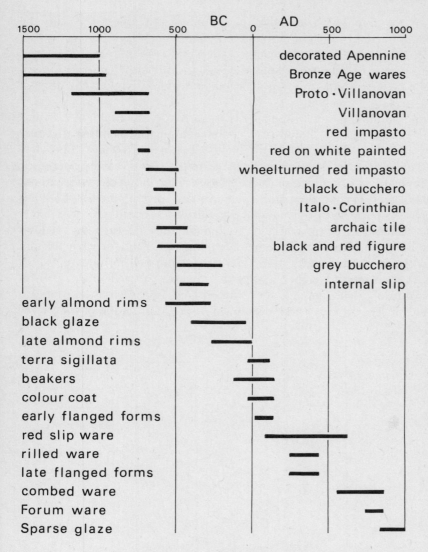

2 The main pottery types current in south Etruria between the Bronze Age and the Middle Ages.

measurement being the percentage variation in the number of sites of each period (after allowance has been made for the differing length of each period). In this way the overall trend towards population increase or decline can be estimated. Secondly, it provides a rough guide to continuities and hiatuses in the growth of the population; for example, a very large number of sites may turn out to have been abandoned at the end of one period, while a great many new foundations were made at the same time. This is in fact the case in some areas at the time of the Roman conquest and implies a substantial degree of mobility (perhaps land-settlement schemes) in the history of the population. Finally, it introduces an objectivity into the treatment of the data which, if inaccurate in detail, does nevertheless provide the best chance of defining the broader pattern of events. Figures for figures' sake are a poor substitute for proper archaeological reconstruction, but used effectively they can add a new dimension to regional studies like that of south Etruria.

Just one additional reservation needs to be made. As Blake (1978) has recently emphasized, we should perhaps be cautious in assuming that best quality fine wares were readily available to all classes of society. The early medieval glazed fabric, 'Forum' ware, for example (the one truly diagnostic pottery type for sites occupied in the eighth to ninth centuries), was without much doubt well beyond the price range of many people; most households must have made do with only unglazed tablewares. Similarly, it is likely that late Roman Red Slip-wares, even though they do turn up on low-ranking sites, were much less commonly marketed than in early to mid Imperial times. Consequently, there is a danger implicit in our analysis of the data that we might weight the statistics towards the sites of the well-to-do—a distortion that can only be compensated by much more detailed knowledge of ceramic types and, eventually, a re-examination of the survey collections.

2
The land

Topography and geology

Italy possesses a landscape of extraordinary variety, reflecting a diverse and complex geological background. A journey down the Autostrada del Sole from Milan to Rome effectively illustrates these contrasts. Initially, it is the monotonous alluvial flats of the Po Valley that dominate the terrain: an unending, intensively cultivated plain, interrupted only by tributary rivers, large farms and the towns and cities of Italy's industrial north. Then at Bologna, 180 kilometres to the south-east of Milan, the terrain abruptly changes, as the motorway begins to climb the foothills of the massive limestone chain of the Apennine Mountains. This great range forms a backbone to the peninsula, extending from Genoa in the north-west to the toe of Calabria in the south-west. It averages between 60 and 80 kilometres in width and in many parts rises to well over 2000 metres, the highest peak, Gran Sasso in Abruzzi, being nearly 3000 metres in height. The Apennines thus create a formidable barrier between east and west, with travel restricted to only a few widely spaced passes down the larger river valleys. The Autostrada employs one of the long-established routes across the mountains between north and central Italy. From Bologna it follows the course of the River Reno towards the summit of the pass and then joins the narrow valley that winds down the south side of the Apennines to Prato and Florence. Here, as in the north, the countryside once again abruptly changes, as we enter the region of Tuscany, ancient Etruria. Demarcated by the valley of the Arno, the sparsely vegetated grey limestone suddenly gives way to the fertile hills and ridges of a typical volcanic landscape.

Two impressions are outstanding. The first is of colour, especially the deep reddish-brown of a soil formed by the weathering of the volcanic tuff (*tufo*). The second is the celebrated fertility of Etruria which provides a sharp contrast with the thinly cultivated Apennine stretch. Most prevalent are rows of vines, olive and nut trees, all juxtaposed within the same field, the so-called *coltura promiscua*; but there are also many hectares of cereals, river-side meadows with good quality grazing and everywhere patches of scrub (*macchia*) which supply both fodder for pigs and abundant fuel. Agriculturally, therefore, Etruria is a land with much to offer and these advantages are further enhanced by large deposits of mineral ores. These are most richly represented in the Colline Metallifere, a range of hills extending west from Siena, with considerable quantities of copper and tin; but there are also sizeable amounts of the same metals at Monte Amiata and in the Tolfa Hills, as well as abundant deposits of iron ore on the island of Elba. Not surprisingly, all these sources of mineral wealth were extensively exploited well before the Roman period and, in combination with the arable potential of the region, do much to explain the early importance of Etruria.

Within the Tuscan area, however, there is little topographical uniformity. Towards Florence the relief is gentle, the countryside rolling and the towns, like Volterra, tend to occupy the crests of hills whose sides are almost completely terraced. Moving down towards Rome, on the other hand, the relief becomes much more sharply defined and the terrain increasingly dissected. The towns, such as Orvieto, generally lie on promontories or low hills, surrounded by steep cliffs, and deep river valleys and volcanic craters are much more common. Often, as at Bolsena or Bracciano, they survive as large lakes incorporated within ranges of hills, which divide the landscape into a series of drainage basins (Pl. Ia). The most prominent range forms, in fact, a linear chain running southwards down towards Rome and beyond, which effectively partitions the lower part of Etruria. It includes the lakes of Bolsena, di Vico, Bracciano and those of the Alban Hills, as well as conspicuous landmarks like Monte Cimino, which rises to a height of 1053 metres. Overall, this range stands several hundred metres above the level of the surrounding countryside and is thus the major watershed of this region. Numerous streams drain its slopes, cutting down through the soft bedrock and thus creating a landscape scarred by deep canyons and gorges. Travel may be difficult as the roads wind tortuously in and out of these valleys but, at the same time, this is a fertile and prosperous countryside, contrasting with the thinly settled and bare Apennines that rise steeply from the east side of the Tiber Valley.

Geology therefore has much to do with explaining the shape of settlement patterns in Italy, especially the regionalism that has been so conspicuous a feature of the country's history. Recently we have begun to learn a good deal more of the sequence and chronology of these geological events. Much of Etruria, for example, has proved to be of very recent formation. Underlying the volcanic tuffs are marine clays, now shown to be of Pliocene date (Alvarez, 1972). In places these have been trenched by river valleys, including the Tiber which originally took a course some distance to the west of its present line (Alvarez, 1973). The volcanic activity began towards the end of the Pliocene and has persisted until as recently as c. 60,000 years ago. There are a number of well marked phases of eruption, interspersed by periods of erosion; thus valleys were created, refilled by *tufo* and then excavated again, so that their walls are lined with spurs of rock derived from older phases of volcanism and the sections show layer upon layer of lava and pumice (Mattias and Ventriglia, 1970). The type of lava varies considerably. Apart from a few outcrops of basaltic *selce*, widely used for paving Roman roads (Pl. VIIIa), there are many areas of very hard rocks (ignimbrites), which are fairly resistant to large-scale erosion, and are much favoured as building stone. Much softer are mud-flow or ash-flow lavas, and in areas where these form the parent rock, such as the Ager Veientanus, the degree of landscape dissection is normally much higher than in regions with an ignimbrite cover, like the western Ager Faliscus. This fundamental lithoid distinction is also reflected in the type of earth cover, since the ignimbrites are generally less easy to plough and tend to produce a stickier, less cultivable soil; for this reason the western Ager Faliscus is mostly given over to scrubland and grazing rather than to the vine and olive growing that predominates in areas to the south and east.

The volcanic craters themselves are very numerous, although they vary considerably in size. The most prominent cluster is the north-south chain mentioned above, incorporating Monte Cimino. This major topographical boundary also includes a large group of *calderae* around Lake Bolsena, the Monti Volsinii, and in the south the complex series of craters focusing upon Lake Bracciano, the Monti Sabatini. In the Sabatini group are several huge craters which are now dry including Baccano (drained in the early Roman period) and Sorbo, as well as many minor *calderae* (Pl. Ia). One small group extends eastwards from the main chain, forming a prominent ridge that stands some 100 to 200 metres above the level of the surrounding countryside. Topographically, this is important since it forms the watershed between the River Treia drainage basin to the north and a much larger group of streams that fall southwards into the Tiber and the Tyrrhenian Sea; and politically it has significance as the natural boundary between the territories of the two major Iron Age tribes of the region, the Faliscans and the Veientes (Fig. 11).

To the west of the Sabatini-Cimini range, the natural boundaries are much less marked. The most prominent topographical feature is the Tolfa Mountains, a tangled group of hills which rise to just over 600 metres. They are composed partly of volcanic *calderae* but the surface geology also includes clays and calcareous deposits. Their main importance lies in the fact that they yield mineral deposits, including copper, tin and iron (Bono, 1971), which may well have contributed to the prosperity of Caere in the early Etruscan period, especially the seventh century B.C. The northern periphery of this group of hills is delineated by the River Mignone, which rises just to the west of Lake Bracciano and drains into the sea half-way between Civitavecchia and Tarquinia. To the north of the Mignone, the countryside, although still volcanic, becomes much more gently undulating and easier to traverse. Tarquinia is the centre of heavily cultivated and fertile farming land which stretches up the coast into the territory of Vulci. The two principal rivers are the Marta and the Fiora, of which the Marta is the major element in the very extensive drainage basin that constitutes the Viterbese. Viterbo itself lies towards the head of the basin, at the junction between the heavily dissected fans of volcanic detritus surrounding Monte Cimino and the more even spread of lava to the west: it is a choice of site that makes best advantage of the local geology and largely explains its rise to regional importance in preference, for example, to nearby towns like Tuscania.

Such, therefore, is a simplified picture of the geological variation to be found in south Etruria. There are of course other important features, such as the alluvial plain that borders most of the Tyrrhenian coastline; the solitary western outliers of the Apennines, like Mount Soracte; and the water-laid travertine deposits which become especially frequent along the western edges of the Tiber Valley, and are widely exploited for building material. But it is the palimpsest of layers of volcanic ash, of varying durability and in a state of continual erosion, that gives the countryside of south Etruria its distinctive shape and character.

Climate, vegetation and land use

The present-day climate of central Italy follows a typical Mediterranean pattern with a wet autumn, cold winters, a damp spring and a very dry, intensely hot summer. The total rainfall over the year varies with elevation but in south Etruria it rarely exceeds 1000 millimetres, with peaks in November and March. This low and sporadic precipitation effects great change in the appearance of the countryside during the year. In the winter and spring months the land is verdant with *macchia*, good pasture and crops; in summer the drought withers the ground to a pale brown, many of the streams dry up and only the xerophytic scrub retains its colour and density. For the farmer, the variability of this regime enforces well defined strategies. Priority is given to high-return crops like grapes, olives and nuts, all of which are well adapted to a Mediterranean climate. Wheat is harvested early but the precipitation levels are too low for more than an average yield and its cultivation has tended to decline in recent years. Livestock are common in the Campagna and generally fare well. Areas of wooded land are maintained near most of the villages to provide pannage for the pigs, and cattle are grazed in the summer on the river-side meadows and supplied with fodder crops in the winter. Sheep, on the other hand, pose rather more of a problem. They are valued for their wool, their *ricotta* cheese and, in the autumn, for young *abbacchio arrosto*, and for these economic reasons have always been a characteristic sight in the Roman Campagna. However, sheep are particularly susceptible to vitamin deficiency if grazed on arid pasture and are in consequence poorly adapted to withstand the summer drought in the Italian lowlands. Their watering requirements are also high, sometimes exceeding five litres per sheep a day. Irrigation would be one answer, but the traditional solution provides a cheaper and much more effective way of husbanding reserves: the practice of transhumance, where the flocks are transported into the upland regions, particularly the Apennines, so that they can take advantage of the fresh grazing brought about by the melting of the winter snows in May. The flocks are then kept in the mountains between June and September and are driven down just before the lambs fall in the early autumn.

This practical and efficient response to the difficulties imposed by a Mediterranean climatic zone is apparently of long antiquity. It is well attested in Roman times (e.g. Varro, *de re rustica*, II.2,9) and a famous inscription from Altilia (*Saepinum*), placed along one of the drove-roads, orders that interference with the passage of the sheep should straightaway cease (*CIL* 9, 2438). Transhumance was also widely practised in medieval times (Barker, 1973) and nineteenth-century travellers provide frequent descriptions of the enormous flocks visiting the summer pastures—Craven (1838), for example, saw sheep 'plodding across the valleys of Abruzzo as far as the eye can reach'. But a most interesting result of recent research has been to demonstrate that the seasonal exploitation of summer pasture must on archaeological evidence have originated with the earliest phases of animal domestication, in the Neolithic (Barker, 1975). The arguments, which cannot be fully reiterated here (although some of them will be mentioned in subsequent chapters), depend essentially upon the discovery of a series of small occupation sites, positioned well above the winter snow-line and yielding a very high proportion of sheep bones. It is probably no coincidence that most of these sites are intermediate between the main lowland and upland pastures and lie on traditional transhumance routes. It would seem that the effect upon livestock of summer aridity in the coastal areas was appreciated from the earliest phases of an agricultural economy in central Italy and that a simple solution was found: once established, transhumance has maintained its importance in the organization of the economy down to the present day.

One of the assumptions behind this argument is that the climatic pattern has been fairly constant in recent times, especially the combination of long dry summers and cold damp winters. That there must have been some fluctuation in the regime is evident from studies in other areas of Europe which suggest a fairly frequent shift in the average annual temperature (Lamb, 1966); but as yet we lack any detailed assessment for this area of central Italy. Amongst the most sensitive indices of climatic change are pollen grains, trapped in stratified deposits of organic material. So far, however, only three sites have been tested in south Etruria (Fig. 1), the Baccano crater (a drained lake), Lago di Monterosi and Lago di Vico (Bonatti, 1963, 1970; Frank, 1969). All are situated on the eastern flank of the Monti Sabatini-Cimini chain of craters and thus are largely peripheral to the main foci of human settlement in the region. The results are nevertheless remarkably consistent in the picture they present. The earliest levels reflect the cold steppe conditions that prevailed in southern Europe during the last glacial. Then, as the temperature rose, a deciduous forest cover was gradually established, with first hazel, then fir and finally oak becoming the dominant species. This corresponds well with Livy's (9, 36) description of the Ciminian forest as 'pathless and terrifying'. But there must also have been some nearby areas of parkland, for the diagrams incorporate a small but consistent percentage of grasses (*Gramineae*). These figures for *Gramineae* and other non-arboreal pollen rise steeply in the upper layers of the lake deposits, and a radiocarbon date of 270 ± 120 b.c. from Monterosi shows that this coincides with the first major period of archaeological activity, in early Roman times (Ward Perkins, 1970a). Evidently, the initial settlers cut down a large part of the forest around the lake to create farmland and before long a major highway, the Via Cassia, had been driven through the area (Harris, 1965; Wiseman, 1970). The prevalence of open ground supporting cereal crops is reflected in the pollen diagrams throughout the Roman period and only declines with a reduction in the number of settlements in the early Middle Ages. But the retrenchment of woodland was only of brief duration for, by the thirteenth century, the growth of Monterosi as a medieval village had re-established the arable pattern, and grass and cereal pollen dominates the uppermost strata of the lake.

The correlation between human activity and the pollen record is thus particularly clear at Monterosi and holds great promise for the results of future work in the more densely settled areas to the east. Certainly the pollen cores studied so far do not show any major climatic fluctuation in recent times although, as we shall see, in the river valleys there may be additional evidence for climatic change. This being the case, we can probably take the present-day system of farming and assume that many of the methods extend back far into antiquity; that contemporary forms of land use are in fact the result of long-established tradition.

River valleys

The valleys have particular importance in south Etruria. For the traveller they represent natural corridors of communication and for that reason were often chosen as transhumance routes; for the farmer they provide areas of river-side meadow for grazing and *macchia*-clad cliffs for firewood; in terms of mineral resources, there are exposures both of building stone and, in the deeper valleys, of beds of clay; and for the settler, there are sites of great natural strength. Not surprisingly, the valleys formed the focus of much of the early occupation of south Etruria, many of the major towns (like Civita Castellana, ancient Falerii Veteres) developing at points where a number of valleys converged. The pattern of river movements within the valleys is therefore a matter of some consequence (especially as valleys take up quite a large proportion of the available territory in south Etruria), and in fact recent work suggests that there have been some major fluctuations in the behaviour of the rivers during the last few millennia. At present, most of the rivers flow in steep-sided channels, incised deeply into a broad and level flood plain. When in spate, the rivers can occasionally flood the surrounding meadows but this is a very rare occurrence; for the most part the tendency is for them to cut down even deeper into the underlying deposits. At the same time there is some very gradual lateral movement, with silt deposition on one bank and erosion of the other. Settlement on the flood plain is largely ruled out by the periodic floods but extensive use is made of the pasture for grazing.

The first studies of older stream sediments in central Italy were made by

Judson (1963a). His principal work was upon a river-side site beside the Fosso della Crescenza, just to the north of the Rome suburb of Tomba di Nerone. Two buildings were identified, one a mausoleum of the early third century A.D. and the other an extensive complex of rooms, dating to the first century (Pl. VIIb). The important feature of this excavation was to demonstrate that this low-lying position had suffered intermittent flooding during the first and second centuries A.D., and then had become liable to more or less continuous inundation thereafter (Ward Perkins, 1964, 14–15). Altogether, nearly eight metres of flood silt had accumulated over the structures, suggesting a build-up of long duration, extending well into the Middle Ages.

Other sites corroborated this result. At Veii, Barri Jones examined a bath-house, the 'Bagni della Regina', situated on the floor of the Valchetta Valley, half-way between the north-east gate and the Piazza d'Armi (Jones, 1960). The building had been constructed in the first century A.D. and refurbished towards the end of the second century. Pottery indicated that it survived in use until c. A.D. 300 but that it then became liable to severe flooding. The total build-up of silt since Classical times amounted to over six metres and the trend was only halted when the stream began once again to cut through the flood plain, re-exposing the Roman building. Similarly, at a valley-bottom site beside the River Arrone, near to the route of the Via Clodia, the bank of the river revealed two layers of occupation debris, sealed beneath thick layers of alluvium (Potter, 1976b). The finds in the debris showed the building to have been of first-century date and it was evidently occupied for only a brief interval between periods of flooding.

The cumulative evidence from these sites provides therefore a remarkably consistent picture: that low-lying valley sites were being occupied in the first two centuries of the early Empire, and were subsequently buried beneath deep layers of alluvium, laid down by the flooding in the late Roman and medieval periods. Ostia seems to have suffered a similar deterioration of conditions (Meiggs, 1973) and, in the Gornalunga valley of Sicily, Judson (1963b) was able to demonstrate a parallel sequence.

The picture was further broadened by Vita-Finzi's study of valley sediments through the Mediterranean region as a whole (Vita-Finzi, 1969). Extensive fieldwork in eight other countries provided close confirmation of the results from central Italy, with numerous examples of valley-bottom alluviation, beginning in the early to mid Imperial period. Vita-Finzi termed this the 'younger fill' to distinguish it from separate and earlier phases of aggradation, the 'older fill', which appears to date to the beginning of the Würm glaciation, as long as 17,000 years ago. But subsequent fieldwork has suggested that the picture may be rather more complicated. In 1970–1, the opportunity arose to carry out extensive excavation and drilling upon the flood plain of the River Treia, immediately opposite the Faliscan settlement of Narce (Cherkauer, 1976; Potter, 1976b). The site was for-tunately chosen since there proved to be abundant quantities of potsherds incorporated in the silts. These sherds ranged in date from the middle

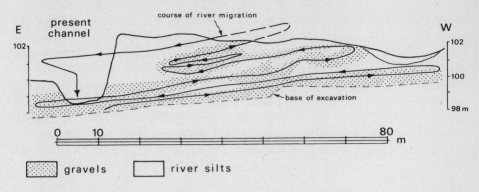

3 Section through the valley at Narce showing the lateral and vertical movements of the river over the last two thousand years. (Source: Cherkauer, 1976)

Bronze Age, *c.* 1400 B.C., down to the present century and provided a fairly clear picture of the chronology of the deposits. The immediately striking feature was the difference between layers deposited within the river channel—normally a bed of gravel, cobbles and sometimes large boulders—and the fine-grained silts that had formed on the flood plain. These two quite distinct types of material were interleaved in such a manner as to leave no doubt that the river had migrated a number of times across the valley floor within the last 2000 years, until it began to cut its present steep-sided channel on the east side of the valley (Fig. 3). Unfortunately, the height of the present-day water-table meant that the detailed sequence could only be reconstructed from *c.* 250 B.C. At that time the river was moving gradually westwards and building a silt bank behind it, a pattern of fluvial aggradation that matches the evidence for the formation of late Republican flood deposits at the Fosso Arrone site, described above. Between *c.* 250 B.C. and A.D. 150, the River Treia changed its regime and started to migrate eastwards, cutting a channel through the older silts and slowly eroding them. The deposition of alluvium was so restricted in this period that there can have been little or no flooding of the valley floor and settlement would have been quite possible. Thus there is close correspondence with the similar 'dry' periods in the Valchetta, Crescenza and Arrone valleys where, as we have seen, buildings were constructed in the early Imperial period on the meadows close to the course of the streams.

The deterioration of conditions at Narce appears to have begun in the second century A.D. Once again, the river reversed its pattern of migration, so that it now moved westwards across the valley and, at the same time, began to deposit large quantities of alluvium on the valley floor. Evidently there was persistent flooding when the river was in spate. The volume of water in the river must also have increased, for the bed was filled with large abraded boulders, some of them weighing several tons, which only a major river could have moved. Medieval pottery incorporated in the flood silts shows that these conditions persisted right through the Middle Ages and perhaps as late as the eighteenth century (with possibly a brief phase of down-cutting at the end of the first millennium A.D.). A radiocarbon date of a.d. 1490 ± 30 (I.6110) from charcoal in the silts also corroborates these dates. Then, c. 1750, the river began to migrate towards its present position near the east wall of the valley, slowly eroding some of the medieval alluvium and cutting down to create its present deep channel—a pattern which once again is closely paralleled by stream behaviour both in other areas of Italy and elsewhere in the Mediterranean (Vita-Finzi, 1969, 101–2).

The pattern of stream movements over the last two thousand years contains therefore a major archaeological implication: that settlement was only practicable on valley floors for a very brief period during the early Empire. Both before and after this period the low-lying ground was heavily water-logged and in winter there must often have been standing flood water. It is unfortunate that we cannot document the history of the rivers in the later prehistoric period, for the relevant deposits lie mostly beneath the present-day water-table; but it is likely that there were also significant fluctuations at that time. The concentration of sites dating to the late second and early first millennia B.C. in the valleys (such as Narce) suggests a period when conditions must have been fairly dry; equally, the construction of the well known drainage *cuniculi* by Etruscan engineers (to be discussed in Chapter 4) argues for a deterioration in conditions from as early as c. 500 B.C. How then are we to explain these riverine fluctuations? Undoubtedly there can be no simple answer, especially as data are now coming to light which suggest a similar sequence from topographically quite different zones like lagoons and the coastal plains (Delano-Smith, 1978). Two main theories have, however, been put forward.

One is an argument which suggests that the phases of high alluviation are initiated by man's agricultural activity: the clearance of forest to create farmland led to accelerated rates of erosion upon the hill slopes, which in turn resulted in much greater levels of silt deposition by the rivers (Butzer, 1974; Davidson, 1976). If so, it is hard to explain why a period of intensive land-utilization, such as the first and second centuries A.D. in south Etruria (cf. Chapter 5), should coincide with a phase of very low silt deposition in the valleys. Alternatively, we can favour a hypothesis which argues that the pattern of fluvial change is due to a more generalized cause, such as climatic change (Vita-Finzi, 1969, 112–15; Cherkauer, 1976, 117–20). This second explanation has a good deal to commend it. It is now realized that climate has fluctuated quite sharply in recent times with, for example, a very warm spell in the thirteenth and fourteenth centuries and a 'little Ice Age' between c. 1550 and 1850 (Lamb, 1966). Whilst such fluctuations appear to be strongly regional, their consequences may well have been sufficiently general to exert approximately synchronous effects over very large territories. Thus a climatic optimum would account for the aridity of the valleys in the early Imperial period, followed by a slow deterioration in subsequent centuries.

Equally, we could argue for a period of high Mediterranean precipitation in the last four centuries of the first millennium B.C.

Even so, it would be facile to pretend that a single explanation will suffice for the complicated geomorphological changes that have taken place in valleys, estuaries and coastal plains over the last few millennia. Investigation of these problems has only just begun and there is a need for a great deal of new data. But the archaeologist cannot afford to ignore this aspect of his study: the fluctuating conditions in the valleys imposed major constraints upon settlement and land use in certain periods, and must be taken into account in evaluating the history of the landscape.

Discussion

The importance of geographical factors in shaping the pattern of human settlement has been recognized ever since Sir Cyril Fox expounded the principles in studies like *The Archaeology of the Cambridge Region* (1923) and *The Personality of Britain* (1932). Sites tend to cluster on the most easily exploited soils and expand on to marginal land only under heavy population pressure. More recently this type of approach has been considerably refined. Due allowance has been made for the effects of a changing climate, which can drastically alter the environment of a site. Similarly various types of settlement have come to be interpreted as representative of mobile societies, whose sites reflect a seasonal movement from one region to another: in the context of central Italy, for example, we can recognize a process of lowland–upland migration—still today an important element in the structure of the agricultural economy. Equally, we need to consider the changing environment of the coastal plain of western central Italy, the Maremma, where conditions for settlement appear to have deteriorated markedly in the late Roman period, as once well drained land became marshy and probably malarial (Ward-Perkins, B. 1978). For these reasons therefore the archaeologist needs both to examine the pattern of ancient sites in the light of the contemporary landscape and to take account of the work of scientists who are attempting to define environmental and geomorphological change.

One of the key words in this context is *territory*, that is the land habitually exploited by a particular group of people. In a primitive but mainly sedentary society it is clear that such territories cannot have been very large. Most estimates (based mainly on studies upon contemporary primitive societies: Chisholm, 1968, 66) agree that a circle with a five-kilometre radius around the settlement nucleus is likely to mark the main limits of the territory exploited by that group. Beyond that point the 'costs of operation rise sufficiently . . . to be seriously detrimental', notes Chisholm (1968, 66). Of course, an effective system of transport, combined with dependent rural farms, can vastly increase the size of the *territorium*: but it is the immediate environs of a site that are of prime importance.

In this context, the settlements of south Etruria were generally well served. Certainly the awkward terrain imposed a paramount need for a network of communications upon any site that wished to support a large population: but most normal requirements lay within easy reach of the settlement nucleus. There was fertile land that served both as grazing and arable; a plentiful water supply in the form of streams and springs; wood fuel and pannage in the *macchia*; and abundant building materials. Moreover, the primitive farmer soon became skilful at improving these resources: land drains (*cuniculi*) for example were devised to reduce soil wash in a high-erosion region and ploughs were developed that could break up the soft bedrock and create new topsoil.

However, there are also major disadvantages in this area. A primary factor is the isolation imposed by the chains of steep and wood-covered volcanic hills—an isolation that persists despite the creation of major highways through the region. Only along the coast of the Tyrrhenian Sea were communications in any way easy and this proved a crucial advantage for the coastal cities. Moreover, there exist few special resources to exploit in the way for example that Etruscan Populonia was to benefit from the iron ores of Elba. The only metal ores in south Etruria lie in the Tolfa Mountains, close to the city of Cerveteri which, significantly, was the earliest Etruscan settlement to grow prosperous. Otherwise, the only major resource in the region is the salt deposits at the mouth of the Tiber: these, equally significantly, were controlled from a very early period by Rome. Rome in fact was well situated. It lay on a navigable river, close to an easily developed port; enjoyed good communications to the north via the Tiber Valley, to the east along the Aniene River, and to the south down the Sacco and Liri valleys; and had easy access to the fertile countryside of Etruria and Latium. These topographical advantages were to weigh heavily in Rome's favour during the period of her emergence, and it is not surprising that when the time came for conflict with nearby Veii Rome was to win convincingly and Veii was slowly to fall into decline. The importance of topography and resources could not be illustrated more tellingly.

3
The earliest settlers

Most of peninsular Italy avoided the successive phases of ice cover that affected large parts of northern Europe during the Palaeolithic period. On the other hand, the advance and retreat of the ice sheets did have an impact both upon the level of the Tyrrhenian Sea and upon the climate of central Italy. The marine sequence seems to fall into five principal episodes in which the melting of the ice sheets in northern Europe caused the sea to rise above the level of the present-day coast, inundating the lower ground. Traces both of older shoreline and of sea-laid deposits have been identified in south Etruria, showing that some of the marine incursions may on occasion have extended as far as the foothills of the Apennine Mountains. Similarly, five cold phases have also been demonstrated, beginning with two episodes that preceded the start of major vulcanism in the region, *c.* 700,000 years ago, and extending in date down to the final withdrawal of the ice sheets, in *c.* 10,000 b.c. (Collins, 1978).

Recent discoveries make it likely that man has been present in Italy for at least one million years, but so far the picture of this very early period remains extremely blurred. In the Rome area there are both pebble tools and a number of handaxes of Acheulean (Lower Palaeolithic) type: but successive volcanic eruptions, interspersed by long periods of valley erosion, have largely obliterated the camps of these early men. One of the major exceptions is the remarkable site at Torre in Pietra (Torrimpietra), which lies 26 kilometres to the north-west of Rome (Fig. 4a). Here Blanc (1958) uncovered the hearths and windbreaks of a small hunters' camp of Lower Palaeolithic date. It was surrounded by flint debris, amongst which were about 350 artifacts, including more than 30 Acheulean handaxes. In addition there were the bones of the hunters' quarry, with horse, cattle, red deer, elephant and rhinoceros all well represented. The camp had been buried beneath a deep deposit of gravel and volcanic ash, containing later forms of stone tool; but unfortunately we lack any unambiguous absolute dating evidence. Our best guide is a figure of 435,000 years ago worked out by the Potassium-Argon method for pieces of volcanic rock incorporated in or immediately beneath the level of the hunters' camp. It is not clear, however, if the rock is contemporary with the camp or derived from earlier layers: indeed one recent assessment argues for a much later period for the Acheulean remains (Collins, 1978).

Our scanty picture of the early phase of the Palaeolithic begins to fill out

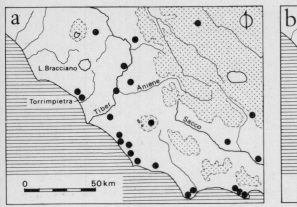
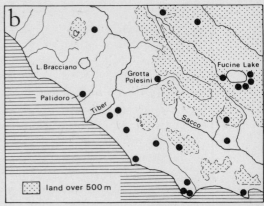

4 Sites in western central Italy of (a) the lower and middle Palaeolithic and (b) the upper Palaeolithic. (Source: Barker, 1975)

only with the main cessation of volcanic activity *c.* 60,000 years ago. The climate at this time appears to have favoured a broad spectrum of game, including large animals like elephant and rhinoceros, as well as red and roe deer, horse, cattle and ibex. This ready source of food seems to have been extensively exploited by the Middle Palaeolithic hunter bands whose cave and open camp sites are widely dispersed through Italy. In the Rome area, the 25 or so sites that are known tend to cluster mainly along the shores of the Tyrrhenian Sea, with a few outliers extending up the major valleys like the Tiber (Fig. 4a). This distribution closely matches the availability of the raw materials used to manufacture stone tools; but it also implies that the food resources, particularly the game, were sufficiently concentrated in this region to encourage only lowland settlement.

After *c.* 40,000 b.p. the climate began to deteriorate and conditions became cold and arid. The consequences of this change were far reaching. The big game such as elephant and rhinoceros became largely extinct in central Italy and animals better adapted to the lower temperatures, like horse and deer, much more prevalent. These animals tend to follow clearly defined seasonal migrations: they generally spend the winter in areas of lowland pasture and then move up along a narrow corridor onto higher ground in the spring, their territorial pattern thus corresponding in plan to the shape of a dumb-bell. Hunter bands, especially those which depended only on a narrow spectrum of game, must soon have come to understand these annual migrations and to evolve an appropriate strategy. The cave sites in the Marina di Camerota, a sea-girt peninsula near Sapri in southern Campania, provides an interesting example. The bones from the caves show that this group of hunters relied almost exclusively upon red deer as their source of meat (Barker, 1975, 114–8). They apparently practised a careful husbandry, culling mainly the young deer (presumably the males), so as to conserve the herd. The Lapps of northern Scandinavia in fact follow an identical policy (Sturdy, 1972), selecting males in their first year for food. In the summer, the deer are likely to have left the lowland pasture to seek fresh grazing in the hills. The topography of the area has only one natural corridor to the uplands: the narrow valley of the Mingardo River, which rises at a height of about 1500 metres above sea level. At the head of the valley are large areas of summer grazing which were no doubt exploited by the deer. Here a number of flint scatters have been identified, yielding tools of identical type to those from the caves: it looks therefore as though the Camerota hunters followed the deer during their annual migration, so as to maintain control of the herd.

This increased sophistication in hunting strategies cannot as yet be paralleled in detail in central Italy but there are some indications of economic adaptation towards the beginning of the Upper Palaeolithic, i.e. c. 35,000 b.p. This phase is clearly marked technologically by the adoption of many new tool forms, most notably the long flint blade, with blunting along one side to facilitate hafting into a shaft, and also the burin, a sharp-cornered flint used mainly for working bone and wood. The distribution of sites yielding these tools shows quite distinct differences from the Middle Palaeolithic pattern, however. The mountainous area of the Apennines, previously almost devoid of settlement, now appears to have been exploited on a fairly extensive scale, with cave sites clustering along the natural corridors provided by the valleys (Fig. 4b). Barker's (1975) suggestion that there were summer camps, created by bands following red deer and steppe horse, carries conviction in the light of the Camerota evidence. Certainly the band that lived in the Grotta Polesini, a large cave in the Aniene Valley near Tivoli, appear to have relied heavily upon red deer for meat and there are hints in the faunal record that they may have practised some herd control (Barker, 1975, 122); moreover their base was well placed, straddling one of the major natural routes towards the upland pasture.

Why there should have been this selectivity of food resources is open to conjecture, but the prevalence of a harsh steppe-like environment during the Upper Palaeolithic (Bonatti, 1963, 1970; Frank, 1969) may well have been a major incentive towards more sophisticated hunting. Moreover, if the number of known sites is in any way meaningful, there was also some population expansion at this time. In the South Etruria Survey region, for example, excavation in the caves that line the river canyons in the vicinity of Civita Castellana and Corchiano has yielded a great many Upper Palaeolithic flint forms (Rellini, 1920; Incardona, 1969). Further west, beyond the Monti Sabatini and Cimini there are also a number of sites, including a large base camp near to the sea at Palidoro (Blanc, 1955) and, further north, many flint scatters on the Monte Argentario peninsula and the island of Giglio (Bronson and Uggeri, 1970). Presumably these represent camps occupied during the winter when the upland pastures were covered by snow.

From c. 15,000 b.p. the pollen diagrams begin to register a gradual change from the steppe conditions prevalent during the Upper Palaeolithic.

Ia *Above* Aerial view of the Baccano crater with, beyond, Lago Martignano and Lake Bracciano. (Photo: *BSR*)

Ib *Right* Narce from the south.

IIa *Opposite top* Narce: oval hut of the twelfth to eleventh centuries B.C., together with a cemetery enclosure of the sixth century B.C.

IIb *Opposite bottom* Villanovan cinerary urns from the Grotta Gramiccia cemetery at Veii. (Photo: *BSR*)

IIIa *Above* Veii, the north-west gate under excavation in 1958. To the left: the city wall, overlying successive timber and stone buildings. (Photo: *BSR*)

IIIb *Right* A typical shepherd's hut in the Campagna. (Photo: *BSR*)

IVa *Above* Cuniculated valley to the north of Veii, drained by the Olmetti *cuniculus*. Note the four vertical shafts. (Photo: *BSR*)

IVb *Left* The Olmetti *cuniculus* beneath Casale Selviata. (Photo: *BSR*)

At first the higher temperatures encouraged only the growth of grassland but from about 12,000 years ago, there was a slow increase in the amount of forest. Soon the landscape was dotted with hazel and fir trees and before long these were supplemented by various species of oak, eventually forming a typical Mediterranean deciduous forest. The effect of these changes in the flora has yet to be properly measured in terms of the game available to man. The steppe horse certainly disappeared in early Post-glacial times but the contention of scholars like Radmilli (1963) that the quantity of large game was very drastically reduced remains to be substantiated. Barker (1975, 126–8) has shown in fact that ibex, red deer and the bones of other large animals are well attested in many caves occupied at this time, and some groups may have altered their way of life very little. But other sites, especially those bordering lakes and the sea, do show a much increased reliance upon fishing and shell collection, implying overall a much more diverse system of economies.

We have had to take a much larger canvas than south Etruria to reconstruct even in the broadest outline something of the mode of life during the Palaeolithic and early Post-glacial period. There is a very obvious logic to this in that the territories exploited by the hunters seem to have been very extensive, being dictated in some periods by the pattern of animal migration to the upland regions during the summer months. But it is also the case that the tangled volcanic countryside of Etruria has so far proved largely barren of flint scatters. This may reflect the limitations of a survey team with an undoubted bias towards remains of the Classical period. Alternatively, it could suggest a preference on the part of Palaeolithic groups for other environments, such as the coastal belt of Etruria. In either case the evidence (particularly pollen analysis) for a detailed assessment is still inadequate and it is better to postpone judgement at this stage.

Neolithic

Radiocarbon dates suggest that the first settlers to practise cereal cultivation and animal husbandry were established in Italy before 5000 b.c. (Whitehouse, 1978) and the form of some of their sites has been richly demonstrated by air photography in the silt lands of Apulia (where more than one thousand sites are now known) and by excavation in the north of Italy (Barfield, 1971, 33–53). But in central Italy, excavation still lags behind artifact studies and we badly need some large-scale work upon individual settlements. In Lazio, for example, we know of less than 20 Neolithic sites and few of these have been sampled on anything like the necessary scale (Fig 5a).

Amongst the more spectacular sites is a cave known as the Grotta Patrizi, situated near to the village of Sasso di Furbara on the lower slopes of the Tolfa Hills. Here, excavations by Radmilli (1954) uncovered a series of burials, accompanied by rich grave-goods. With the tombs were flint blades and scrapers, a number of querns, decorated bone work and a group of

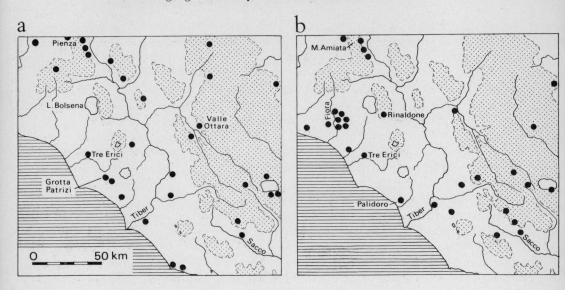

5 Sites in western central Italy of (a) Neolithic and (b) Copper Age. (Source: Barker, 1975; Renfrew and Whitehouse, 1974)

pottery cups and large jars. The form of the vessels indicates a date in the early phases of the Neolithic and points to stylistic links with the so-called Fiorano culture of the Emilia region of Italy. Rather similar sherds have also been found at an open site in the Tolfa Hills at Tre Erici (Ostenberg, 1967), for which there is a radiocarbon date of 3445 ± 80 b.c. (St. 1344), and at Pienza, just north of Monte Amiata. Pienza provides us with our best evidence for the early development of agriculture within the region. Not only are there plant remains of wheat and barley but the faunal sample is dominated by the bones of domesticated animals, especially sheep but also cattle and pig. Pienza therefore was a settlement where a fully integrated agricultural economy was developed, exploiting the light, easily farmed soils that form the environs of the site (Barker, 1975, 146–7). But this is only one side of the picture. Excavations at caves like that in the Valle Ottara, near to the town of Rieti, suggest a parallel but quite differently based economic system. Here Acanfora (1962–3) found that the faunal sample consisted mainly of the bones of red deer, indicating more or less complete dependence upon hunted meat. A Neolithic date for this site was demonstrated by both the pottery and a radiocarbon date of 3440 ± 145 (Pi 28); but the flint work, as Ostenberg has underlined (1967, 162–3), harks back much more to the traditions of the early Post-glacial period than to the types popular at Neolithic sites like Tre Erici. We seem therefore to have two main cultural groups in central Italy at this time, one continuing a long-established mode of life based upon hunting, and the other reflecting the innovations of sedentary agriculture.

Too little is known of the overall distribution of these Neolithic sites to examine this economic dichotomy in terms of territories and settlement patterns. Indeed it is one of the surprising results of the ground survey work in south Etruria that no Neolithic site has yet come to light. It is quite possible that Neolithic potsherds have escaped identification, for there are Neolithic levels in some of the Faliscan caves (Rellini, 1920) and the region cannot therefore have been completely unexploited; but it is equally likely that the open sites of this period have been totally obliterated by the overlay of later settlement and the intensive agriculture that this entailed. It is significant that the Neolithic levels at Tre Erici lay buried beneath more than five metres of overburden (Ostenberg, 1967, 34) and it may be that much of this early landscape is similarly hidden.

Eneolithic (Copper Age)

Towards the end of the third millennium B.C. objects of copper make their appearance in central Italy. The range of artifacts is initially small, preference being given to simple flat axes, halberd blades and some types of small daggers, amongst them a form with a midrib and rounded butt, fastened by means of rivets to a haft. But they mark a significant advance in technology and the first beginnings of a major Etrurian school of metalworking. The source of the ores was fairly clearly local, for the sites with copper objects tend to cluster in the vicinity of the main metal-bearing regions like Monte Amiata (Fig. 5b); yet most of the sites consist not of domestic settlements but of rock-cut burial chambers or simple trench tombs, richly furnished in grave-goods (Renfrew and Whitehouse, 1974). In cultural terms they take their name from a tomb found at Rinaldone, near Montefiascone; but the main groups of burials lie to the west in the Fiora Valley, to the north in central Tuscany, and in Lazio to the south of the Tiber. There are also two outliers, situated high in the Apennines.

The copper weapons, flint daggers and arrowheads, and stone 'battle axes' found in these graves have been interpreted as evidence for an incursion of warriors, who broke up the agricultural sedentism of Neolithic life and created a nomadic society, based on pastoralism, that endured throughout the Bronze Age. This hypothesis was formed at a time when the presence of Bronze Age agricultural settlements had not been recognized, and does not now carry the credence it used to (Renfrew and Whitehouse, 1974). But settlements of Eneolithic date remain only poorly represented in the archaeological records, especially in western central Italy. Sites like Conelle, a promontory village defended by a wide ditch, situated near to Arcevia in Marche (Trump, 1966, 96–7), show that there were substantial settlements at this time, but the few known occupation sites west of the Apennines consist almost entirely of caves. An important exception is Tre Erici (Ostenberg, 1967) where the Neolithic levels were overlain by a deep Eneolithic deposit and the remains of a hut. This building is dated by three radiocarbon figures, falling between 2075 ± 100 b.c. (St. 2042) and 1850 ± 80 b.c. (St. 1343). The pottery styles change comparatively little between the Neolithic and Chalcolithic and the impression of population continuity that this suggests is matched by the stratigraphies at other sites like Palidoro (Peroni, 1965) and the cave at La Romita di Asciano near Pisa (Peroni, 1962–3). Indeed it seems likely that, as more radiocarbon dates become available, we shall find that many of the Neolithic sites persist in occupation into the early second millennium B.C., with little sign of cultural change, except for the adoption of metalwork.

The Bronze Age

The advent of bronze technology early in the second millennium B.C. did not have an immediate widespread impact. There was, it is true, a gradual diversification of the range of objects and a certain amount of technological improvement, but the evidence of excavated settlements indicates that the use of bronze tools did not become in any way common until the late second millennium B.C., the period of the Late Bronze Age. Our best source of information about these artifacts remains, in fact, the contents of hoards buried either for safety or perhaps as votive offerings. Significantly, most of these hoards cluster in the vicinity of the ore-bearing deposits, such as Monte Amiata, closely following the distribution of the Rinaldone burials (Trump, 1966, 106). Perhaps the heirs to this Copper Age group exercised a monopoly over the metal ores—a monopoly that was only broken when the potential of the Colline Metallifere deposits was discovered sometime in the Late Bronze Age.

Despite the restricted use of bronze tools and weapons, the Bronze Age culture of Italy exhibits in other ways an extraordinary uniformity. This is an impression conveyed most clearly by the pottery but it applies also to other artifacts such as flintwork and bone objects. The most distinctive ceramic forms consist of a series of carinated cups and bowls, often provided with elaborately modelled handles, some of which resemble animals. The fabric of the vessels varies from a dark brown or black to a bright red, of which the surface has been burnished to a bright lustre. Usually the upper part of these pots was decorated with deeply incised geometric designs, including both rectilinear and circular motifs; the incision was then filled with a paste, normally a white gypsum, to bring out the pattern.

This distinctive tableware is distributed over most of the Italian peninsula and, while displaying some regional variation (Trump, 1958), is nevertheless immediately recognizable throughout the country as a hallmark of the Bronze Age. This implies schools of professional potters, who appear to have disseminated their wares over wide market areas. In central Italy, for example, identical shapes and motifs occur on sites more than 100 miles apart (Potter, 1976a, 200). The chronological development of these forms remains, however, to be closely defined. Such evidence as we have suggests that the earliest Bronze Age decorated wares drew heavily upon Eneolithic designs and that these were rapidly elaborated into the profusion of ornament which characterizes Middle Bronze Age decorated pottery. Towards the latter part of the second millennium B.C. the quantity and quality of the designs appear to fall away, before being replaced by a new set of motifs, heralding the spread of Urnfield cultures (Potter, 1976a): but it has to be said that our stratified sequences where such developments can be recognized are still lamentably small. What is not in question, however, are the typological changes in the handles. Trump, (1958, 1966) has demonstrated very clearly how Eneolithic prototypes are the preferred form in the Early to Middle Bronze Age, and that these give way to the plastic types with horns and animal heads. These later Bronze Age handles provide in fact a very clear index of settlement in the later second millennium B.C., a chronology that can be very well demonstrated at the important stratified site at Luni-sul-Mignone (Ostenberg, 1967), to be discussed in detail below.

The presence of such distinctive pottery types on Bronze Age sites in Italy greatly aids the reconstruction of the second-millennium landscape. Bronze Age sherds are easily identified in a surface collection and approximate dates can be assigned to them. Moreover, this appears also to have been a period when settlement began to expand on a significant scale. Lowland sites became many times more numerous, compared with the fourth and third millennia, and exploitation of the upland region is equivalently increased. In fact, the quantity of sites discovered in the mountains (Fig. 10) is so large that the term the 'Apennine culture' has been coined to describe the Bronze Age of Italy (Puglisi, 1959; Trump, 1958). This label first became current in the 1930s but it was the publication of Puglisi's critical study of La civiltà appenninica in 1959 that laid the basis for most recent interpretations of the archaeological record. Puglisi skilfully demonstrated from the evidence of the animal bones and the widespread occurrence of Bronze Age 'milk-boilers'—vessels used to separate curds and whey for the producing of ricotta cheese—that the basis of the second-millennium economy lay in pastoral nomadism, with sheep and goats as the principal domesticated animals. The mountain sites—most of which lie far above the height of the winter snow-line—he explained as shepherds' summer camps whilst the lowland sites represented the winter bases, occupied only during the cold months of the year. His arguments were backed up by ethnographic parallels, most notably from Italy itself, where transhumance is still, as we have seen, widely practised (Fig. 6).

Underlying this elegant explanation of the archaeological record lies an important cultural assumption: that the sedentary life explicitly represented by the Neolithic farm and village communities had been broken up by the incursions of Eneolithic warriors, attested by the Rinaldone burials. Pastoralism was seen as the consequence of political change rather than as a response to environmental constraints. In the 1960s, however, this view came under scrutiny as a result of the excavation by the Swedish School at Rome on a site beside the Mignone River in the Tolfa Hills, at Luni-sul-Mignone (Ostenberg, 1967). Luni comprises an elevated promontory of volcanic tuff, 550 metres in length and 140 metres wide (Fig. 7). It is readily accessible only by means of a narrow ridge joining the plateau from the

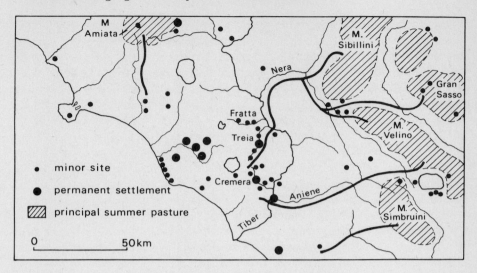

6 Western central Italy: Bronze Age sites and pre-war transhumance routes to the summer pastures. (Source: Barker, 1972)

west, and is strongly protected by cliffs which fall sheerly into deep river canyons on either side. It constitutes in fact a natural fortress and was utilized as such in both Etruscan and medieval times.

The surprising discovery of the excavation, however, was the existence of a long period of prehistoric occupation. The sequence began with a series of superimposed huts and occupation deposits, sited on rather lower ground to the east of the main acropolis. This area, known as Tre Erici, had been first inhabited from as early as the fourth millennium B.C. and occupation continued intermittently into the Iron Age. But in the second millennium B.C. the main nucleus had shifted onto the plateau of Luni itself, taking advantage both of the greater area of available land and of the natural defences provided by the cliffs surrounding the site. The buildings of the Bronze Age village were concentrated in the central part of the plateau and consisted of three deep trenches, laid out in a line across the site (Fig. 7). The largest measured 42 metres in length and 4 metres in width, and averaged 2 metres in depth: a second, not completely excavated, was c. 30 metres in length and 4 metres wide, and a third was much smaller, measuring 7 × 4 metres in plan and between 1.2 and 1.4 metres in depth. In addition, the north end of what was probably a fourth trench was excavated at the south side of the plateau, and could have been just over 20 metres in length.

At first sight, these trenches look very much like a ditch system, crossed by causeways, and designed to cut off one end of the promontory. Very similar protective measures can be found on many of the medieval sites in the region. But there seems very little doubt that these trenches were in fact

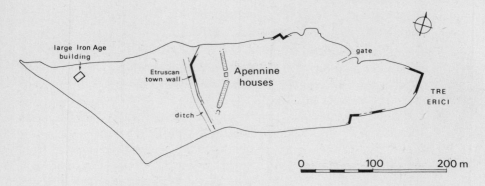

7 Plan of the Apennine Bronze Age and Iron Age settlement at Luni-sul-Mignone in the Tolfa Hills. (Source: Ostenberg, 1967)

permanent habitations, covered with a roof to make long houses. Inside the trenches were properly laid floors and hearths made of sherds and clay, and a build-up of refuse that had accumulated on the floors rather than as a series of tips from outside. In addition there were well defined entrances where the bedrock had been worn down and post sockets had supported a porch. The collapsed remains of dry-stone walls were also found, incorporated into the upper fill of the trenches. Thus we can reconstruct these buildings as the remains of long houses with deeply sunken floors, low stone walls and probably, given the absence of vertical supports, a simple, slightly inclined roof of thatch.

The excavations sampled only part of the plateau and we cannot assume therefore that these were the only Bronze Age houses on the site. In any case other buildings may well have been more ephemerally constructed and less well adapted to survive the effect of subsequent centuries of occupation. Thus we cannot do more than guess at the size of this community beyond recognizing it as a 'nucleated' settlement. Nevertheless, it is clear that defence had some priority. This is implicit in the choice of this inaccessible site and confirmed by the linear arrangement of the houses which would, in effect, have constituted a near-continuous wall across the promontory. Later, an identical strategy was to be adopted by the inhabitants of medieval villages. This emphasis upon defence is an interesting feature that is duplicated in numerous other Bronze Age settlements both in central Italy and elsewhere, and is a matter that we shall return to later.

The finds from these houses provide us with both a useful cross-section of domestic objects and with an idea of the way in which artifact styles evolved during the Apennine Bronze Age. Ostenberg (1967) classified his material into four chronological phases, of which I–III were represented by the long houses and IV was best illustrated by late Bronze Age levels from Tre Erici. During this time there were clearly marked typological changes in the pottery, described briefly above, and fluctuations too in the relative frequencies of different forms: decorated wares, for example, became much less common after Luni Apennine II, although the styles and motifs remain similar. But it is worth emphasizing that this division into periods, although based principally upon distinctions in the stratigraphy, does not imply any hiatus in the population. We seem to be dealing with a continuously inhabited settlement, where the different periods reflect only minor events in the history of a single building.

The provision of dates for this archaeological sequence depends upon two sources, one a series of radiocarbon dates and the other a small sample of five imported potsherds. The sherds are very clearly differentiated from the usual Bronze Age wares by their cream fabric and decoration in orange-red paint and clearly were not made locally. Professor Furumark believes them to be imports from the Mycenaean world—a plausible suggestion since Mycenaean finds are widely distributed through southern Italy (Fig. 10: Taylour, 1958; Biancofiore, 1967)—and has assigned one to Mycenaean IIIA (c. 1400–1230 B.C.), two to Mycenaean IIIB (c. 1300–1230 B.C.) and two to IIIC (c. 1230–1000 B.C.). But not all scholars are happy that sherds as small as this (none is larger than a few centimetres across) can be dated with quite this precision and we should perhaps be cautious about the way we use this evidence. This leaves the radiocarbon dates, the most meaningful of which relate to Luni Apennine II: these are 1170 ± 75 b.c. (St. 2045) and 1245 ± 75 b.c. (St. 1345). Interpreted literally these dates would support the excavator's contention that Luni Apennine II fell in the period between 1250 and 1150 B.C. But we now know that radiocarbon years are generally much younger than their equivalent in calender years and, consequently, need to be calibrated so that they approximate to their true value. Calibration (Potter, 1976a, 313) would in fact suggest a date of c. 1500 B.C. for Luni Apennine II and other values would also have to be adjusted accordingly. A more probable chronology for Luni might therefore be as follow:

	Ostenberg 1967	Adjusted (B.C.)
Luni I	1350/1300–1250	1800–1550
Luni II	1250–1150	1550–1400
Luni III	1150–1000	1400–1200
Luni IV	1000–800	1200–1050

This scheme also has the advantage of lessening the gap between the Eneolithic deposits of Tre Erici, dated by radiocarbon to 1850 ± 80 (St. 1343) and Luni Apennine I, for, as Barker (1975, 146) has underlined, there are close similarities between the pottery of the two periods.

This excursus into the complexities of Bronze Age chronology highlights the difficulties that confront us while there are few radiocarbon dates, a very approximate index of calibration and little in the way of imported datable objects from Apennine sites in central Italy. We are obviously far from establishing a reliable dating sequence for sites of the second millennium B.C. and are well advised to be cautious at present. Nevertheless, whatever the precise chronological development, it is clear that at Luni we are dealing with a village settlement, permanently occupied throughout the year. This is borne out by a quantity of plant remains, showing that club wheat and barley were cultivated, and a number of millstones, some of them still *in situ* on the house floors. The skeletal remains indicate that the stock kept by the inhabitants of Luni included cattle (45–53 per cent), sheep (22–26 per cent) and pig (20–25 per cent), a range that matches modern animal husbandry in the area, although there is reason to think that these percentages for cattle may be exaggerated (Barker, 1972, 186–7). The mortality data show that the cattle were normally full-grown when slaughtered and most must have been maintained as ploughing teams: indeed, the plant remains included horse bean and grass pea which are both widely used as fodder crops. The pigs were raised into the second and third years, presumably after fattening in the woodland around the site. In fact, pork appears to have formed a staple element in the meat diet, for the mortality figures indicate that there was not the large-scale slaughter of lambs that is practised today and consequently it is likely that many of the sheep were kept to produce cheese. Indeed, milk boilers were commonly represented in the range of pottery vessels. The presence of these flocks indicates, however, that there must have been some mobility in the management of the stock, for, as we have seen, the lowland sites are normally incapable of supporting domestic animals throughout the year. Transhumance would therefore have been obligatory for the shepherds and it is likely that, like their modern counterparts, they followed the *tratturi* (Fig. 6) up through the Faliscan region to the confluence of the Tiber and Nera and then into the mountain pastures east of Terni (Barker, 1972, 193–6). But we need not assume, as Puglisi's pastoralist model demands, that all the population moved with the flocks. Most of the villagers would presumably have stayed in the lowland to harvest the crops, prepare for the autumn sowing and maintain the remaining livestock. We must argue therefore for a dual economic system, in part involving mobility and in part requiring sedentism, a practice that is maintained in south Etruria down to the present day.

We must now turn to the South Etruria Survey and see how the results of excavations and surface fieldwork correspond with this model for the settlement at Luni. The Bronze Age, as we saw earlier, is the first period to be well represented by surface finds in the survey region. Nearly 20 sites have been identified (Ward Perkins, 1968, 14–17), to which we should add seven or eight caves with Apennine pottery located by Rellini (1920) in the vicinity of Civita Castellana. Despite all the limitations of such survey work, the overall distribution of sites (Figs. 6, 12) does present a remarkably consistent pattern: with very few exceptions, the Bronze Age finds derive from four major valley systems, the Tiber, the Cremera, the Treia and the Rio Fratta. They suggest the use of quite restricted corridors through the region and this is borne out by the pollen analysis from the area to the west, where deciduous woodland appears to have survived largely intact until the Roman period (Bonatti, 1963; Frank, 1969). Only at Monterosi is there

any hint of change, with the appearance of chemical changes, dated to *c.*
1000 B.C., from which Hutchinson (1970, 165) inferred 'a small amount of
human activity'. The sites themselves consist for the most part of small
scatters of pottery and (less often) flint, occurring at intervals of between
one and two kilometres. The recognizable pottery types include horned
handles and other late Apennine forms, suggesting a date in the latter part
of the second millennium B.C. Most of the sites appear to have been very
small and would conform well with Barker's suggestion (1972, 195) that
they represent the overnight stopping places of shepherds following transhumance routes to and from the summer pastures. But some may have
been winter base camps or permanent settlements, like the large site on the
right bank of the River Cremera at Pisciacavallo, near Formello (Anon,
1954–5; Peroni, 1959, 248). One such site, where detailed excavation has
taken place, is situated by the River Treia close to the Faliscan town of
Narce (Potter, 1976a). The Treia, a fast-flowing perennial stream, enters
a wide, flat-bottomed gorge immediately to the south of the settlement and
heads northwards down the valley towards Civita Castellana and the River
Tiber (Fig. 8). The site, part of which has been destroyed by fluvial erosion,
was identified in the river bank on the east side of the valley. It proved to
consist of a deep stratigraphy, which had built up between the Middle
Bronze Age and Roman times. Altogether ten main building phases were
represented, the first three being of Bronze Age date.

The earliest settlement, period I, consisted of little more than a temporary
encampment, constructed in a clearing on the valley floor. Traces were
found of branches, thorns and berries, burnt during the initial clearance of
the site, and there were stake-holes indicative of tents or light huts. Near
by were rubbish pits and spreads of refuse containing Middle Apennine
pottery and fragments of bone. Before long, however, the settlement took
on a more permanent aspect. Much of the sloping ground to the east of the
building area was levelled out with rubble, and a palisade, made of stout
timbers, was constructed (Fig. 9). Within this fence, remains of part of a
rectangular building were identified. At foundation level it was built of dry-
stone walling but the superstructure was made of timber verticals, probably
filled in with wattling and daub. Close by were the post sockets of another
wooden structure and a number of hearths.

The solid nature of these structures leaves little doubt that this was a
permanently occupied settlement, quite possibly of some size. This is
corroborated by the survival both of seeds of emmer wheat and of millstones,
showing that, like Luni, cereal cultivation was practised within the vicinity
of the site. The stock economy also implies a stable base with quite high
proportions of pig (15 per cent) and cattle (30 per cent). Barker (1976)
believes that cattle may have been maintained both as ploughing teams and
for their dairy produce, but were unimportant as a meat source. Pigs on the
other hand were generally raised for pork in both the Roman and medieval
periods (Jones, 1966a, 382) and it is likely that this was also their main
purpose in a prehistoric community. They have the advantage of high rates

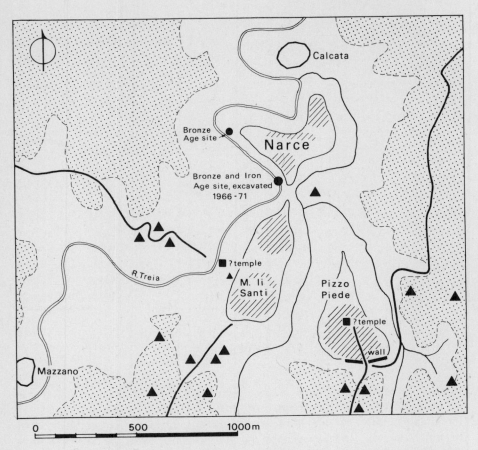

8 Plan of the Bronze and Iron Age settlement at Narce. The main settlement nuclei are shown by diagonal hatching. Triangles indicate cemeteries.

of reproduction and require little more than areas of scrub or woodland for pannage, of which there must have been a good deal near to Narce. But the faunal samples in both period II and the succeeding phases are dominated (as in other Bronze Age sites) by the bones of caprines: as today, large flocks of a hundred or more sheep, led by a few goats, must have been a common sight within the environs of the settlement. The mortality data suggest that, as at Luni, their main importance was for cheese products, for the slaughter of lamb played only a small part in the management of the flocks. But the wool must also have been used extensively, since items of weaving equipment—loomweights, spindle whorls and bobbins—were a common find in the occupation deposits of almost every phase.

This picture of a rather isolated agricultural community, living close to the land, corresponds very much with one's impression of village life in this region within recent decades. Even today, the villages near to Narce, Mazzano Romano and Calcata, have an astonishingly high proportion of

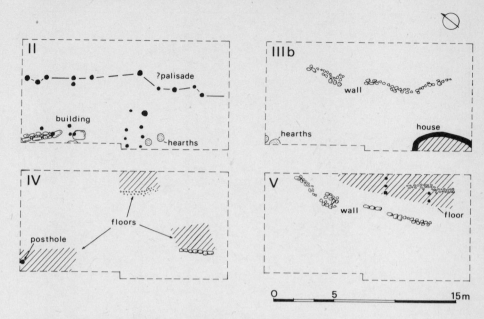

9 Plans showing successive phases of occupation by the River Treia at Narce. II: *c.* 1200 B.C.; IIIb: *c.* 1100 B.C.; IV: *c.* 1000 B.C.; V: 900 B.C.

inhabitants who have visited neither Rome nor the sea. The outside world has only recently begun to make any substantial impact upon contemporary life in the Narce area and much the same sort of isolation is indicated by the finds from the Bronze Age site: metal objects, for example, are extremely rare and imported pottery (possibly excepting the 60 sherds—a tiny proportion—of decorated Apennine 'tableware') more or less absent. Despite the mobile element imposed by the need for transhumance, the eastern part of south Etruria seems to have remained something of a backwater in the middle Apennine period.

The actual calendar dates for this phase in the history of the settlement cannot be established at all closely. There is a radiocarbon date of 1055 ± 100 b.c. (St. 2397) which can be calibrated to *c.* 1325 B.C., and a few bronzes of the same general period; but we cannot do more than suggest very tentatively a bracket of between *c.* 1400 and 1250 B.C. for the first two periods at Narce (although links in pottery styles between Luni and Narce would support this dating). There seems moreover to be a stratigraphic break between phases II and the next phase on the site, which probably falls between *c.* 1250 and 1150 B.C. (Potter, 1976a, 313–14). An insufficient area of the site survives to determine whether the gap reflects an abandonment of the settlement or (as seems more likely) the nucleus shifted to another spot; but there are significant changes both in the architecture of the houses and in the styles of some of the pottery. The houses of phase III consist of oval buildings (Fig. 9; Pl. IIa), with a width of 4 to 4.5 metres internally. They were built of dry-stone walling but, as in phase II, probably had a superstructure of wattle and daub, supported by wooden uprights. In the centre of the house was a large clay hearth.

These oval buildings can be paralleled at a number of other sites. At Luni a house of similar plan was built over the most southerly of the Apennine Bronze Age long houses (Ostenberg, 1967, 104–5) and there are identical buildings at San Giovenale (Boëthius and Ward Perkins, 1970, Fig. 8 and Plate 2). But the most striking analogies are with the ceramic models of huts that were widely used in south Etruria and northern Latium for the interment of the ashes of the dead in the late second and early first millennium B.C. (Gierow, 1966; Hencken, 1968, 462–4). These models show buildings with rounded corners, wide jutting roofs, a single door and, very often, details of a window. The Narce houses of phase III seem to provide a clear antecedent for this style of construction, both in terms of the plan and in the use of timber for the superstructure. Even though foreign parallels, from Crete for example (Müller-Karpe, 1959, 45–74), have been cited for these hut urns, it may well be that they are simply a translation into miniature versions in clay of house types current in Lazio during the late second millennium B.C.

Phase III at Narce is also marked by other changes. Whilst the valley-bottom settlement itself does not seem to have expanded—a roughly built perimeter wall made of lumps of volcanic tuff delimited the main area of occupation, much as the palisade did in period II—there is evidence in the form of plant remains for a much increased emphasis upon cereal cultivation. Seeds of emmer wheat and barley were especially abundant in the layers of refuse around the buildings and, if fortuitous preservation can be ruled out, suggest that a great deal more land was brought into arable use at this time. Stock management, on the other hand, followed lines that were identical to the previous phase, although, if the size of the sample is any guide, the actual number of animals was increased. We might conclude therefore that there was a sustained effort to raise the level of agricultural productivity from c. 1250 B.C. and it argues for a population that was beginning to expand. It is here that the evidence of surface work becomes particularly useful. Above the valley-bottom site is a hill surrounded on all sides by steep vertical cliffs; like Luni, it is a natural acropolis (Fig. 8, Pl. Ib). Examination of the surface yielded very large quantities of potsherds, mainly of Iron Age type but including some earlier material. There was one decorated handle of Apennine type (Potter, 1976a, Fig. 69, no. 62) and many more fragments datable to the later second millennium B.C. The hilltop seems therefore to have become an additional focus of occupation in the Late Bronze Age and it seems likely, on analogy with Luni, that this was the site of the main settlement. There was, moreover, some confirmation for this conclusion from the excavation in the valley. One trench was dug on the hill slopes immediately under the lowest cliff. In this layer were a few sherds of Middle Bronze Age pottery and a much larger quantity of late Apennine forms. These point very clearly to the presence of a substantial

10 Bronze Age sites in peninsular Italy.

community upon this well protected hill overlooking the valley of the River Treia.

Luni and Narce show, therefore, both a common cultural tradition and a choice of site where natural defences played an important part. The factors that compelled the occupation of such inconvenient citadels have still to become clear, but what is certain is that this was a widely established practice in Italy during the later second millennium B.C. (Fig. 10). In other parts of the Tolfa Hills, for example, sites with strong natural defences have been identified—at San Giovenale, Monte Rovello and Sant' Andrea—while to the south of Rome at least three Iron Age nucleated settlements appear to have originated in the Apennine period (Potter, 1976a, 315–17) and should probably be classified with the Etrurian sites. Further south, the phenomenon is still more marked, as Ruth Whitehouse (1973) has pointed out. A number of villages along the coast of Apulia appear to have been fortified with stone walls in the late second millennium and, if

the results of recent excavations upon the hilltop site of Gravina-in-Puglia
are at all typical, there was a move to settle naturally defended positions
in the interior of Apulia as well. The Bronze Age material from Gravina
(still unpublished) is all late Apennine in date and is sufficiently abundant
to imply the existence of a substantial village. Many of the coastal sites
appear, on the other hand, to have been of quite modest size. Porta Perone,
for example, which lies on a small peninsula jutting into the Gulf of
Taranto, was only about 50 metres across (Lo Porto, 1964) and the nearby
settlement of Torre Castelluccia was not a great deal larger (Drago, 1953).
The importance of these sites is nevertheless quite clear. Porta Perone was
enclosed within a very substantial stone wall, which was nearly four metres
thick and provided with bastions; there was also an external ditch. The
houses were comparatively simple, consisting of rings of timber uprights,
two or three metres across, and fronted by a concave façade; but the
occupation levels yielded large quantities of painted pottery of c. 1500–1100
B.C. imported from Mycenaean Greece. These finely decorated vessels
(Taylour, 1958; Biancofiore, 1967) indicate sustained maritime trade with
the Aegean and, to judge from the overall distribution of Mycenaean pottery
in Italy (Fig. 10), reflect a process from which many of the coastal sites of
Apulia and Sicily profited. There are also some sherds of Mycenaean
pottery from the islands of Ischia and Vivara in the Bay of Naples and, as
we have seen, five possible sherds from Luni-sul-Mignone. What is not
clear is the nature of the goods that the Italians were selling in return for
the Greek vases. Cereals, slaves and *Murex* shells for making a popular
purple dye have all been suggested, whilst the sherds from Luni (which,
whether Mycenaean or not, unquestionably indicate familiarity with Greek
styles of pottery manufacture) raise here the interesting possibility of
exploitation of the metal ores of Etruria. Further work may well show that
the Mycenaeans had a much closer interest in central Italy than the available
evidence allows. Meanwhile, it is worth recalling that the larger settlements
of Bronze Age Greece are characterized by the use of elaborate fortifications,
typified by Mycenae itself, and it may be that the defended Apennine sites
of southern Italy owed something to these Aegean architectural trends.
Equally, the acropolis sites of Luni and Narce, while a far cry from their
sophisticated contemporaries in the south, do seem to fall into a pattern
which extends far beyond the boundaries of Etruria.

   In the closing centuries of the second millennium B.C. Italy came within
the orbit of quite different but ultimately more pervasive cultural changes.
The most striking feature is the adoption of a new burial rite where the
dead were cremated and the ashes interred in a cinerary urn. But there was
also a wide diversification of bronze objects, including the development of
a long slashing sword and flanged axes with side wings, as well as numerous
smaller objects: amongst these are two-sided rectangular razor, brooches
shaped in the form of a violin bow, and various forms of decorated pins
(Bietti Sestieri, 1973). At the same time, a new range of pottery shapes
appears, most notably a bag-like biconical vase with a flared rim (often

used to contain cremations) decorated with a medley of incised motifs, geometrically arranged.

Many of the changes may well have originated north of the Alps, within a belt stretching eastwards from Germany into Austria, Hungary and beyond; here the adoption of Urnfield cremations can be traced back through much of the second millennium B.C., and there are analogies for many of the pottery shapes and decorative styles (Hencken, 1968, 440–6). Some of the Italian metalwork can also be paralleled in this central European region. Yet, we cannot be certain how to interpret the widespread adoption of Urnfield religions and artistic practices. Some scholars think that there must have been major folk movements in the later second millennium B.C. —perhaps resembling the Germanic migrations at the close of the Roman period in northern Europe; others would prefer to explain the Urnfield traits as the results of a gradual diffusion of ideas, probably influenced by the travels of mobile craftsmen. The short answer is that archaeological evidence for population movement is often a poor substitute for proper historical documentation; yet the Italian evidence does have a certain consistency. In the north of Italy, Urnfield cemeteries first appear towards about 1400 B.C. and rapidly become established as the principal ritual for the burying of the dead (Barfield, 1971, 81–103). Some appear to be associated with a series of small defended settlements, the *terremare*, which cluster on low-lying ground along the eastern margins of the Apennines between Piacenza and Parma. Others are concentrated in the southern lea of the Alps in an area which seems to have supported an inventive metalwork industry, typified by the finds from Peschiera (Bietti-Sestieri, 1973), on Lake Garda. Further south, urnfields used in the late second millennium extend as far as Torre Castelluccia near Taranto and on the north and east coasts of Sicily. Some of these cemeteries appear to be in use by 1200 B.C. but the majority of the burials are likely to date to the eleventh and tenth centuries, with an overall tendency to become more frequent during that time. In other words, a diffusion model best explains the evidence as we know it at present, although we should not rule out the possibility of some settlement from either the north of Italy or further afield.

In Etruria, the earliest known urnfields cluster in a remarkable concentration upon the hills of the Tolfa-Allumiere district. There are at least 14 of these cemeteries and some, like Poggio La Pozza (Peroni, 1960), may have been of considerable size, since for this site alone we have notes on over 40 burials. The majority of the interments were placed in pits (*pozzi*) cut into the volcanic rock. The ashes were contained in a biconical or globular urn, around which were placed other funerary vessels. Metalwork, especially brooches, was sometimes buried in the grave and, in a few instances, the tomb group was interred within a circular coffin (*custodia*), made of stone. What is much less certain is the date of these cemeteries. Metalwork characteristic of *c.* 1200 B.C., like violin-bow brooches, is lacking and there are no datable imported objects, such as Mycenaean vessels: they look, therefore, to be later than the twelfth century B.C., and some scholars have argued for an eleventh-century span for many of the interments (Hencken, 1968, 468–9; Peroni, 1960). But many of the burials closely parallel the funerary rites employed in the ninth to eighth centuries by the Villanovans of Etruria (see pp. 52–3) and it is considered that some of the urns have been turned on the wheel (Ostenberg, 1967, 45–9), a technique that does not appear in central Italy until the eighth century B.C. It looks then as if some of these burials—often described as 'Proto-Villanovan'—are in fact contemporary with the Villanovan culture and represent a survival of an archaic cultural tradition. What then is the date of the earliest Urnfield interments in the Tolfa Hills? Our best evidence derives from Luni-sul-Mignone, where the Swedish excavations disclosed the remains of buildings associated with large quantities of 'Proto-Villanovan' pottery (Wieselgren, 1969; Hellstrom 1975). There are two radiocarbon dates for this period: 835 ± 70 b.c. (St. 1346) and 915 ± 80 b.c. (St. 1340). The corrected values for these dates would be c. 1035 and 1135 B.C. which suggests that the burials in the Tolfa area may span a period of three centuries or more, beginning in the eleventh century B.C.

Further east, within the area of the South Etruria Survey, we so far lack any 'Proto-Villanovan' cemeteries. But there is now some important new evidence for this period from the recent excavations at Narce where, as we have seen, there was a large Apennine settlement. The river-side settlement on the valley floor yielded prolific amounts of 'Proto-Villanovan' pottery, with a range of forms that can be closely paralleled in the Urnfield cemeteries. Two of the commonest shapes were biconical jars and wide bowls with an everted rim and a sharp shoulder. Many of these were elaborately decorated, preference being given to zigzag designs, drawn in a wide variety of ways. Later there was further diversification of the ornament with the introduction of different sorts of stamp, including concentric circles, shields and cord-impressed designs: everything attests to a lively and accomplished local pottery industry.

The importance of the Narce site in this context is the association of these wares with a deep stratigraphy: their evolution can be measured quite closely. The first examples of 'Proto-Villanovan' types occur in very small quantities in deposits of phase III, a period that probably falls during the twelfth and eleventh centuries B.C. By phase IV, datable to the eleventh to tenth centuries, Apennine decorated wares had largely disappeared and 'Proto-Villanovan' styles had taken over completely (although Apennine coarse-ware forms continued to be used). Moreover, just as at Luni, these increasingly archaic designs continued to provide the main decorative inspiration down into the first millennium and probably as late as about 750 to 700 B.C. There seems to have been therefore a process of assimilation whereby Urnfield styles of pottery were gradually adopted by the Apennine people of Narce until the indigenous and intrusive traditions were more or less completely blended. Much the same is true of the metalwork. Unlike the Tolfa area, there are Peschiera, Terramara and early 'Proto-Villanovan' bronze objects from the excavations at Narce, including fragments of violin-

bow brooches, winged axes and decorated pins. Their presence in a later
Apennine context demonstrates the spread of north Italian technology in
much the same way as does the pottery. After the eleventh century B.C. the
metalwork finds tend to be much more local types, dominated by simple
domestic objects like needles and awls, which are likely to have been made
in the vicinity of the site.

The evidence of the artifacts is therefore clear and consistent: it suggests
close contact between the late Apennine settlements of south Etruria and
the Urnfield world of north Italy, resulting in a gradual adoption of 'Proto-
Villanovan' styles by the populations at sites like Luni and Narce. This
was apparently accompanied by a decisive swing towards the custom of
burial by cremation. We cannot on the other hand point to any conclusive
body of evidence for new settlement by people from outside Etruria. There
was little or no attempt to colonize virgin areas nor any obvious hiatus in
the stratigraphies of Narce or Luni. Whilst it is unsatisfactory to talk of
'influences', this would seem the most appropriate way to describe the effect
of the Urnfield world upon south Etruria in the late second millennium B.C.
The contrast between this and a period of major population expansion will
become readily apparent when we consider the events of the ninth and
eighth centuries in the next chapter.

It will be helpful at this stage, however, to draw together the main
threads that we have traced in Bronze Age south Etruria during the second
millennium B.C. Even allowing for all the deficiencies of field survey and the
still modest volume of excavation, the impression remains of a sparsely
populated landscape, where woodland and forest covered much of the
countryside. The few available pollen cores register little or no interference
by man and most of the known sites cluster in the vicinity of a few major
river valleys: in all probability they mark the line of the main cross-country
routes. The sites themselves tend to be small and can be best explained as
temporary camps, set up by shepherds travelling between winter and
summer pastures. A great many summer camps have now been identified,
situated high in the mountainous areas of central Italy, and the finds from
them, especially the animal bones, leave no doubt that these were occupied
by shepherds. On modern analogy we can expect them to have been occupied
between June and September, followed by a return to lower ground with
the onset of autumnal conditions.

Some of the permanent lowland bases have also now been identified and,
at Luni and Narce, treated to detailed excavation. Arable farming appears
to have played an important part in the economy of these settlements, with
pork and dairy products as the other main sources of protein. The size of
these communities remains open to question but the location of the main
nucleus shows a clear preference for strong natural defences, particularly
in the mid to late Apennine period. This is a trend that is repeated on a
much more elaborate scale in other regions of Italy, especially the south:
here the visits of Mycenaean traders may have influenced the construction
of sophisticated stone defences. At the same time, Urnfield influences began

to permeate the northern areas of the country and slowly spread southwards. In south Etruria, the last two centuries of the second millennium saw the adoption of burial by cremation, and the acquisition both of 'Proto-Villanovan' metalwork and pottery. Gradually, a blend was effected between these two diverse cultural traditions although, on present evidence, we cannot detect any appreciably new element in the indigenous population before the first millennium B.C.

4
The population explosion: south Etruria in the first millennium B.C.

The first millennium B.C. takes us for the first time into a period in which the archaeological evidence becomes relatively abundant and we can match it against a substantial body of written material. Initially, the picture is blurred, although it is clear that in the ninth century there was a massive expansion of both nucleated and open sites. But later the focus sharpens, with the foundation of the Greek colonies in the south of Italy from *c.* 775 B.C., the emergence of the powerful Etruscan federation in the seventh century and, from the fifth century, the gradual ascendency of Rome. By the end of the millennium, all Italy had been Roman for two centuries or more, and modes of life that had become traditional were more or less completely swept away with the transition from a small republic to a vast empire. This therefore was a period of utmost historical significance in which south Etruria played a considerable rôle, and for this reason alone the archaeology of the region assumes a special fascination. At the same time these clearly marked historical phases furnish a well defined framework for the archaeological data so that we can, at any rate in theory, measure historical change against the material evidence—a theme that will underlie this and subsequent chapters of the book.

The landscape of the early first millennium

Of the one hundred or so urnfields known from Italy, the great majority belong to the cultural group that takes its name from the Villanova cemetery near Bologna. This was the first Italian urnfield to receive archaeological attention, the earliest excavations taking place in 1856. The most distinctive find was the ossuary itself. This normally took the form of a biconical urn where the neck and body were sharply differentiated as though the vessel had been made in two separate sections (Pl. IIb). The neck and shoulder were usually decorated with geometric designs, made up with bands of parallel lines: popular motifs included meanders, rectangles and swastikas. The shoulder was commonly provided, too, with a pair of horizontal handles, one of which had often been broken off at the time of burial.

These 'Villanovan' urns were to become a frequent discovery as exploration was extended to the necropoli of well known Etruscan cities like Vulci and Tarquinia. But the associated grave-goods soon made it apparent that these cemeteries were a great deal older than the elaborate tombs of the Etruscan period, and eventually it became evident that they represented the burials of the founders of these settlements. The earliest graves consisted of circular shafts, cut deeply into the rock. The urn was usually inserted into a small pit at the base of the tomb and was accompanied by a number of accessory vessels, together with some objects of bronze. Later, many sites witnessed a gradual swing towards burial by extended inhumation, where the body was laid out in a rectangular rock-cut trench. Grave-goods were placed either beside the corpse or within a small cavity or *loculus*, cut into the side of the trench. They included a much increased number of metal objects (amongst them some intricate jewellery, often made in precious materials) and some tombs yielded painted vessels, imitating Greek geometric wares of the eighth century. Here, therefore, was a crucial fixed point, suggesting a span of *c*. 800–700 B.C. for the trench-grave inhumation and, by implication, a ninth-century *floruit* for the shaft-tombs.

The relationship between the graves of the Villanovan and Etruscan periods continued to remain enigmatic but the researches of the nineteenth century left no doubt that all the major Etruscan cities possessed Villanovan antecedents. The principal divergence was in terms of overall distribution since the Villanovan urnfields were spread far more widely than the urnfields of Etruria. One substantial group clustered along the edges of the Po Plain, immediately beyond the foothills of the Apennines, and other typical cemeteries have come to light in recent years both at Fermo, near the Adriatic coast in Marche, and at a number of sites in Campania (Hencken, 1968, 472). Thus the dense group of Villanovan sites in southern and central Etruria has to be seen in the context of a much wider penetration of the Italian peninsula by this Urnfield group and it could well be that their main areas of activity will turn out to be even more extensive than the present evidence allows. Nevertheless we ought to note the presence of a number of other well defined groups of the early first millennium, such as the Latium culture (where cremations were often placed in model houses) or a series of groups, for example in Umbria and large parts of Campania, whose preference had always been for burial by inhumation. These divergent trends argue for a complex overlay of populations which absorbed the cultural developments of the period at many different levels. South Etruria, as we shall see, reflects this situation in microcosm, which makes it a particularly valuable area in which to study the first millennium landscape.

In cultural terms, we seem to be dealing with three main groups. The most archaic tradition is represented by sites like Narce and Luni, where, as we have seen, Apennine Bronze Age settlements gradually acquired 'Proto-Villanovan' characteristics, most notably the burial rite of cremation and various artifact types. The evidence of recent excavation suggests that this metamorphosis took place over the last two centuries of the second millennium but apparently did not involve any significantly new element in the population (Potter, 1976a). The subsequent development at each site runs remarkably parallel. The pottery, for example, continues to model itself upon 'Proto-Villanovan' forms right down into the eighth century and

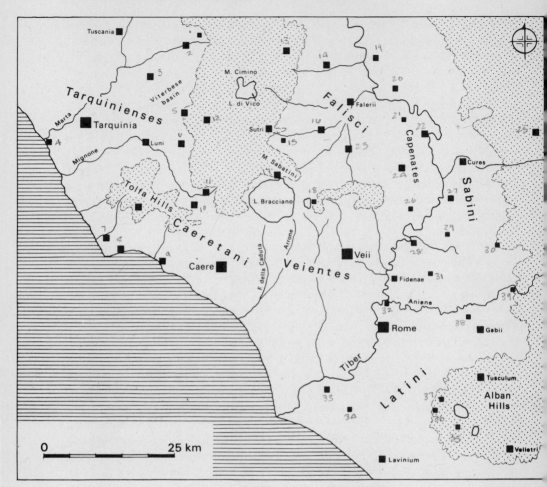

11 The principal Iron Age sites and tribes in western central Italy.

perhaps later, arguing very clearly for population continuity. Only the occasional Villanovan import (Wieselgren, 1969, 38; Potter, 1976a, 314) and a certain number of metalwork types hint at external contact; otherwise these regions seem to preserve a strong cultural independence. These cultural distinctions came eventually to be expressed in terms of local tribes. Narce, for example, lies centrally within the region of the Faliscan group whose territory (to judge from the distribution of Faliscan inscriptions) extended over the greater part of the Treia drainage basin (Fig. 11). It was an area clearly demarcated by its natural boundaries—the prominent volcanic ridges of the Monti Cimini and Sabatini—and it came during the first millennium to support a number of nucleated settlements and a substantial rural population. If the evidence from Narce is at all representative then we can conclude that the Faliscans owed their origins to the Apennine Bronze Age settlements of the second millennium, a genesis that sets them apart from all the other tribal groups of Etruria. This goes a long way towards explaining why the historian Strabo (v.2.9) refers to the Faliscans as a 'special and distinct tribe' who 'spoke a language all of their own'. The Faliscans had their roots deep in prehistory and preserved their independence partly because of the peculiar topography that delineated their territory. Luni and the other sites in the Tolfa Hills were on the other hand rather less favoured. No tribal name is preserved for the region and it seems likely that it came within the orbit of Cerveteri at an early phase of Etruscan history. There was in fact a clear hiatus between the 'Proto-Villanovan'' and Etruscan levels at both Luni and San Giovenale suggesting that these sites were annexed militarily, and it is a plausible guess that the region was taken over for its metal ores. Many of the sites remained in occupation but the inhabitants were now unmistakably Etruscan, as their inscriptions and artifacts clearly attest.

These areas of 'Proto-Villanovan' survival are quite sharply differentiated from the regions occupied by the second main cultural group, the Villan-ovans. The two groups unquestionably share a family relationship, as the similarity in burial rite and grave furniture make clear: but few would disagree that the variations are sufficiently numerous to suggest a related but divergent cultural tradition. Not surprisingly some 'Proto-Villanovan' artifacts do occur on Villanovan sites; for example, there is a grave-group from Veii (Vianello Córdova, 1968), while at Sasso di Furbara, on the southern fringes of the Tolfa Hills, 'Proto-Villanovan' and Villanovan tombs are found within the same cemetery (Brusadin Laplace, 1964). But explicit examples of overlap are on the whole comparatively rare, indicating very clearly defined boundaries between these groups. There seem in fact to be three main Villanovan territories within the most southerly part of Etruria (Fig. 11). Immediately to the south of the Faliscan tribe lay the region controlled by Veii, a major nucleated settlement that was positioned equidistantly between the Monti Sabatini and the River Tiber. These prominent topographical features provided clear-cut natural boundaries to the north and east; but the extent of the territory under the surveillance of Veii to the south and west is much less apparent. Most probably the limits fell somewhere in the tangled ridges to the south of Lake Bracciano, where the Fosso Arrone and Fosso della Caduta provide the main drainage outlets. But the division between the territory of the Veientes and their Villanovan neighbours to the west, the Caeretani, is likely always to have been blurred. The Caeretani themselves built their main settlement, Caere (Cerveteri), on slightly elevated ground at the junction between the coastal flats and the volcanic mantle of the Bracciano system. The Tolfa Hills provide a backdrop to the settlement and underline how easily the Caeretani could exploit the mineral wealth of that area. It was in fact an ideally selected position with on the one side the fertile Maremma and a long seaboard, and on the other the rich agricultural land of the Campagna. Not surprisingly Caere was to achieve prosperity ahead of almost all of the other Etruscan cities. Its neighbour to the north was Tarquinia, which occupied a rectangular territory stretching far into the flat Viterbese and flanked by two major river systems, the Marta and the Mignone. As at Caere the site was located at the interface between the volcanic bedrock and the coastal alluvium, where maximum advantage could be made of the dual environments. The paintings of the Maremma in sixth-century burial chambers like the Tomb of Hunting and Fishing leave no doubt of the abundance of fish and game along the coastal plain, just as the acres of cornland on the ridges behind present-day Tarquinia demonstrate the agricultural wealth of this part of its territory. These were environments with much to offer the primitive farmer, and when the time came to develop a share in the world of Mediterranean commerce, both Caere and Tarquinia were to find even greater advantage in their position.

The creation of the territories of Veii, Caere and Tarquinia introduced a quite novel factor into the distribution of settlement in south Etruria. All of these sites appear to represent new foundations, and, with the exception of Veii, largely ignore the foci of Apennine Bronze Age and 'Proto-Villanovan' sites. We earlier laid stress on the divergent cultural traditions and this finds confirmation in the distribution of the Villanovan sites: they seem to reflect a process of colonization where there was a substantial influx of settlers who brought into occupation large areas of new land.

These clearly defined Villanovan territories were bordered to the south by a third group which maintained a cultural homogeneity quite as pronounced as that of its neighbours. It is known as the Latian culture (Colonna, 1974) and corresponds directly with the Latin-speaking peoples whom Rome came to weld into a powerful military and political force. Latium has none of the cohesive geography of south Etruria. It consists essentially of a long volcanic ridge running parallel with the Tyrrhenian Sea and the Apennine Mountains, and flanked by a wide coastal plain to the west and a major river valley, the Sacco-Liri system, to the east. All these topographical features converge upon the Tiber Valley, making the site of Rome the natural focus of the region. The known settlements of Latium are evenly distributed through this area, exploiting both the volcanic uplands of areas like the Alban Hills and the lower ground nearer the coast. Sites like Lavinium and Ardea are in fact placed at the same interface between the alluvium and the volcanics as Cerveteri and Tarquinia. But, with the exception of Rome, the territories of these Latin towns seem never to have become as extensive as those of their Villanovan neighbours, the pattern remaining that of small town units linked within a broader tribal framework. As we shall see, this is precisely the pattern that emerged within the Faliscan region and is in fact just one of a number of close similarities between these two areas. Linguistically, for example, Faliscan and Latin share both an Indo-European origin and many other traits in common (Giacomelli, 1963). Culturally, too, there are a good many analogies, amongst them an early preference for the rite of cremation, and certain similarities in favoured styles of pottery. At Narce, for example, there are a number of reticulate vessels that closely recall one of the most prevalent of Latian styles. But the most telling link is undoubtedly provided by the demonstration in recent years that some of the Latian sites share with Narce and Luni an origin in the Apennine Bronze Age. Ardea, Satricum and Lavinium all fall within this category and we may suspect that some of the other settlements will eventually yield similar evidence. The implication is that the Latian Iron Age owes its main genesis to the Bronze Age population of the area, even though artifact styles underwent fairly drastic modification during the late second millennium B.C., and mainly on a very regional basis.

Rome itself provides an additional example. It is not always realized that the original topography of the central area covered by the city consisted of a highly dissected landscape, divided by stream valleys. The Capitoline Hill and possibly the Aventine were entirely isolated by low-lying ground, while the Quirinal, Viminal, Esquiline and Palatine Hills were part of a series of long and uneven ridges, extending rather like the fingers of a hand towards the Tiber. Even though the relief has been smoothed out by many centuries of building, drainage and infilling, the original landscape cannot have looked so very different from the present-day topography of areas like Narce. In other words, Rome was a site with the same defensive potential as other acropolis settlements in the volcanic region. Inevitably, our picture of the earliest phases of the city is limited to the results of small-scale trenching beneath monuments of the Roman age—even Boni's excavation in 1902 of 41 cremation and inhumation graves in the Roman Forum only examined an area of c. 10 × 10 metres—and there are manifest dangers in assuming that one sample is representative. Moreover, we cannot yet claim to be able to date either the burials or the remains of the earlier domestic sites with any sort of precision, despite the variety of chronological schemes that have been advanced in recent years, recently summarized by Colonna (1974). We do know, however, that there were houses at the west end of the Palatine ridge, where excavations in 1949 by Puglisi (1951) disclosed the remains of several buildings with sockets for timber uprights, while other structural traces were found by Boni a short distance to the south-east. They presumably belong to a fairly extensive promontory settlement (sometimes interpreted as having several separate nuclei) which, to judge from the associated finds, was occupied from early in the first millennium B.C. Burials of the same general period have been discovered beneath the Roman Forum, which was laid out across the narrow valley dividing the Palatine and Capitoline Hills. Other graves have been identified some distance to the north-east, distributed along the crest and slopes of the Esquiline ridge. They imply a separate settlement nucleus, cut off from the Palatine village by another small stream valley. Differences in the burial rite between the two cemeteries, combined with recurrent references by the Roman historians to a Sabine element in the population of early Rome, have inclined a number of scholars to interpret these different settlements as representative of diverse ethnic groups. In fact, as we shall see, it was not uncommon for the major sites of Etruria to possess several nuclei—both

Veii and Narce provide ready examples—and it is much more probable that the occupation of several hills in Rome reflects nothing more than the expansion of a fast-growing population. But we cannot as yet pinpoint the position of the original nucleus. The only indications come from excavations beside the church of S. Omobono, which is situated on low-lying ground near to the Tiber Island. In Classical times much of this river front was taken up with the quays of the Forum Boarium, Rome's cattle market, but the excavation by the church disclosed the remains of two early temples, apparently dedicated by Servius Tullius and rebuilt in 212 B.C. The reconstruction of these temples had been preceded by a drastic levelling of the ground, for which large amounts of soil were brought in from elsewhere. The layers of make-up yielded a significant volume of sherds, amongst them characteristic pieces of the middle and late Apennine Bronze Age. Wherever the sherds came from—and the Capitoline, Palatine and Aventine Hills are all possible sources—they nevertheless imply that Rome, in common with several other Latian sites, had its origins in the second millennium B.C. Indeed, it would be entirely consistent with what we know from other nearby settlements to envisage a community upon one of the hilltops commanding the valley of the Tiber: but the scale of rebuilding in this central part of Rome has been so massive and continuous that it is most unlikely that we shall ever know for certain.

The burden, therefore, of what we have said so far is that we can distinguish two related tribal entities with origins in the Apennine Bronze Age, in the Faliscans and Latini, and three new tribal groups, the Veientes, Caeretani and Tarquinienses, who on present evidence come into being at the beginning of the first millennium B.C. Given the diversity of artifact styles between the Villanovan tribes and their indigenous neighbours, it is tempting to see the Villanovans as arrivals from outside the region (e.g. Hencken, 1968, 631–46). Indeed, there is a body of written evidence (although largely a compilation of legends) that can be interpreted to show folk movement into western Italy from the east Mediterranean within this general time period (e.g. Heurgon, 1973, 233–9). Yet this explanation does seem to oversimplify a much more complex problem. It does not account for the family relationship of 'Proto-Villanovan' and Villanovan urns nor does it identify a homeland for these settlers: unlike, for example, the Saxon settlers of late Roman and early medieval England, whose origin in the Elbe-Weser region of north Germany can be demonstrated archaeologically, it appears that Villanovan 'culture' evolved on Italian soil. This does not exclude a foreign element in the population (many nations have been built up through a process of immigration that leaves little trace in terms of artifacts) but it does suggest that we should look at the internal situation rather more closely.

The South Etruria Survey provides just such an opportunity. We cannot claim that our data for the early first millennium (period II of the scheme outlined in Chapter 1) are full, nor can we attach very precise dates to the sites: but at least there is sufficient evidence to pick out some of the factors

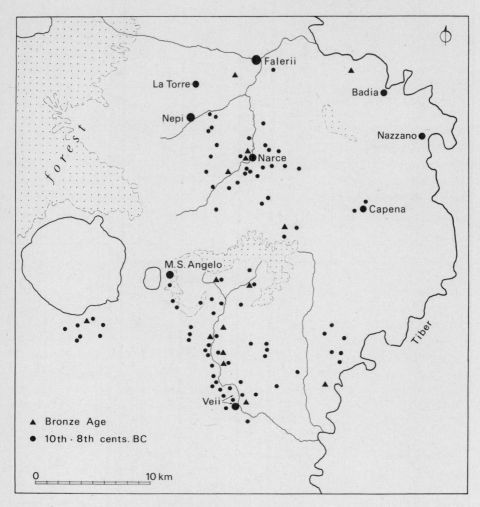

12 South Etruria Survey: sites of c. 1500–700 B.C.

at work in the formation of this landscape. Certainly, the most obvious and striking feature is a metamorphosis in the scale and density of settlement (Fig. 12). The number of nucleated sites, for example, rises from the one or two occupied in the Bronze Age to nine or more which had grown up by c. 750 B.C. There is also a concomitant increase in rural settlement with more than 70 sites coming into being during the same period. Everything points therefore to a dramatic rise in the population throughout the greater part of the survey region.

The consequences of such population growth upon food supplies can only have been very considerable and it is therefore interesting to see that the archaeological evidence illustrates efforts to raise production in two ways. First, we can see from the distribution maps how the major settlements

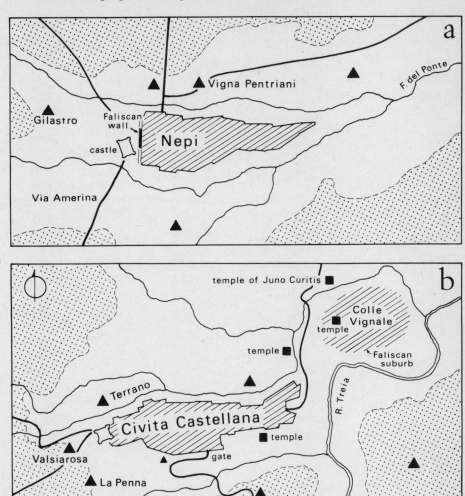

13 Comparative plans of (a) Nepi and (b) Falerii Veteres (Civita Castellana).

created a number of farms within their environs so as to extend the area under cultivation. At Veii, for example, a dozen or so sites were established on the ridges and plateaux that fell within a five-kilometre radius of the settlement. Beyond this point (and in accordance with Chisholm's model for site exploitation areas) the number of find-spots drops sharply until we reach the *territorium* of the next major settlement on Monte S. Angelo. This interdependence between what were presumably rural farms and the 'urban' centre is a novel feature in south Etruria: in the Bronze Age, for example, we saw how sites tended to congregate along the natural com-

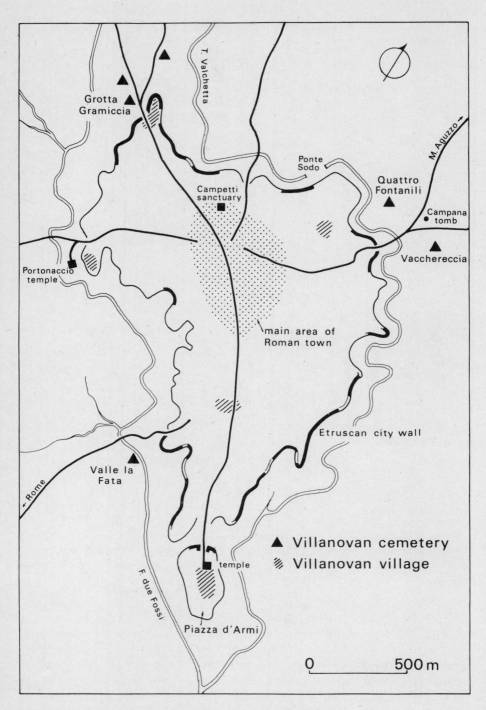

14 The Etruscan and Roman town of Veii. (Source: Ward Perkins, 1961)

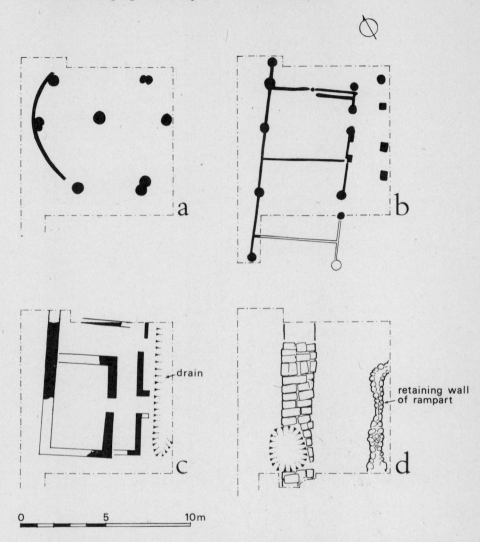

15 Plan of successive structures by the north-west gate of Veii. (a) Round timber house, ninth to seventh centuries B.C. (b) Timber house, sixth century B.C. (c) Stone house, sixth to fifth centuries B.C. (d) The Etruscan city wall, fifth century B.C. (Source: Ward Perkins, 1959a)

munication routes; now they were much more directly connected with the nucleated settlement. Secondly, some useful botanical evidence comes from the excavations beside the River Treia at Narce where, in the ninth-century levels, the quantity of cereals showed a sharp rise. At the same time, as Jarman (1976) has demonstrated, there was an equivalent increase in the sample of noxious weeds of cultivation; her conclusions—that the period of fallow was being much reduced—is, if right, a further illustration of the pressure upon the land nearest the nucleated settlements. The available resources were simply insufficient to support an increased population and the eventual outcome was an extension by means of rural sites of the land under cultivation around the main nucleus.

Most of the settlements themselves still await the extensive excavation that is needed to disclose the plans of individual buildings and their overall layout. Yet certain common factors appear. Most conspicuous is the choice of situation: just like the founders of Narce and Luni, the builders of these later settlements invariably selected positions of great natural strength. These varied from small pedestals of rock like La Torre dell'Isola, or a hilltop situation such as Monte S. Angelo (which forms part of the western rim of the Baccano crater), to the occupation of a whole plateau, as at Veii; but, whatever the size of the site, it is the defensive potential that unites this group of settlements. The point is made most impressively by the sites of Nepi or Civita Castellana (ancient Falerii). Both occupy the eastern tip of long promontories flanked by very deep gorges with sheer cliffs (Fig. 13). Easy access is thus restricted to a route along the ridge from the west and, equally, can be denied by the simplest defences stretched across the plateau. As Livy recalls in his story of the siege of Falerii in 394 B.C. (5.26.5), even the great Roman general Camillus encountered the utmost difficulty in conquering so impregnable a position, being forced to camp outside the town for a long period until the treachery of a Faliscan schoolmaster paved the way for victory. Yet the area available for settlement on these plateaux was considerable: the promontory at Falerii, for example, was nearly 400 metres in width and nearly a kilometre in length.

Thus the impression from many of these sites is that of a substantial community. At Narce, for instance, the evidence of surface finds indicates that there were nuclei both upon the summit of Narce itself (the isolated hill in the Treia gorge) and on the promontory of Monte li Santi, immediately to the south (Fig. 8). Veii, on the other hand, reminds us that by no means all the area available for settlement was in fact occupied. This is the conclusion from systematic survey of the 2000 hectares enclosed within the Etruscan walls (Ward Perkins, 1961, 20–5). This survey disclosed that the Villanovan buildings clustered in five discrete nuclei around the periphery of the plateau (Fig. 14). The largest group, excavated by Stefani (1944), lay on the Piazza d'Armi, the natural *arx* at the southern end of Veii; here traces were found of a number of irregular depressions, representing the sunken floors of small houses, sealed by layers of domestic refuse with numerous Villanovan sherds. Other buildings were examined by Stefani (1953) on the slopes of the plateau above the Portonaccio temple and included a large oval structure, nearly ten metres in length and six metres wide. More recent excavations investigated the area on either side of the Etruscan north-west gate (Ward Perkins, 1959a; Murray-Threipland, 1963), and a sequence of buildings that terminated with the construction of the fifth-century rampart was identified (Fig. 15). The earliest structure consisted of a circular house, built partially with a continuous wall trench and partially with post-holes. The building was *c*. four metres wide and

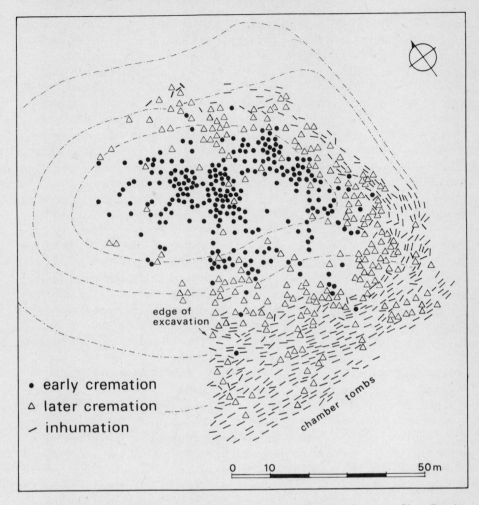

16 Plan of the Villanovan cemetery at Quattro Fontanili, Veii. (Sources: Close-Brooks, 1965; QF, 1963–72)

was associated with a scatter of pottery that should date to the ninth and eighth centuries. It was eventually replaced by a large rectangular house, again constructed of timber. This measured *c.* 11.50 × 4.50 metres and was fronted by a portico held up by solid wooden uprights (Pl. IIIa). Cross-walls divided the building into three rooms, recalling the seventh-century tripartite houses at Aquarossa near Viterbo (Ostenberg, 1975), and access was provided at two points. Later, some of the timbers were replaced and the two entrances converted into a single doorway, to be followed in a subsequent phase by a complete reconstruction of the building in stone.

These excavations, together with the sherd scatters that mark the sites of the other two nuclei, provide a tantalizing glimpse of the layout of Villanovan Veii, with most of the interior given over to agriculture, farmed

Va *Above* Etruscan road-cutting on Monte Aguzzo, to the north of Veii. (Photo: *BSR*)

Vb *Right* Part of the Etruscan name *Larth Vel Arnies* to be found on the side of the road-cutting leading west from Corchiano. (Photo: *BSR*)

VIa *Above* The Porta
Vecchia at Sutri. The
gate has at least four
phases of construction,
the oldest of which may
well date to the late
Etruscan period.

VIb *Left* Early Roman
bridge carrying the Via
Amerina over the Fosso
Tre Ponti. (Photo: *BSR*)

VIIa *Above* The Via Amerina to the south of Nepi. (Photo: *BSR*)

VIIb *Right* Excavation of a villa and mausoleum, sealed by late Roman and medieval silts, in the Fosso della Crescenza. (Photo: *BSR*)

VIIIa *Above* A Roman
paved road, preceded by
a track with numerous
ruts, at Vallelunga.

VIIIb *Left* The keystone
of a Roman bridge near
Formello, built *in privato*
by T. Humanius Stabilio.
(Photo: *BSR*)

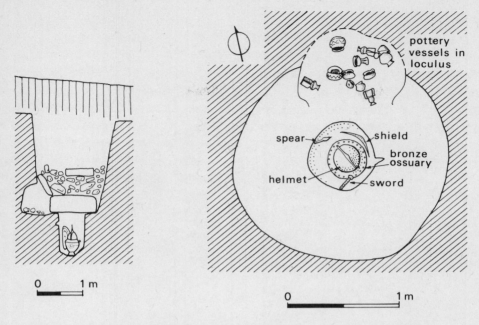

17 Section and plan of tomb AA1 at Quattro Fontanili, Veii. (Source: QF, 1970)

from small villages distributed around the perimeter of the plateau. This is not the pattern of settlement of other Villanovan sites: at Tarquinia, for example, Villanovan sherds are spread over most of the acropolis (Hencken, 1968, 7). But it does suggest a situation where a small community on the Piazza d'Armi gradually expanded from their original nucleus.

What is intriguing about the sites at Veii is that each village had its own cemetery, situated in every case upon the far side of the river valleys demarcating the plateau. Many of these cemeteries have been subject to extensive excavation but the most complete picture has been built up from a long-term study in recent years of the Quattro Fontanili necropolis, on the north-east side of Veii (QF, 1963, 1965, 1967, 1970, 1972, 1975). The site lies on a small knoll at the east end of a long ridge which flanks the valley of the River Valchetta (Fig. 14). The knoll itself is not large—its width is barely more than 100 metres—but is densely packed with burials, many of which are cut into earlier graves (Fig. 16). So far, details have been published for 597 tombs, of which 184 consist of cremations and the remainder of inhumations placed in trench-graves. Indeed, if this density of burials were to be maintained over the whole cemetery than the total number would exceed 2000. Many of the graves contained an enormous wealth of objects, of which tomb AA1 (QF, 1970, 296–308) will provide us with an example. This was a circular pit-grave, dug over three metres into the bedrock (Fig. 17). The cremated remains of the body had been interred in an elaborately decorated bronze ossuary, set into a small hole

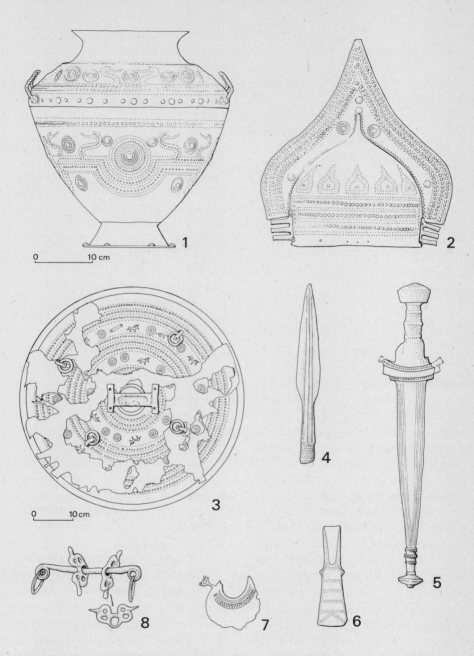

18 Some of the objects from tomb AA1 at Quattro Fontanili, Veii. They are likely to date
to between *c.* 760 and 730 B.C. (1) Bronze ossuary; (2) Bronze helmet; (3) Bronze shield
with an iron rim; (4) Bronze spearhead; (5) Iron sword with an ivory and bone hilt and a
bronze scabbard; (6) Bronze axe decorated with metal strips; (7) Bronze razor; (8) Bronze
and iron horse bit. All but no. 1 are drawn at the same scale. (Source: QF, 1970, 296–308)

at the base of the tomb (Fig. 18, 1). Covering the ossuary was a magnificent bronze helmet and other objects (including a shield) and the pit was sealed by a round lid carved of tuff. Other grave-goods were placed beside this lid and also in a specially cut cavity, set into the wall of the tomb. Altogether, there were 59 objects accompanying the burial. Sixteen of these were pottery vases while the remainder divided mainly into military equipment—the helmet, shield, two spearheads, a short sword, an axe and two horse bits—and various personal possessions and jewellery—a razor, several bracelets, rings, six brooches, earrings in the form of spirals, glass beads and an Egyptian-type scarab in greenish faience. The range and quality of these grave-goods leave no doubt of the affluence of a community that could afford to bury their dead in this extravagant manner, although the use of a bronze ossuary and helmet, rather than the much more commonly employed versions in clay, mark this tomb out as that of a high-ranking personage. Yet it is surprising to see just how numerous such wealthy tombs are in the Quattro Fontanili cemetery: imported materials such as gold, silver, lead and amber are by no means uncommon and the quality of the metalwork is especially high. We would dearly like to know how representative such cemeteries are of the total population, for they imply a society with a level of economic success considerably beyond that of the simple agricultural people indicated by their domestic remains.

The importance of Quattro Fontanili is not restricted to its individual burials, however. Far more valuable from an archaeological standpoint is the fact that we can trace the development of the cemetery by means of a horizontal stratigraphy. This is the outcome of a burial policy where the earliest graves (all of them cremations) were set into the crest of a knoll while subsequent interments (mainly inhumations) gradually extended down the hill slopes (Fig. 16). Thus, with a few exceptions, the latest tombs are found only along the furthest periphery of the cemetery. This concentric arrangement of burials, where the chronological position of one grave vis-à-vis another is normally quite clear, has enabled a detailed reconstruction of the history both of the burial rite and the individual artifacts (Close-Brooks, 1965). Thus, we can follow the gradual swing from cremation to inhumation and, at the same time, plot the changing fashions in the grave furniture. The results are best set out in the form of a diagram that shows the occurrence of individual types—for example, a particular vase shape—in successive tombs (Fig. 19). The first impression is one of continuity: inhumation appears to supplant the rite of cremation in a very gradual way, just as new types of artifacts achieve popularity at an equally slow pace. There are, on the other hand, diagrammatic suggestions of minor watersheds (perhaps indicating no more than the creation of new workshops) which furnish something of a framework for classification. Close-Brooks (1965) has termed them Veii I, IIa, IIb and III, following Pallottino's, (1939) more generalized scheme for Etruria as a whole. In the earliest phase, most of the burials consist of richly ornamented Villanovan ossuaries, covered with simple lids and accompanied by a few functional objects of

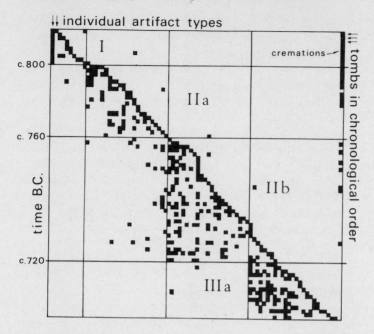

19 Diagram listing the occurrences of individual artifact types in the tombs at Quattro Fontanili, Veii. They cluster into four main periods. (Source: Close-Brooks, 1965, 1968)

bronze. These graves cluster on the summit of the hill and are likely to represent the burials of the first settlers of this part of Veii. In the next phase, IIa, cremation begins gradually to be superseded by trench-graves containing inhumations. At the same time, the range of objects increases significantly, with the appearance of elegant decorated bronze belts, bronze helmets, a variety of new forms of fibulae and elaborate horse bits. There is also some use of iron, especially for brooches and knives, and a diversification in the shapes of the funerary vessels. But the most informative discovery in the IIa graves has been the recovery of a number of twin-handled *skyphoi*, painted with horizontal bands on the body and chevrons just below the rim (Ridgway, 1968). The distinctive cups are typical of Middle Geometric styles in the Euboean-Cycladic region of Greece where they date to the early eighth century. It is not yet clear whether the Veientine examples (or the similar cups from Campanian sites like Capua, Ponte-cagnano and Cumae) are imports or copies but in either case they mark the earliest phases in what was to become a trading market of far-reaching importance, especially in metals. Before long the Greeks were to found colonies on the island of Ischia (*c.* 775 B.C.), at Cumae (*c.* 750 B.C.) and along the east coast of Sicily, with the eventual outcome that Etruria was to be flooded with objects from all over the Mediterranean world. The chevron *skyphoi* from Quattro Fontanili—together with the occasional scarab and faience figurine—mark the earliest stages in that process.

The subsequent phases in the cemetery at Quattro Fontanili reflect both a widening trade market and an increasing sophistication in the artifacts. Iron becomes relatively common and its use is extended to objects like axes and swords: imported materials like amber, faience and gold are now well represented; and there are numerous painted vases, many of which imitate Greek styles. The contents of the later graves provide us in fact with a document that describes the transition from parochialism to an involvement with a much wider world. But before examining the consequences of these developments, we must define the absolute chronology of the Quattro Fontanili cemetery. This has been studied by Joanna Close-Brooks (1968), whose scheme hinges in part upon the occurrence of Middle Geometric *skyphoi* in the IIa graves and also upon the presence in well dated contexts at the Greek colony of Pithecusa on Ischia of typical IIIa artifacts, especially fibulae and a distinctive form of amphora, decorated with spirals. These 'fixed points' suggest that following chronology:

I	?–*c.* 800 B.C.
IIa	*c.* 800–*c.* 760
IIb	*c.* 760–*c.* 720
IIIa	*c.* 720–?

Not all scholars would agree in detail with these dates and we should exercise caution in using them. Moreover, we cannot be sure that funerary assemblages reflect the sort of changes that were taking place in domestic artifacts. But we cannot deny the importance of the Quattro Fontanili cemetery as a mirror of social and economic change for the early centuries of the first millennium B.C.—a period of measurable population expansion, increasing wealth and widening commercial horizons.

The orientalizing period and its aftermath: *c.* 750–500 B.C.

The foundation of the Greek colonies in the south of Italy, outlined above, created a watershed in the archaeology of the peninsula. The Greeks introduced a catalyst with far-reaching social, economic, artistic and technological implications, into the ordered society of late prehistoric Italy. Out of this mingling of indigenous and foreign elements came writing and, with it, named peoples; a vastly increased emphasis upon Mediterranean trade; a monumental architecture; and a novel range of artifacts where technological advances, such as the potter's wheel, were matched by the adoption of quite new artistic conventions. We use the term the 'orientalizing' to describe this period, since the transformation of much of Italian culture closely imitates a parallel development in the east Mediterranean—so much so that the Etruscan heirs of the Villanovans have, since the days of Herodotus (I.94), been seen by many as an élite who migrated from a shadowy homeland in Asia Minor to settle the coastlands of Etruria. Few would

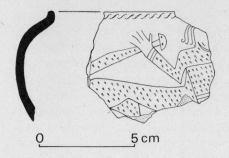

20 Fragment of a jar engraved with a centaur, from Narce *c*. 650–25 B.C. (Source: Potter, 1976a)

now accept this view of Etruscan origins without major reservations—Dionysius of Halicarnassus (I.30) believed them to have been an indigenous people—but, equally, we cannot discount the very strong foreign influences at this time.

The Greek colonialists were undoubtedly responsible for much of this. We have already seen how Greek-type objects first appeared in graves at the Quattro Fontanili cemetery at Veii in the early eighth century and became increasingly common after that time. Much the same pattern applies to the finds from other sites in south Etruria, even in more remote districts like the Faliscan territory. From Narce, for instance, we have two vessels where the mythological encounter between Hercules and the centaur, Nessus, is represented (Torelli, 1976). They probably date to the period between 650 and 625 B.C. One of the pots comes from the recent excavations beside the River Treia (Potter, 1976a). This sherd, part of a small jar, is made in a dark brown coarse ware of local manufacture (Fig. 20). It shows a bearded centaur who is brandishing a sword and presumably fighting with Hercules. Yet, what is interesting about the piece is that the artist has confused some of the details of the legend: the sword should be held by Hercules rather than by Nessus, who traditionally is always armed with a bough. Evidently the myth was sufficiently well known for the artist to want to draw it (although in the locally favoured technique of incision) but he had not heard an authentic account of the story. This epitomizes quite precisely the effect of Greek influence in areas such as the Ager Faliscus: there was eager absorption of these novel ideas but they are sufficiently diluted to imply only second-hand contact with the Greek world. Even so, some settlements came to be thought of as Greek foundations. Falerii (Civita Castellana), for example, was believed by Cato to have been first settled from Argos in Greece (Pliny, *Nat. Hist.* 3.51), while Dionysius of Halicarnassus (1.21) compared both the spears and shields and some of the ritual employed in the temple of Juno Curitis at Falerii with Argive tradition.

The importance of this Greek influence cannot therefore be ignored and it is reasonable to suppose that there may have been some settlement in the mercantile towns along the coast. The legend of Demaratus, for example, has a ring of truth about it: he was a Corinthian who, according to Polybius, was forced to leave his home town after a coup. He had become prosperous through trade with Etruria and chose to settle at Tarquinia, together with a number of craftsmen, especially potters. There he married an Etruscan princess, whose younger son was to become Lucius Tarquinius Priscus, king of Rome between 616 and 579. The recent identification of a very large number of Greek inscriptions from a sixth-century site at Gravisca (Torelli, 1971), a coastal settlement close to Tarquinia, is archaeological confirmation of the general burden of the Demaratus story. So too are the enormous number of Greek vases which appear in Etruscan tombs from the orientalizing period onwards.

What was the motivation behind these close Greek contacts with Etruria? It is evident from the volume of Greek objects in Etruscan contexts that there was a great deal of trade, much of which may well have been in perishable goods that leave no archaeological trace. But Etruria's most saleable commodity was unquestionably metal ores—copper, tin, and iron—and it is a fair presumption, in a world of expanding metallurgical technology, that these represented a primary interest of the Greek traders. Nor is this solely speculation, for recent excavations at the colony of Pithecusa on Ischia have confirmed the Greek exploitation of the central Italian metal ores in a quite remarkable way. The evidence comes from the Mazzola site, which lies below the main acropolis, close to the present village of Lacco Ameno. Here, Professor Buchner and his associates have brought to light a complex of rooms, dating to the eighth century B.C., where the principal activity was the working of metals. Amongst the finds were fibulae discarded because of poor casting and of a type exactly paralleled in late Villanovan Etruria. Furthermore it has been shown by spectroscopy that the metal ores themselves derived from the Etrurian deposits, especially the iron of Elba. Here therefore is evidence both typological and spectrographic for a direct trading link between Etruria and the earliest of the Greek colonies in the west Mediterranean, and we can hardly doubt that this was a major catalyst in the cultural metamorphosis that followed in the Etruscan area (Ridgway, 1973).

We must now turn to the survey region of south Etruria and examine the effect of the orientalizing period in terms of the archaeological evidence upon the ground. The task of defining the early Etruscan landscape is to some extent simplified by the appearance of widely distributed and easily recognized pottery styles during this period. Painted wares in a fine cream clay are a common surface find upon sites occupied in the seventh and sixth centuries and appear to represent the products of thriving local industries. Coarse wares in highly burnished red and brown fabrics continue, however, to form the bulk of the pottery but their general date is clear both from the shapes (which evolve into a very wide range of forms from the late eighth century) and from the tell-tale horizontal lines, indicating the use of a slow wheel. At first the wheel was often used only to add the rim and pedestal base of a vessel, and perhaps to smooth the overall contours, but before long much of the fine-ware was being turned. One distinctive product was 'red impasto', a coarse-ware fabric where the external part of the vessel was dipped in a slip, burnished to a high sheen and then fired under oxidizing conditions. Sometimes painted decorations was added, the techniques ranging from a simple use of white or yellow paint to a more elaborate process where motifs in red or black were placed upon a white or yellow ground. The designs initially reflect the geometric ornament of eighth-century Greek vases but during the seventh century orientalizing motifs became increasingly fashionable, especially the painting of bizarre animal forms. The Faliscans also favoured, as we have seen, the technique of incision for the drawing of such themes.

The vessel shapes were also widely influenced by foreign forms so that by the sixth century the tableware was dominated by fashionable Greek types such as *kantharoi*, *skyphoi* and *oinochoe*. Although burnished impasto was quite often used, the most favoured ware in Etruria was bucchero (Ramage, 1970). This is a hard black fabric, with highly polished surfaces, and a core that has also been completely reduced. Bucchero (with all the technical skill that the quality of the fabric implies) seems to have been an invention of Caere, *c.* 650 B.C. The earliest products, superbly exemplified by the vases in the Regolini-Galassi tomb, were of exquisite quality—a wafer-thin ware, skilfully turned, finely decorated and perfectly fired. By the beginning of the sixth century the quality had begun to deteriorate: the wall of the vessels was thickened, the reduction less perfect and the shapes less precise. At the same time, bucchero became much more common and it is clear that it was no longer the product of a small body of skilled craftsmen but of a large-scale manufacturing industry. Probably there were centres other than Caere (although without the requisite thin-section work we cannot tell for certain) for, with more than 250 site finds from the South Etruria Survey alone, it is evident that bucchero had come within the reach of the ordinary man. As such, it constitutes an excellent index of the extent of sixth-century settlement—especially as the colour and quality of bucchero tends to alter again after *c.* 500 B.C.—and, in combination with the wares already described, allows us to build up a quite detailed picture of the early Etruscan landscape (Fig. 21).

The first and overwhelming impression is that of a sustained population increase, most tellingly demonstrated by the figures themselves (Table 2). We need of course to interpret these statistics in a very judicious way, since we cannot be sure of the number of sites within a period bracket that were occupied simultaneously: there could be quite startling fluctuations that are disguised by these totals. Yet, this trend for a sharp increase in the number of sites is so consistently repeated from area to area that we can hardly doubt its overall significance. Everything points to a steep rise in the size of the rural population, combined with a major expansion of areas under cultivation. The focal point for this growth appears to have been the nucleated settlements. In the Faliscan region, for example, sites like Narce

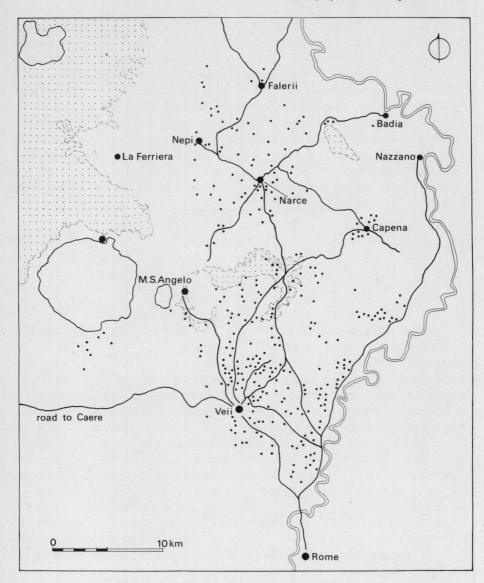

21 South Etruria Survey: sites of the seventh to sixth centuries B.C.

show an enlargement both of the inhabited area and of the cemeteries (where the chamber tomb is the most prevalent form of grave) and this is mirrored by an equivalent rise in the number of small open sites in the environs of the main settlement. A similar history is implied by the graves from Falerii and Nepi where chamber tombs with orientalizing period objects become increasingly common from the late eighth century. At the same time, a number of new nucleated settlements came into existence, amongst them Corchiano and Vignanello on the northern fringes of the

Treia basin and a small hilltop site at La Ferriera (Duncan, 1958), near to Sutri. The contents of the tombs leave no doubt that these were affluent and successful district centres, where trade must have played an important part in their prosperity. There seems, on the other hand, to have been little overall reorientation in what we might term 'settlement strategy'. Sites like Narce and Falerii, together with most of the dependent farms, remain in occupation without any obvious hint of a hiatus in their growth while the new foci select territories that to all intents and purposes were virgin ground. There is a logic to their development that argues above all for continuity rather than for change.

Area	Number of Sites	
	Period II (10th–8th cents B.C.)	Period III (7th–6th cents B.C.)
Ager Faliscus	27	72
Ager Veientanus	16	137
Ager Capenas	4	39
Sutrium	0	1
Craven	6	34
Hemphill	26	31
Total	79	314

Table 2

To the east of the Faliscan area, on the far side of the great ridge that carries the Via Flaminia down to the Treia gorge at Civita Castellana, a separate tribal entity came into existence (Fig. 11). This was the Capenates, a group that recurs frequently in Livy's account of the early wars between Rome and Etruria. The principal settlement was Capena itself, which is a now deserted promontory site, some four kilometres to the north-east of Morlupo (Fig. 22). According to Cato (Servius, *Aeneid* 7, 697), the settlement was founded by young men sent out by an otherwise unknown king of Veii, called Propertius; but the archaeological evidence from the cemeteries indicates otherwise. The earliest graves, which belong to the eighth century (Paribeni, 1906; Stefani, 1958), show much closer links with contemporary Faliscan sites than with the cemeteries of Veii and quite clearly stand apart from the Villanovan cultural tradition. These affinities persisted and became stronger in later centuries. Inscriptions in Faliscan (rather than Etruscan) dominate the epigraphic record and imply that this was the main dialect in this region, while the centuries preceding the conquest of Rome saw frequent military liaison between Falerii and Capena. Culturally, too, they favoured similar styles of artifact, amongst them the distinctive impasto vases decorated with animals drawn in a graffito technique, of which there are many examples in the Capena cemeteries.

Comparatively little is known of the settlement itself at Capena although the site was first identified in the mid eighteenth century and many of the cemeteries have been extensively explored (Jones, 1962, 134–45). The defences built in the late Etruscan period enclose an elongated area of *c.*

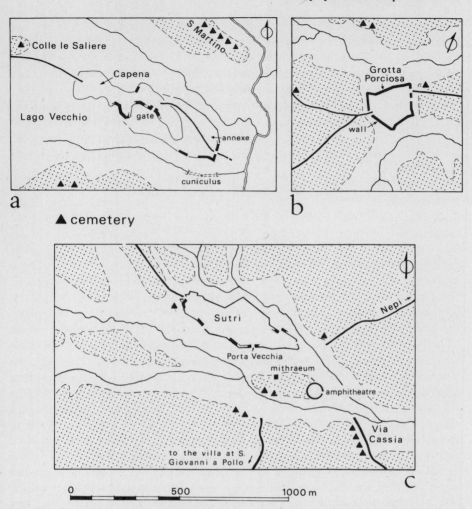

22 Comparative plans of (a) Capena, (b) Grotta Porciosa and (c) Sutri. (Sources: Jones, 1962; Frederiksen and Ward Perkins, 1957; Duncan, 1958)

700 × 100 metres but the position of the buildings remains to be identified and we have no clear idea of the historical development of the town. Nevertheless, the size of the site and the rich contents of the graves leave no doubt that this was a large and influential community and there is nothing inconsistent with its interpretation as a tribal capital. There seem, however, to have been several other nucleated settlements within the Ager Capenas (Fig. 21), so that the overall regional pattern closely resembled that of the Ager Faliscus. All of these sites occupied hills or spurs close to the Tiber Valley, whose fertile alluvium and advantages as a natural corridor must have been an influential factor in the selection of these positions. The most northerly were Badia (Jones, 1963, 105–6) and Nazzano (Jones, 1962, 107–8), both of which seem to have been first occupied in the

eighth century. In the southern part of the tribal territory there were two other nucleated sites, Fontanile di Vacchereccia and Grotta Colonna (Jones, 1962, 151–5). These were minor settlements located on the far tip of ridge spurs, where the provision of a ditch across the neck of the promontory made the position secure. Like the other villages in the Ager Capenas, both of these settlements have yielded pottery of the eighth to seventh centuries B.C.: thus the overall pattern from the region does appear to have a remarkable consistency, in that most of the major sites appear to have grown up at about the same time, matching the contemporary expansion in the Ager Faliscus.

On the other hand, there is much less evidence for rural settlement amongst the Capenates than in the territory of their neighbours. Barri Jones's survey (Jones, 1962, 1963) brought to light a small number of open sites in the vicinity of Capena, Fontanile di Vacchereccia and Grotta Colonna but the great majority of the region appears to have been devoid of countryside farms. The temptation is to interpret this as an indication of a sparse rural population, but the pattern is so much at odds with the results from survey of adjoining areas that there may be other factors at work and the picture a misleading one. In the Ager Veientanus, for example, the distribution of early Etruscan sites is astonishingly even over the whole of the surveyed territory, and there can be no doubt that most of the land was under cultivation or grazing by the sixth century (Fig. 21). Where the Veientine pattern differs from that of its neighbours is in the complete absence of any other nucleated settlement apart from Veii itself. All the rural sites consist of scatters of pottery and tile, spread over the crest of a ridge or small hill, in positions where defence had no priority. None of these sites has been excavated and we know nothing of their layout, architecture or economic function. The only hint comes in the form of the occasional millstone, spindle whorl or loomweight, all of which are types common from the Bronze Age. But there is little reason to think that the essential economic pattern can have changed much since the second millennium nor that the buildings were any more elaborate than the rectangular timber houses of the Villanovan period. These must have been very largely the homes of single family units whose surplus produce was channelled directly to Veii: significantly the quantity of sites does in fact become much greater within the environs of the town.

Of early Etruscan Veii itself (Fig. 14), we still know comparatively little, despite the fact that there is no overlay of modern or medieval building: what excavation has taken place has been largely directed at the exploration of the Etruscan sanctuaries, most notably the Portonaccio complex on the west edge of Veii (Stefani, 1953), the temple on Piazza d'Armi (Stefani, 1944) and the sanctuary buildings in Contrada Campetti in the northern part of the plateau (Torelli and Pohl, 1973). These well known sites were all laid out in the course of the sixth century with footings in substantial *opus quadratum* masonry and elaborate terracotta revetments. They provide an impressive insight both into Veii's affluence and into the skill of her craftsmen, especially in clay modelling. On the other hand, they tell us little of the overall layout of the town. Piazza d'Armi was certainly the focus for an important complex of buildings, for Stefani (1944) located the remains of at least three rectilinear houses facing onto an open square. A street left the square from one corner, and part of a second street was identified at right angles to it: but claims of a planned civic centre of the sort that was being laid out at this time in the Greek colonies of southern Italy and elsewhere (Ward Perkins, 1974) would seem to go far beyond the available evidence. The Etruscans seem to have utilized a regular street grid only in a few sixth-century cemeteries such as Orvieto (Bizzari, 1966), and in the new towns that they later built outside Etruria, like Marzabotto. Within Etruria, the settlements seem to have grown directly out of the Villanovan nuclei, without any real attempt to rationalize the layout of the town. Thus at Veii the scatter of surface finds implies a loose-knit arrangement of buildings, linked only by a main street that ran along the crest of the ridge between the north-west gate and the Piazza d'Armi, and by a number of side-roads. Four of these roads met on the summit of a low knoll in the northern part of the town and it is possible that this formed something of a town centre (as it was later to do in Classical times). The proximity of the Campetti sanctuary adds credence to this idea, but as yet the only other structures to be excavated in this part of the site are a complex of houses, set into the sloping ground to the north (Stefani, 1922). The lowest rooms of these buildings were cut directly into the bedrock while the upper walls were made of large blocks of tuff, so that they were in effect terrace houses. A rather similar arrangement has been excavated by the Swedish School at San Giovenale in the Tolfa Hills (Wetter, 1962). The front rooms of these houses opened directly onto a minor service road which in turn joined the main street heading westwards up the hill. Both roads were flanked by drains, a sensible provision in an area where the run-off of surface water must have been considerable during the autumn and winter storms.

We cannot date these houses excavated by Stefani at all closely although the presence of bucchero points to a fairly early date. But we do know from work by the north-west gate that the timber buildings on that site were reconstructed with stone foundations in the sixth century (Ward Perkins, 1959a; Murray-Threipland, 1963), and there were certainly stone domestic houses at other settlements in Etruria, such as Acquarossa (Ostenberg, 1975) and San Giovenale (Wetter, 1962), at this time. Very often the superstructure must have been built of timber in the traditional manner; but the use of substantial masonry blocks for the socles implies that there was large-scale quarrying of the volcanic *tufo* for purposes other than the construction of public buildings and monuments.

The most major investment of labour and materials was unquestionably in the construction and furnishing of the tombs in the vicinity of the city. The cemeteries of Veii may not exhibit the same overall level of munificence or architectural elaboration as, for example, the well known Banditaccia necropolis at Cerveteri: but some individual tombs are closely comparable, and the cemeteries just as numerous. The dominant form of grave was, as on other Etruscan sites, a tomb with one or more chambers, carved out of the rock. The deceased was laid upon a funerary bed, also normally shaped in rock, and surrounded by grave-goods. Naturally there were many variations in the style of the architecture both from site to site and within a single cemetery: but there was much more variation in wealth and scale than in burial rite. It is the homogeneity of the tomb types rather than their diversity which is the surprising feature of early Etruscan cemeteries.

The Veientine necropoli (Fig. 14) clustered mainly along the seven main roads leading out of the city. Most of the tombs therefore lie well outside the inhabited area, anticipating the tradition of Classical times; but there were also cemeteries such as the Macchia della Communità (Colini, 1919) or Casalaccio (Vighi, 1935) where the graves encroached onto the lower slopes of the main plateau. Some of these burials may date as early as the eighth century and it is quite possible that their proximity to the city indicates the growing pressure upon land for agriculture and settlement. For the most part, however, the cemeteries grew out of Villanovan nuclei in a manner that implies a continuously developing funerary tradition, uninterrupted by any major hiatus. At Quattro Fontanili, for example, the periphery of the Villanovan necropolis (and especially the upper part of the cliffs around the ridge) is honeycombed with chamber tombs which, from their position and contents, would seem to represent a last phase in the history of the graveyard. Significantly, the earlier burials remained undisturbed by later tombs, as if their location was still remembered and accorded respect. Much the same is true of the other Villanovan cemeteries: the growth of the necropoli is characterized by a systematic development from the original nucleus along quite ordered lines.

The exception to this pattern is a series of remarkable burials, capped by massive tumuli. Such tumuli are by no means uncommon in early Etruscan necropoli: we have only to think of the Banditaccia cemetery at Cerveteri, where group after group of enormous mounds extend along either side of a funeral road for over a kilometre. At Veii the individual tumuli are no less impressive but they tend to stand in isolation from other tombs, often in a position of special prominence. The so-called Chigi tomb, for example (which yielded an exquisite Proto-Corinthian *aryballos*, the Chigi Vase), is situated high on Monte Aguzzo, north-east of Veii, where it still forms a conspicuous landmark. This is just one of a number of tumuli to be found several kilometres from the city itself and it is clear from their size that people of special importance were buried in them. Similarly, the two painted tombs which have been found at Veii, the Tomba Campana (which lay on Monte Michele, close to the north-east gate) and the Tomb of the Ducks (one of the graves in the Oliveto Grande necropolis) also stand out as exceptionally elaborate: they are likely to date to the first half of the sixth century B.C., a little later than most of the tumulus tombs. But most of the chamber tombs are much more modest structures, best interpreted as the burial vaults of the well-to-do but ordinary family. Many of these tombs were constructed as separate entities, entered from a long dromos; but another common type comprised an open rectangular court, sunk into the bedrock and giving access to a series of underground chambers. Here again we may have a reflection in architecture of divisions in social rank.

There is still an enormous amount to be learnt of the layout and development of Etruscan cemeteries (although the evidence is undergoing an alarming erosion at the hands of the *clandestini*); even so, it is quite clear from what we already know that the Etruscans exercised very considerable skill in the construction of their necropoli. No less remarkable, however, was their achievement in related fields of engineering, especially those of road building and drainage schemes. Both were innovations of far-reaching importance. In agricultural terms, the construction of roads made available to centres like Veii the produce of a much greater area of land; at the same time the quality of the land itself could be substantially improved by the construction of drainage shafts, connected by horizontal tunnels, known as *cuniculi*. Consequently, the potential existed to raise the level of agricultural production very considerably and there is little doubt, to judge from the increased number of rural sites, that this did in fact happen. Equally important, however, were the implications of more sophisticated communications upon the development of trade. The major centres of Etruria were soon linked by roads adapted to wheeled transport and before long the network had been extended to minor settlements as well. As a result the flow of goods from the coastal ports to the hinterland was (as the contents of the cemeteries clearly indicate) very greatly accelerated; equally, there must have been an equivalent stimulus upon the products of inland centres such as Veii and the Faliscan towns. Indeed, the very deep penetration of orientalizing traditions into Etruria may well have been largely due to the development of this network of roads.

South Etruria is a particularly critical area in which to study the evolution of the road network. One important reason is that many of the innovations—especially the design of road-cuttings—undoubtedly originated in this region, coinciding with its development as a focus of trade in the early orientalizing period. A more surprising reason is the way in which much of the evidence is still very well preserved. The chief reason is that any engineer given the task of constructing a road across the volcanic terrain of south Etruria has to devise a way of crossing innumerable deep river valleys with vertical cliffs: the only effective answer is the creation of winding cuttings, taking the road down to the level of the valley floor. Fortunately, the volcanic rock is sufficiently soft to make the removal of large quantities of *tufo* a practical proposition, and the result is that the roads of south Etruria are invariably characterized by massive excavations at the junctions with the river valleys, forming a scar upon the landscape that is all but indelible. The difficulty comes in assigning a date to these cuttings, since a continuous process of erosion necessarily creates a need for constant maintenance, either by lowering the road level or by recutting the groove: thus the routes out of long-established towns invariably display a baffling multiplicity of recuts that normally defy reasoned interpretations. The key to the decipherment of the pre-Roman elements in the road network comes principally from sites which, through historical accident, were abandoned during or after the Roman period. Veii, for example, went into a steady decline after its conquest by the Romans in 396 B.C. and was bypassed when the Via Cassia was constructed in the mid second century (Harris, 1965). Similarly Falerii Veteres, Capena, Narce and a number of other major pre-Roman centres were also largely ignored when the Roman road network was laid out across the territory of the Faliscans and Capenates. Thus the pre-Roman pattern of roads (although sometimes modified in the medieval period when many Iron Age sites were reoccupied) is often fossilized in the vicinity of those centres. Overall, therefore, we are in a position to reconstruct a quite comprehensive road map for the pre-Roman period and, in so doing, to shed a good deal of light upon the Etruscan and Faliscan accomplishment in this area of engineering (Fig. 21).

Two main phases in the development of the communication network can be immediately discerned. The earlier relates to the development of tracks that in the main followed the line of natural features such as ridges and river valleys. Few of them represent more than pack-trails, providing access to the countryside immediately surrounding the settlement; but some were long-distance routes, connecting the major sites. The Valle la Fata road (Ward Perkins, 1961, 13), is a good example. It began as an inconspicuous series of gullies, evidently belonging to several periods, that climb out of the valley on the west side of Veii. These gullies turn into a single narrow cutting, unsuited as anything more than a mule track, towards the crest of the valley, and the road then winds its way south-westwards towards the Via Cassia. There seems little doubt that its ultimate destination was Rome, probably, as Ward Perkins (1961, 14) has suggested, along the line of the Via Triumphalis. However, we can infer an early date since the initial stretch of the track is lined with Villanovan graves and traces of contemporary occupation sites. Another early route, based entirely upon a natural feature, was the track that led south-west from Veii, down the Cremera Valley (Ward Perkins, 1968, 57–8). Its destination seems to have been the Tiber crossing commanded by the town of Fidenae, from where there must have been well defined routes both towards Rome and the Tiber mouth and also east into the mountains via the Aniene Valley. The latter was until recently a much used line of transhumance (Barker, 1972) and the Cremera trackway may well have originated in this way—a suggestion that finds support in the Bronze Age camps that line its course. The Treia Valley, the natural corridor through Faliscan territory up towards the Tiber Valley, seems to have been used in much the same way. In the Bronze Age these valleys appear, as we have seen, to have been relatively dry and free from any sustained flooding: they must have afforded the traveller an easy journey for most of the year.

By the second half of the second millennium B.C., however, climatic conditions seem to have deteriorated so that the rivers began to alluviate;

the valley floors must have become marshy or under standing water for much of the winter and it is hard to envisage them as much used trackways at this time. Instead, alternative routes came into existence where special provision was made for drainage of low-lying ground, as we shall see shortly. The tracks that developed along the ridge-tops, on the other hand, remained in constant use and in a number of cases developed into major highways. For example, the crest of high land that still carries the Via Flaminia up through Ager Veientanus, over the Monti Sabatini and on down through the Treia drainage basin, is a route that seems to have been employed (on the evidence of nearby sites) from very early in the first millennium B.C.; so too was the line taken by the Via Cassia, which gave access to the Villanovan settlement on Monte S. Angelo, high in the Monti Sabatini, and to the Villanovan sites to the west. What is interesting about the ridgeways is that their natural focus lay not at Veii (as one might expect) but much closer to the Tiber at Prima Porta, just to the north of Rome. This underlines the conclusion that we have already inferred from other sources of evidence: that Veii was very much a secondary element in the growth of settlement patterns in south Etruria, and was forced to adapt its communication network to a pre-existing layout of ridge and valley tracks, in use since the Bronze Age or before.

This system of country tracks appears to have prevailed down to the seventh century, by which time two factors had emerged to create an incentive for change. One was the development of trade during the orientalizing period, when there appears to have been a very extensive passage of goods. The other was the widespread adoption of wheeled transport in Etruria and elsewhere during the seventh century. Vehicles had of course been in existence from considerably before the orientalizing period (Piggott, 1965, 92) and there are some fine pottery *askoi* from several Villanovan sites in Etruria, which show plump birds riding along on four wheels (Hencken, 1968, 525–30). But the orientalizing period is remarkable for the number of carts and chariots that appear in graves of that time. There are examples both from the major sites like Caere (e.g. Regolini-Galassi tomb: Pareti, 1947), Populonia and Vetulonia, and from smaller settlements such as Narce (Pasqui and Cozza, 1894, 396–8). Even though the surviving remains are generally those of ceremonial chariots (such as the famous sixth-century example from Monteleone di Spoleto) there is little doubt that a more modest cart or trap (perhaps resembling the *carpentum* of Livy and Ovid: Heurgon, 1964, 132–3) came to be widely used at this time. As a result, many of the pack-trails that had sufficed in the Villanovan period had to be replaced by roads that were designed to take vehicular traffic. At the same time, the elementary network based upon natural corridors was extended by the construction of cross-country routes, where the engineers were forced to surmount natural obstacles of considerable magnitude. Indeed, it was only by the construction of such sophisticated communications that a site like Veii was able to diminish the disadvantages of its position and build up a very extensive *territorium*.

There is little direct evidence for the date of these engineered roads. A few of the cuttings bear makers' signs, like the celebrated example (*CIE* 8379) near Corchiano which records in Etruscan letters 33 to 36 centimetres high the name *Larth Vel Arnies* (Pl. Vb). There are also some pre-Roman chamber tombs (in almost every case robbed of their contents) inserted into the side of the road-cutting. These, however, do not prove anything more than a pre-Roman date for the construction of the road. There is, on the other hand, a considerable body of indirect evidence in the form of the sites that line the road. These may not give us a date of construction based on stratigraphy; but we can assume with a fair degree of certainty that the period at which sites appear along the whole length of a road also indicates its period of completion. What makes this argument convincing is the extraordinary consistency of the results. If we take the engineered roads of presumed Etruscan date in both the Faliscan and Veientine territories and compare the period of foundation of the adjacent sites, then it emerges that the great majority, on surface evidence at any rate, originate in period III, the seventh to sixth centuries B.C. There is thus a strict chronological coincidence with the appearance both of a wealth of imported goods and the remains of wheeled vehicles in the tombs. We can conclude that the orientalizing period saw a substantial attempt to modify and extend the existing network of communications.

The results are in engineering terms much more dramatic and impressive than is sometimes allowed. The principal aim was the creation of roads where the gradients would allow the passage of vehicles which, in many cases, meant a complete remodelling of the network. The road linking Veii and Caere provides a good example (Hemphill, 1975, 126). The earliest route between these centres followed a winding and irregular course that dipped in and out of the valleys that extend southwards from Lake Bracciano. It was a track that had all the advantages of directness but was suited only to foot and mule traffic. The road that replaced it was quite different in character. Its most noteworthy feature is the way in which it picks a course around the head of the steepest valleys, such as the Rio Galeria and the Fosso Arroncino; the route was somewhat longer but there was compensation in that the worst gradients were more or less completely avoided. Other sharp slopes were smoothed out with road-cuttings and the result was a road-line that, in the form of the Via Clodia, has survived down to the present day. This road demonstrates the priorities of the Etruscan engineer very clearly: his principal concern was the provision of a route negotiable by carts and waggons, even though it may have involved a detour. Alternatively, where no other option existed, he was prepared to create huge cuttings to carry the road across natural barriers. These massive excavations still form the most enduring feature of the Etruscan landscape. The main road linking Falerii Veteres and Nepi had, for example, to cross the precipitous gorge of the Fosso Maggiore, and we can still see the trench, 15 metres deep and 200 metres long, that carried the road down to the level of the river (Frederiksen and Ward Perkins, 1957, 141–2). A similar cutting then wound its way up the cliffs on the far side of the valley onto the ridgeland beyond, its sides lined with Faliscan chamber tombs. It is an impressive demonstration of the importance that was attached to the creation of a road link between these two nucleated centres.

At the same time, we should note that these expensive projects were by no means confined to the major highways. Properly engineered roads that served only areas of farmland were given equal priority in the construction programme. We can take as an example the route that left the north-east gate of Veii and climbed north-eastwards onto the high ground around Monte Aguzzo (Ward Perkins, 1968, 30–6). Even though this road can have been designed for no other purpose than to bring farm produce to the markets of Veii, it is nevertheless laid out with all the skill and attention to detail of the long-distance roads. Cuttings smooth out the steeper inclines (Pl. Va), *cuniculi* are used to divert streams and thus facilitate a valley crossing, while the line chosen displays over all a high degree of careful planning—an impressive demonstration of the close relationship between town and country.

What were the techniques of road construction and maintenance? The cuttings themselves vary quite considerably in shape and scale, ranging from V-shaped gashes in the landscape to narrow tunnel-like passages which broaden out only at road level. Some are laid out straight, such as the crossing of the Fosso delle Sorcelle between Falerii Veteres and Corchiano (Frederiksen and Ward Perkins, 1957, 147), but more often the gradient was eased by the use of a winding route. There was normally room for two vehicles to pass, assuming a wheel width of *c*. two metres, but the passage must have been hindered by the soft and friable nature of the road surface. Nothing short of paving could have prevented continual wear and erosion of the road surface. Some of the effects of soil erosion were minimized by the use of a gutter placed either centrally or along the edges of the road; but in the long term the only effective solution was to lower the surface and eliminate the ruts. That this was often done is quite clearly shown in a number of cuttings, where successive working levels are indicated by steps and ledges.

Once in the valley bottom there were a number of ways of crossing the stream. The simplest expedient was to use a ford, created by one of the shelves of harder rock that are interleaved in the volcanic *tufo*. Many contemporary tracks still cross rivers by this means, but for wheeled traffic such routes are generally impracticable in winter, when the streams are in spate. Bridges must therefore have been devised at an early phase in the history of road construction and there is little reason to doubt that they were widely used. Few of these bridges can have been very elaborate—a single span of timber would have been quite sufficient for most streams—but we can cite an excavated example in the Pietrisco Valley, just to the east of the San Giovenale acropolis, to illustrate one of the more solidly built structures. The principal surviving remains were of the two bridge abutments, massively built in *tufo* masonry (Hanell, 1962, 304–6). The northern

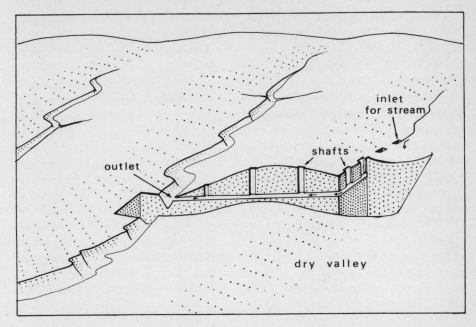

23 Diagram illustrating a field *cuniculus* diverting a stream from one valley to another. (Source: Judson and Kahane, 1963)

abutment still stood to a height of *c.* six metres and had a width of more than seven metres; the southern abutment was smaller, but no less solidly constructed. The total span was nearly ten metres and must have been bridged by at least two sets of timber, probably supported by piles: very similar bridges can still be found in the Campagna today. Masonry abutments of this sort are still surprisingly common finds in the survey region (cf. Frederiksen and Ward Perkins, 1957, 147) and, while not closely dated, they imply that many bridges may have been given stable foundations.

Alternatively, the road builders could employ *cuniculi* as a means of diverting a stream or draining the valley. That such *cuniculi* were widely used in this way is now quite apparent. We can take as an example the so-called Pietra Pertusa road, which provided a link between Veii and the Tiber Valley, just to the north of Prima Porta (Ward Perkins, 1968, 47–50). It has been interpreted as a military road of fifth-century date, intended to keep open a line of communication with Gabii and Praeneste, after the Tiber crossing at Fidenae had fallen to Rome (Ward Perkins, 1962b, 1640). Certainly, it is remarkable for its directness and for its skilful engineering: no less than four valleys were drained by *cuniculi* over a four-kilometre stretch, providing in effect a series of bridges, and the culmination was an enormous tunnel, some 300 metres in length and over 2 metres wide, that was driven some 40 metres below ground level, through the Flaminia ridge. Nothing could provide a more impressive example of the scale and complexity of some of these Etruscan roads.

The *cuniculi* themselves consisted of a horizontal shaft with a flat bottom and rounded roof. Their dimensions are such that they would just accommodate a small man, standing upright—in other words the minimum working space with a pickaxe (marks of which often survive). The normal practice was to drive the *cuniculus* along one side of a valley, leading the stream underground by means of a vertical shaft. Other vertical shafts, spaced at regular intervals of *c*. 30 metres, provided additional drainage. In this manner a stream could be led into another valley or several parallel valleys could be drained into a single stream at right angles to them (Fig. 23; Pl. IVa). Their length varies considerably but Judson and Kahane (1963), in their catalogue of more than 70 examples, cite many which extend for several hundred metres and one remarkable *cuniculus*, in the Fosso degli Olmetti, near Veii, which has a total length of 5,600 metres (Pl. IVb). Their distribution is wide but there are especially dense clusters in the vicinity of the Alban Hills, where over 45 kilometres are recorded, and in the environs of Veii, which has more than 25 kilometres of *cuniculi* near to the city. Further north, they are much less well represented but the known examples tend also to be found close to the nucleated settlements, and there seems little doubt that they were created in the main as public works.

The function of the *cuniculi* has received a great deal of attention both in antiquity and in recent literature. It is clear that they must have served a good many purposes. Livy (5, 19–21), for example, describes how the troops of Camillus ended the seige of Veii in 396 B.C. by cutting a *cuniculus* beneath the defences and gaining access into the citadel. Shortly before, the Alban Lake had been drained by the same device (Livy, 5, 15) and earlier still there is the tradition that the Cloaca Maxima in Rome—which may well have originally taken the form of a *cuniculus*—was of Etruscan construction. These could also, as we have seen, be used as road tunnels and, in an urban context, they were certainly employed both for drainage and water storage purposes (Stefani, 1944, 260–5; Fraccaro, 1919). Equally, they were used to bring water to a settlement, there being a fine example at the north Faliscan settlement of Ponte del Ponte (Frederiksen and Ward Perkins, 1957, 123–5). This small Faliscan town was situated on a low hill beside a fast-flowing stream, the Rio della Tenuta. One hundred metres to the north-west of the settlement is a substantial stone-built aqueduct, 9.50 metres wide at the base and still standing to a height of 10 metres (Fig. 24). It spans the entire width of the small gorge in which the stream flows, the course of the river being diverted not through an arch (as the Roman engineers would have done) but through a *cuniculus*, inserted into the hill on the south side of the valley. The aqueduct itself apparently tapped a nearby spring, the water being collected by a *cuniculus* that opened out into the aqueduct. Once across the valley, the water then entered a second *cuniculus* which headed along the side of the valley down to the site of the settlement.

This wide range of uses for *cuniculi* should not disguise the fact that

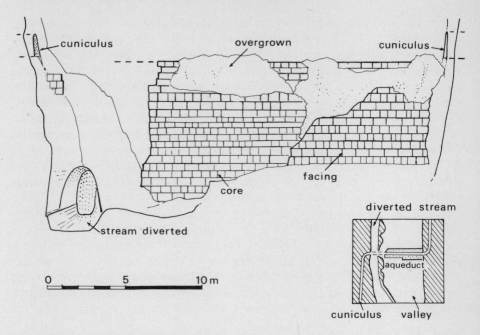

24　The Faliscan aqueduct near the site of Ponte del Ponte. (Source: Frederiksen and Ward Perkins, 1957)

their most general use was undoubtedly for drainage of ground that was liable to erosion or was low-lying. The band of cuniculated valleys that lie north and east of Veii corresponds very closely, as Judson and Kahane (1963) have pointed out, with the distribution of the poorly drained brown Mediterranean soil with mesophytic vegetation. They reason that this clayey land would have been of little agricultural value without extensive land drainage and this argument is strengthened when we recall the evidence (discussed in Chapter 2) for a sharp increase in valley-bottom waterlogging in the second half of the first millennium. With a growing population and a continuous need to increase agricultural production, there must have been a considerable incentive to bring even marginal land into cultivation. In fact, the few *cuniculi* for which we have dates do seem to belong mainly to the fifth and fourth centuries B.C. There are examples from Veii at both the Portonaccio sanctuary (Stefani, 1953, 87–93) and the north-west gate (Ward Perkins, 1959a; Murray-Threipland, 1963), which fall within this time bracket, and another dated example from Narce (Potter, 1976a, 79–80). Similarly, Ward Perkins (1961, 49–50) has argued for a period before the late fifth century for the construction of the most famous of all *cuniculi*, the Ponte Sodo at Veii. The enormous tunnel (enlarged partly through erosion and partly by several subsequent alterations—Judson and Kahane, 1963, 92–3) carried the Valchetta stream through a spur projecting from the northern part of the plateau of Veii. It was probably designed to drain and provide access to the extensive flood plain in this part of the valley, all valuable agricultural land; but, whatever its purpose, it very clearly was built before the construction of the late fifth-century wall (whose line is weakened by the existence of the *cuniculus*) and, significantly, cuts through an earlier system of drainage tunnels. Everything points therefore to the fifth century as the main period of construction for these land reclamation schemes—coinciding, it may be noted, not only with the deterioration of conditions in many valley bottoms, but also with the development of the remarkable drainage and hydraulic schemes in the Etruscan 'new' towns of northern Italy, such as Marzabotto and Spina.

To what extent the road-building programme (with its use of cuniculated bridges) and land reclamation schemes were planned in tandem is unclear and difficult to prove. The Pietra Pertusa road, as we have seen, makes use of at least four *cuniculi* for stream crossings, and may, with its directness of line, point to a deliberate liaison between the two projects. Otherwise there is no direct evidence for the relative chronology, beyond the fact that both roads and drainage schemes quite clearly reflect the control and organization of a major city, setting its *territorium* in order.

The fifth century

With the building of *cuniculi* we have come chronologically into the late Etruscan period, when Rome began gradually to extend its territory. Thus Fidenae was to fall in the period 435–416 B.C., Veii in 396–388, Capena in 395, Nepi and Sutri between 390 and 373 and then, considerably later, Falerii and the remaining Faliscan territory in 241 B.C. We shall trace the consequences of this gradual enlargement of Rome's territory in the next chapter; meanwhile we should first examine the settlement patterns in the period immediately prior to the Roman conquest of south Etruria.

It is fortunate that the discovery of an enormous deposit of pottery at Casale Pian Roseto, just to the north of Veii, gives us a fairly clear idea of the sort of wares in use at this time (Murray-Threipland and Torelli, 1970). The site came to light in 1965, during the building of a private race track. It proved to consist of a large subterranean building, measuring 8.20 × 3.60 metres and built of massive *tufo* blocks. It was entered from a flight of steps in the north-east corner and must have been the cellar (or possibly the cistern) of a suburban farm. Its main archaeological significance derives from the fact that it was filled up in a single operation with a dump of pottery and other rubbish. Amongst the finds were closely dated imported wares of the period 430–380 B.C. and it seems likely therefore that its demolition followed the conquest of Veii and the re-organization of the countryside that this seems to have entailed. The deposit included a minimum of a thousand vessels, many of them tablewares either in grey bucchero or in a cream fabric, sometimes decorated with bands of red and orange paint. Amongst the common forms were various sorts of jug, drinking cups, bowls and platters. But there were also kitchenwares, including a distinctive type of jar with an everted rim and a thick cream slip on the inside of the vessel

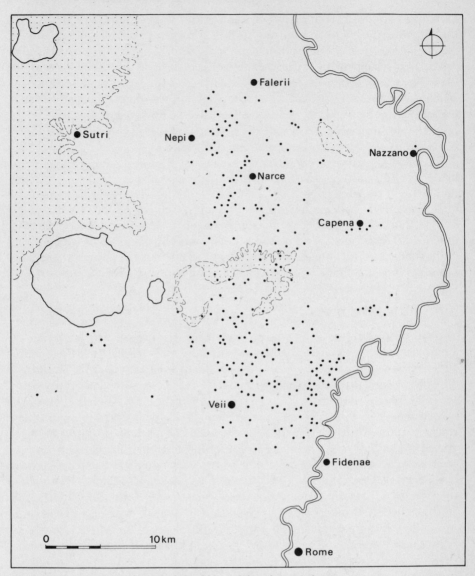

25 South Etruria Survey: sites of the fifth and fourth centuries B.C.

(presumably to make it watertight: the so-called internal slip-ware), as well as large mixing bowls reminiscent in shape of Roman *mortaria*. In addition, there were portable cooking ovens of a form that had been in use since the Bronze Age, and a few large *dolia*, employed for storage purposes.

Many of these shapes—for example, the *skyphoi*—represent popular forms of tableware that had been current since at least the sixth century; but the sharp deterioration in the quality of most of the fabrics provides a clear guide of the date of these later pieces. The everted-rim jars, on the. other hand, while being a form that is at least as early as the sixth century, do not seem to become at all common until *c.* 450 B.C. or later; nor is the use of a thick internal slip known before that date. Once adopted, however, they seem to have become a standard form of cooking jar that appears, on both surface and excavated evidence (Potter, 1976a, 276–7), to have been widely distributed over south Etruria; like the grey bucchero and the finer cream wares, they must have been produced for a much wider market than the immediate environs of Veii. At the same time we can be quite clear that it was Etruscans rather than Romans who used the Casale Pian Roseto pottery, since there were nearly 30 graffiti scratched into the side or base of different vessels, presumably to mark ownership; only one inscription in this large group betrays any hint of Latin influence.

The importance of this dump of pottery is that it provides us with a closely dated fixed point for the range of domestic wares in use about 400 B.C. At the same time, these wares are sufficiently abundant to provide a very useful idea of the extent and density of settlement in this period (Fig. 25). The figures in Table 3 are on the whole extremely telling: for most areas they present a picture of expansion both in the total number of sites and in the amount of land that was under cultivation. It is clear that the size of the rural population was rising in most districts and, in consequence, that a good deal of marginal land came into occupation. Yet, there are also signs of the political tensions of the period. In the Ager Faliscus, for example, many of the open sites tend to cluster either within the environs of the main settlements or occupy areas that were comparatively remote from the main northern highways, like the Flaminia and Cassia ridgeways. Moreover, many of the larger sites situated in less defensible positions seem to have been abandoned at this time; amongst them the western Faliscan centres of La Ferriera (Duncan, 1958, 119–20) and Trevignano (Stefani, 1913), while further south the remote but nevertheless vulnerable settlement of Monte S. Angelo (Pasqui and Cozza, 1894) was also apparently now deserted. In their place, there grew up a settlement perched upon a rocky knoll at Sutri (Duncan, 1958), a strategically placed town that commanded the natural route between the Monti Sabatini and Cimini into central Etruria (Fig. 22; Pl. XIa). The importance of this town is emphasized by the fact that the Romans annexed it, together with Nepi, over 150 years before they took over the Faliscan territory to the east. Eventually it became a *municipium* and, by the end of the first century B.C., it had been further promoted to the status of a *colonia* (Duncan, 1958, 68). Strabo (5,2,9) knew it as one of the larger towns of south Etruria, a munificence that was undoubtedly enhanced by its position on the Via Cassia, a major highway that appears to have been laid out in the mid second century B.C. (Harris, 1965). But, above all, Sutri's importance as an early Roman town reflects the care with which its Etruscan founders selected their site—a choice that combined strong natural defences with the advantages of easily developed communications.

Sutri, like so many of the nucleated settlements of Etruria, has remained an inhabited centre down to the present day and, in consequence, we know

	P III (7th–6th cents B.C.)	P IV (5th–4th cents B.C.)
Ager Faliscus	72	104
Ager Veientanus	137	127
Ager Capenas	39	22
Sutrium	1	1
Craven	34	59
Hemphill	31	32
Total	314	345

Table 3

virtually nothing of its layout in Etruscan times. However, the existing stretches of defensive wall indicate many different phases of construction, normally by the simple process of building the new wall back to back with the old; thus at the south gate there are no less than five main periods of masonry, all in quite distinct style (Pl. VIa). The oldest consists of dry-stone walling with massive blocks laid as headers and stretchers. This is a technique well attested in late Etruscan times and should date to the fifth or fourth centuries B.C. (Blake, 1947, 75). We can trace masonry of this type at several other points in the wall circuit (Fig. 22) and, taken together, they imply that the enclosed area was of very similar dimensions to the medieval nucleus, with a total area of over 100,000 square metres, the size of a substantial town.

The difficulty comes in deciding whether these walls are of Etruscan or Roman construction, given a conquest date between 390 and 383 B.C.; they have yet to be tested by excavation, and close dating by masonry styles is notoriously inexact. Yet, if we compare Sutri with other Etruscan and Faliscan nucleated settlements of this period, there does seem to be a consistent trend towards the construction of defensive circuits immediately prior to the Roman conquest. The list of sites within the south Etruria region is numerically an impressive one: it includes Capena, Fontanile di Vacchereccia, Falerii Veteres, Corchiano, Ponte del Ponte, Grotta Porciosa (Fig. 22), Nepi, Narce and Veii (Potter, 1976a, 22)—a list that incorporates virtually all the larger Etruscan and Faliscan settlements within the region. Many of these mural defences were substantial and imposing. At Capena for example (Jones, 1962, 135–7) the main plateau was enclosed within a wall built of very large *tufo* blocks, laid as at Sutri in headers and stretchers (Fig. 22). The dimensions of the blocks were also very similar at the two sites. At Capena the positions of at least three gates are known with certainty (although there are no details of their construction) from which streets paved with limestone flags led into the town. In addition, there was also a small extra-mural settlement located on rather lower ground to the east. Whilst this may originally have grown up as a separate, undefended entity, it too was eventually enclosed within its own wall. This was by comparison with the main town defences a relatively modest structure, being just one course wide and less than a metre across: but many of the blocks of *tufo*

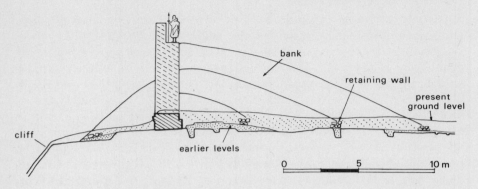

26 The defences of Veii in the fifth century B.C., as revealed by excavations by the north-west gate. (Source: Ward Perkins, 1959a)

were individually quite massive and the construction technique was once again that of headers and stretchers. This suggests it to be an Etruscan construction and its date is confirmed by the contents of a well that had been filled up to make way for the wall. Apart from a large quantity of rubble—presumably intended to prevent subsidence—the wall contained a group of sixth- and fifth-century pottery. We can conclude therefore that the wall—probably built with a certain amount of haste—was put up shortly before the Roman conquest of Capena in 395 B.C., after which time the site was largely abandoned.

What makes this conclusion particularly interesting is that it closely matches the date of the main mural circuit of Veii (Ward Perkins, 1961, 32–9). This was a quite enormous scheme of defences which extended for a distance of over six kilometres (Fig. 14). It divides into two parts. One separate wall, partly explored by Stefani (1922, 390–404), enclosed the natural citadel of the Piazza d'Armi. This was entered from the main plateau through a gate with a large guard-chamber, with at least two phases of construction. The wall itself, so far as can be judged from Stefani's excellent plans, consisted of a rubble core with an ashlar facing; in addition there appear to have been a series of towers or buttresses built along the inside edge of the wall. This technique of construction differs significantly from the type of defences that enclose the main plateau and may imply a rather earlier period of construction. The principal defensive circuit, on the other hand, is of uniform build over its whole length and appears to represent only one phase of construction. It consisted of a massive earthen rampart with a width of more than 20 metres, revetted in front by a strongly built stone wall (Fig. 26). This was between 1.50 and 2 metres in width and was constructed, as at Capena and Sutri, in the header and stretcher technique. In places, this wall has survived to a height of nearly six metres—an impressive demonstration of its solid and durable character: but, at the same time, it is clear from such sections that only the upper part was intended to be visible. This is apparent from the rough and unfinished appearance of the lower courses as distinct from the smooth and well jointed masonry of the upper sections of the wall. Ward Perkins (1961, 34–5) suggests that there must have been a small glacis covering the lower part of the front of the wall, probably designed to act both as a buttress and to steepen the angle of the slope between the defences themselves and the lip of the gorge. It is a convincing argument and one that underlines the sophisticated nature of this defensive circuit, carefully designed and skilfully executed, with considerable attention to detail. Fortunately, we can assign a reasonably close date to this circuit. The evidence derives principally from excavations beside the north-west gate (Fig. 15; Pl. IIIa) where a domestic house had been levelled to make way for the wall and rampart (Ward Perkins, 1959a, 66–7). The pottery incorporated within the rampart terminates in the mid to late fifth century B.C. (Murray-Threipland, 1963, 60–1), so that a date for the wall in the decades that immediately preceded the conquest of Veii in 396 B.C. is very probable. If so, we can hardly doubt that it was the northern expansion of Rome, beginning with the fall of Fidenae in 435–416 B.C., that provided the incentive for this massive investment in artificial defences: indeed, that these were the walls that for ten years held out against continuous seige by Camillus and the Roman army (Livy, 5, 23).

Similarly, we should probably interpret the mural defences of the other settlements in south Etruria (together with the abandonment of the less well fortified positions) as an equal reflection of the political struggles of the period. That these were in part the culmination of a long phase of population growth during the first millennium, combined with a sustained and ever increasing pressure upon land, is the conclusion implicit in the archaeological data. The landscape of south Etruria was transformed during this period. Numerous settlement foci where dispersed sites clustered around nucleated centres replaced the sparse population of the Bronze Age. Tracks and roads linked the centres and schemes were put in hand to improve the agricultural potential of the land. Trade brought in foreign goods, and a monumental architecture superseded the simple buildings of the second millennium. It was a transformation whose scale and speed can only impress.

5
The Classical period

The Roman conquest

The Roman conquest of south Etruria brought about a major hiatus in the history of the region, which entailed many far-reaching changes. As the frontiers of Rome's territory were gradually extended during the fourth and third centuries, so was the structure of Etruscan life gradually eroded. It began with the decline—and in some cases the abandonment—of many of the Etruscan and Faliscan towns that had for so long formed the focus of each pre-Roman *pagus* or tribal subdivision. In some cases, new towns were created, like Falerii Novi: but much more often the inhabitants of the nucleated sites were dispersed into the countryside, to found new farms and raise the level of the rural population. It was a deliberate policy of decentralization, aimed in part at destroying potential foci of resistance, like Falerii Veteres, and in part at raising levels of agricultural production. This was further fostered by a programme of road building that lasted for much of the period of the Republic. Major arterial highways were laid out, like the Viae Clodia, Amerina and Flaminia, all creations of the third century, and the Via Cassia, which was probably built in the 150s B.C. Significantly these roads tended to bypass many of the old pre-Roman centres, such as Veii and Falerii Veteres, as if confirming their redundancy in the new order of things. Instead, there were new foci for settlement, especially the road-stations which began to grow up at many of the important junctions. By the end of the Republic, the settlement patterns within south Etruria bore comparatively little relationship with the pre-Roman layout; in less than four centuries a quite new landscape had been created, one which was to persist right through the Roman period.

It would be wrong, however, to exaggerate the pace of this change. Veii, for example, may well have been temporarily abandoned immediately following the success of the Roman armies, but Propertius' claim (4, 10, 29–30) that all to be heard within the walls of the city was 'the horn of the idle shepherd' and that the land was given over to cornfields is much more true of the site today than in Roman times. The archaeological evidence makes it quite clear that there was little permanent disruption in the life of the city during the Republican period. Not only do all the sanctuaries (except for that on the Piazza d'Armi) survive in use after the conquest (Ward Perkins, 1961, 54–5; Torelli and Pohl, 1973), but there are large amounts of Hellenistic black glaze pottery from most parts of the site. Despite its eventual isolation from the major highways, it evidently continued to flourish as a thriving market town, with an important local rôle to play. Indeed, in the reign of Augustus, it was created the *Municipium Augustum Veiens*, a status that was usually conferred only upon a large pre-existing settlement.

The implication is therefore that in this early phase of expansion, the Romans were prepared to maintain something of the *status quo*, and this is borne out by the history of towns such as Capena, Sutri and Nepi, all of which fell to Rome in the early fourth century, soon after the capture of Veii. Capena for example was, like Veii, created a *municipium* and, on the evidence of inscriptions, persisted in occupation until well into the third century A.D. (Jones, 1962, 124–5). But all the evidence of archaeology—scant though it is (Jones, 1962, 141–5)—points to a gradual but marked decline in the fortunes of the town after its conquest. Approached just by minor roads, the site has yielded only small quantities of Republican and Imperial pottery and no indication of any major public buildings. Once again its rôle can only have been as a parochial centre, serving the needs of farms in its immediate vicinity. Nepi and Sutri, on the other hand, fared considerably better. Both enjoyed positions of considerable strategic importance—they were 'loca opposita Etruriae et velut claustra inde portaeque': 'places sited to face Etruria and, as it were, both its barriers and its gateways' (Livy, 6, 9, 4)—and there was thus every advantage in maintaining these Roman outposts in Etruscan territory. Both towns received Latin colonies shortly after their conquest and then became *municipia* after the Social War. Sutri was further elevated to the status of a *colonia* after the death of Caesar and was compared by Strabo (5, 2, 9) with the larger towns of Etruria like *Arretium* (Arezzo) and *Perusia* (Perugia) as distinct from smaller towns like Nepi and Falerii. Its importance must have been enhanced by the construction of the Via Cassia in the mid second century B.C., the main long-distance route from Rome up into northern Etruria and, not surprisingly, it remained prosperous throughout the Roman period. Nepi, too, benefited from the laying out of the Via Amerina, which led north-eastwards, up into southern Umbria, and remained an important route down into the Middle Ages. Like Sutri, it seems to have been an affluent settlement right through the Roman period and indeed into post-Roman times.

As far as the towns were concerned, therefore, the Roman policy in the early fourth century seems to have been to maintain the *status quo* and, where there was strategic advantage, actively to promote certain settlements. In the countryside too the scale of disruption seems initially to have been muted. In the part of the Ager Veientanus to the north and north-west of the city, for example, Ward Perkins (1968, 145) concludes that two out of every three farm sites continued in occupation after 396 B.C., while in the adjoining area south of Lake Bracciano, the figure for continuity is even higher, 71 per cent (Hemphill, 1975, 155). This is in close correspondence with the literary evidence. We know that four new tribes were created—Stellatina, Tromantina, Sabatina and Arniensis—and, as Livy (6, 4, 4) tells us, amongst those who received the franchise were the Veientes,

Capenates and Faliscans who had come over to the Romans during the wars. Evidently, the indigenous element in the population of this newly conquered territory was a high one, with many people carrying on in much the same way as before.

On the other hand, there must also have been a significant proportion of new settlers, derived either from the cities or from outside south Etruria. We know from Livy that new citizens were allotted plots of land and we can attempt to identify their farms on the basis of surface scatters of Republican pottery. The principal clue to the dating of such sites is the black glaze pottery which, from the fourth century, became the customary tableware for even the most modest families (Lamboglia, 1950; Taylor, 1957; Morel, 1965). The range of forms is so very standardized that it is clear that we are dealing with commercial manufacture on a large scale: but, equally, we can be certain that many of the kiln sites provided pottery purely for local consumption, as a means of cutting down transport costs and wastage. Thus, there appear to have been manufacturing centres both at Narce (Potter, 1976a, 161, 273) and at Falerii Veteres (Del Chiaro, 1957; Pasqui, 1903a), and it seems likely that many of the black glaze vessels of Rome and the Ager Veientanus were supplied by potteries exploiting the clays of the Tiber Valley. The variety of forms was very considerable. In a domestic rubbish pit from the vicinity of Sutri, for example, there were at least 17 different shapes among the 74 vessels (Duncan, 1965). The most common types were bowls and cups (a trend consistently repeated in the groups of black glaze ware), but jugs, platters, lamps and many other forms were also widely produced. They must also have been fairly cheap, for in the Sutri group they accounted for over 20 per cent of the total pottery assemblage—a high proportion that can be paralleled elsewhere. Thus they constitute very common site finds and provide a useful index of Republican settlement.

The difficulty comes in defining the chronology of individual types. We do have a number of dated groups of black glaze within the Republican period—for example from the Roman colony at Cosa, founded in 273 B.C. (Taylor, 1957)—and these provide us with some idea of the way different shapes evolved during the Republican period. There is moreover a very clear *terminus ante quem* of c. 30 B.C. when the red slipped fabrics of Arezzo, Puteoli and elsewhere completely took over the market for fine quality tableware. But we need to exercise a great deal of caution in applying close dates to individual black glaze forms. In the Ager Faliscus, for example, a study of the very large surface collections by J.-P. Morel showed that no less than 75 per cent of the datable forms were of types normally dated to the third century. Much the same observation was made in a preliminary study of the black glaze wares from Veii (Ward Perkins, 1961, 56–7), and the pattern is similar in other regions of south Etruria. Yet the danger is to interpret these statistics too literally and argue (for example) for a massive depopulation of south Etruria in the last two centuries of the Republic—an argument which is manifestly untenable.

	Period IV	Period V (sites with black glaze)	Period V (sites with no earlier material)
Ward Perkins (1968)	127	242	131
Hemphill (1975)	32	63	34
Craven (unpub.)	59	66	23
Duncan (1958)	1	32	32
Jones (1962, 1963)	22	90	69

Table 4

Much more plausible is an explanation which takes into account the conservatism which often prevails in regional potteries: once popular, an individual form such as the simple bowl (Lamboglia, Form 27) may well have continued in manufacture for a very considerable period of time; indeed a glance at the bowl forms in use in the fourth century at Narce and in the second century at Sutri assures us that they did. The inference must be that we should be exceptionally circumspect in interpreting the evidence of the black-glazed wares: they tell us that a site was occupied in the Republican period but it is all too rarely that we can identify an individual century (Brunt, 1971, 352).

What then can we learn of the new settlers in the Ager Veientanus and Ager Capenas after the Roman conquest? There are very few new sites that can with confidence be dated to the fourth century but there is an enormous body of evidence for a gradual intensification of rural settlement during the Republican period. Quite apart from the Etruscan farms that appear to have continued in occupation after the conquest, there is in every area a very high percentage of new foundations. The figures for the respective survey areas, given in Table 4, convey a striking and consistent picture: that during the 350 years that followed the Roman conquest there was a steady influx of new farmers, who gradually brought into cultivation even the most marginal land. It is unfortunate that we cannot achieve any more detailed breakdown of these statistics but, given Livy's reference (6, 4, 4) to grants of land for newly enfranchised citizens, it seems likely that the trend began early in the fourth century, and then slowly accelerated.

Just how dramatic the change to the landscape could be is illustrated by Duncan's survey of the Sutri area (Duncan, 1958). This hilly terrain along the eastern slopes of the Monti Cimini had, as we have seen, always been thinly settled in prehistory: there are hardly any known prehistoric sites and the pollen diagrams show a virtually uninterrupted pattern of forest growth. Sutri's foundation, probably in the fifth century B.C., initiated a programme of land clearance, but progress must have been slow since as late as 310 B.C. the Ciminian Forest could still be compared with the 'impassable and terrifying' woods that the Roman soldiers were to encounter in Germany in Livy's day (Livy, 9, 36, 1). Yet, by the late first century B.C., dramatic changes had been effected. Matching Sutri's own internal growth, a belt of forest had been cleared for as much as four kilometres to the north

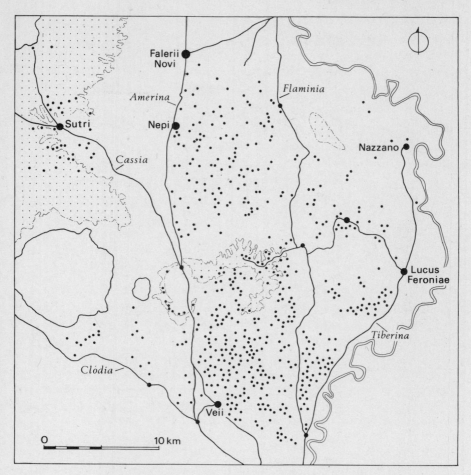

27 South Etruria Survey: the Republican period.

and south of the town; in addition, some attempt had been made to open up a route to Lago di Vico, seven kilometres to the north-west, perhaps to bring the produce of the lake down to the town. Duncan located a total of 38 sites with black glaze pottery (Fig. 27) within this cleared belt of woodland and, while we cannot assume that all were in occupation at the same time, it is nevertheless quite clear that a sustained effort was made to open up the countryside to farming. Once under way, it must have been a process that accelerated both under its own momentum and from the stimulus of new settlers. In 210 B.C. for example the Senate required that certain Campani should be moved *in Veiente Sutrino Nepesinove agro* where, according to Livy (26, 34, 10), land was still available: it was in fact a measure that was never carried out, but it nevertheless shows that conscious efforts were being made to exercise control over rural development. The sum result was a landscape which in a comparatively short period since the Roman conquest had altered to an unprecedented degree.

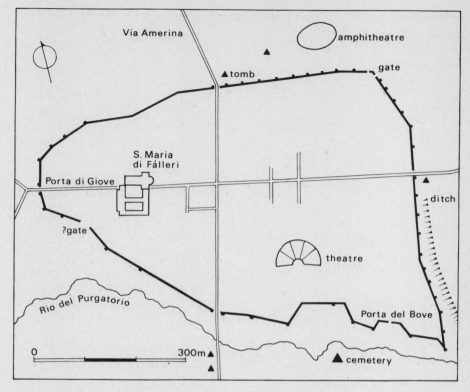

28 Plan of Falerii Novi, S. Maria di Fálleri. (Sources: Frederiksen and Ward Perkins, 1957; Castagnoli, 1974)

Our analysis of Rome's policy towards the territories that were annexed in the early fourth century suggests therefore that at first there was little concern with long-term change: there was no dramatic difference between the landscapes of the fifth and the fourth centuries. The third century, on the other hand, saw the adoption of a much more ruthless strategy, epitomized by the treatment of the Faliscans. Since the end of the fourth century the Faliscans had been under a truce with the Roman state, broken only by some minor infractions. The treaty expired in 242 B.C. and the following year the Romans marched into Faliscan territory. The war was soon over. Six days after the campaign had begun, 15,000 Faliscans had been killed and their principal city, Falerii Veteres, had fallen. The Roman reaction to the capitulation was harsh: half the Faliscan territory was confiscated and in addition it was decided to move the population of Falerii Veteres out of this citadel onto the nearby plain, where a new town, Falerii Novi, was built (Zonaras, 8,18).

The severity of these measures—previously unparalleled in south Etruria—is not hard to detect in the archaeological record. The clearest evidence comes from the remarkably preserved town of Falerii Novi, which was presumably built soon after the conquest of 241. The site lies five kilometres to the west of Falerii Veteres, on a stretch of flat ground between the Rio Crue and the Rio del Purgatorio (Fig. 28). Its walls were laid out in the form of an irregularly shaped triangle, so that the area enclosed was about 750 metres in length and at maximum 500 metres in breadth: it was planned therefore as a large town and an impressive symbol of *Romanitas*, even though it appears to have been, in a formal sense, independent rather than (as one might expect) a *colonia* (Frederiksen and Ward Perkins, 1957, 162). The walls and gates still survive in many places to a height of over six metres. They are built of good quality *tufo* blocks and are pierced by four principal gates, as well as by four minor exits. There are also rectangular bastions at regular intervals along the exterior, recalling the not dissimilar arrangement at Cosa. Inside the town the greater part of the site now consists of open fields, under regular cultivation. The medieval overlay is confined to the church and monastery of S. Maria di Fálleri, now a farm, which lies close to the west gate, the well known Porta di Giove. These ecclesiastical buildings incorporate a good deal of Roman masonry and it is clear that the remains of the classical town have suffered extensively at the hands of stone robbers. This has been confirmed by the excavations that have taken place at sporadic intervals since early in the nineteenth century, identifying, amongst other things, the site of the theatre, close to the south gate. More systematic work began in 1898, when Mancinelli-Scotti (Pasqui, 1903b) traced the broad outlines of the street plan (which seems to have been laid out in the form of a regular grid) and also partially explored several domestic houses, representing various phases of construction. More recently, the Superintendancy of Antiquities has cleared the greater part of an *insula* immediately to the west of the main road junction (probably the site of the forum), bringing to light the remains of a podium built in monumental masonry; it is presumably the base of a temple and gives every prospect of extremely important discoveries in years to come.

There is nothing from the site of Falerii Novi to suggest occupation any earlier than the mid third century and we can assume that the town was planned and built entirely upon Roman initiative, as a new focal and administrative centre. Falerii Veteres on the other hand seems to have been very substantially depopulated, its well defended site, strengthened by massive walls (Frederiksen and Ward Perkins, 1957, 135–6), providing the potential for an unacceptably dangerous focus of opposition. This much is clear from the very large sherd collections from Colle Vignale, an area of Faliscan suburb to the north-west of the present-day town of Civita Castellana; amongst this pottery there are no pieces which can be dated securely to the post-conquest period. Much the same is true of the main nucleus, although there are sporadic Roman finds, including graves and pottery kilns of the early Imperial period (Pasqui, 1903a). Continuity of domestic occupation seems therefore to be largely excluded by the evidence as we know it and there is certainly no question that Falerii Veteres went into a sharp decline as an urban centre. Its sanctuaries, on the other hand, do seem to have been maintained for some considerable length of time after 241 B.C., illustrating a tolerance towards religious practices that the Romans were later to employ widely through the Empire. Falerii Veteres had numerous sacred buildings both within and outside the city (Frederiksen and Ward-Perkins, 1957, 129–33; Andrèn, 1940, 80–151). The best known is the temple dedicated to Juno Curitis, which was situated on low-lying ground in the valley to the north of Colle Vignale. The plan of the temple seems to have conformed to the normal Etruscan type as described by Vitruvius—with three cult rooms and a large portico in front—and the building was handsomely decorated with terracottas. These divide into two main groups, one datable to the late fourth or early third centuries B.C. and the other to the second or early first century B.C. (Andrèn, 1940, 88). Whether the later terracottas represent a refurbishing of the temple or whether they belong to a completely new building is unclear from the report of the nineteenth-century excavations; but they do show that the site did not lapse after the Roman conquest. Indeed, Ovid, writing in the last quarter of the first century B.C. (*Amores*, 3, 13) provides us with a very full description of the festival for the goddess as it was in his day—a ceremony that he witnessed since his wife was born in the 'fruit-bearing Faliscan town', presumably Falerii Novi. Similarly, several other temples seemed to have remained in use into late Republican and early Imperial times, amongst them the important sanctuary complex dedicated to Mercury as Sassi Caduti, which has yielded a fine *acroterion* depicting two warriors in combat. Only the archaic temple built within the suburban area of Colle Viginale does not appear to have survived the Roman sack of the city.

The sharp decline of all but the religious sanctuaries of Falerii Veteres is clear testimony, therefore, of the severe treatment meted out by the Romans upon the conquest of Faliscan territory. But these measures did not stop at the forced evacuation of the principal city. All the available evidence points to a similar decline at the great majority of the other nucleated sites as well. At Narce, for example, extensive excavations of the cemeteries and a systematic search for surface finds on the main centres of occupation have failed to yield any diagnostic material of the second and first centuries B.C. We can infer that the population must have been more or less completely dispersed following the fall of Falerii Veteres. Similarly, in the northern Ager Faliscus, the settlements at Corchiano, Grotta Porciosa and Ponte del Ponte all seem to have been abandoned at the same period and must also have suffered the same treatment. Only at Vignanello (Giglioli, 1924), an isolated outpost in a sparsely populated region of the north-west Ager Faliscus, is there any evidence for occupation into the second century; and even here the site had apparently been abandoned by the end of the Republican period. The conclusion must be that the Romans (who, according to Zonaras, confiscated one half of Faliscan territory) decided to evacuate almost every large settlement and to redistribute the population.

Moreover, it is now equally clear that they did not restrict these harsh measures to the towns. Unlike the areas conquered in the early fourth century, when many Etruscan farms appear to carry on in occupation without appreciable interruption, the rural sites of the Faliscan region present a quite different picture, one of hiatus or total abandonment. More than 80 per cent of the 104 late Faliscan farms located in surface survey appear to have gone out of use about the time of the Roman conquest and close on 50 per cent were never occupied again. Even allowing for all deficiencies of evidence collected from the surface, these figures are impressive. At the same time, we should note that the few farms where surface collections indicate continuity of occupation (there are no more than 15) cluster almost without exception within the environs of Nepi which, while a Faliscan town, had been made a Latin colony in the early fourth century. It is a pattern of distribution which can hardly be fortuitous, and is very reasonably to be interpreted as marking the *territorium* of the colony which was exempt from the consequences of the war.

We do not know what may have happened to the Faliscans who were dispossessed of their farms. All that can be inferred is a well defined hiatus that betokens measures of exceptional severity. Yet the disruption can only have been brief. Before long new farms were founded—68 per cent of them on completely new sites—and the size of the rural population began to rise sharply. The total of Republican sites (i.e. of period V) is almost a third greater than that of the late Faliscan period (period IV) and there is little doubt that these figures are a true reflection of the much greater exploitation of the land at this time. The conquest of the Faliscan area was followed therefore by a pattern of development which closely matches that of neighbouring regions: urban decentralization combined with rural growth. It was a formula that was to recur frequently as Rome's Empire began gradually to expand.

The road network

By the time of the Roman conquest of south Etruria, the Etruscans and Faliscans had, as we have seen, already laid down a network of communications (Fig. 27), linking the major settlements of the region. These roads were not intended as long-distance routes (although they could serve as such) but were created primarily to meet the requirements of local traffic. Thus they were in many cases as relevant to the Roman landscape as to the Etruscan, and must often have remained in use with little or no modification. At the same time, there gradually emerged a need for roads that were specifically designed to afford access to central and northern Etruria and further afield and it was with such considerations in mind that the great 'consular' roads that radiate from Rome were laid out. The Roman engineers were well equipped to build such highways. Not only could they draw upon the experience of their Etruscan predecessors but they had the great advantage of knowing how to construct bridges with masonry arches, a technique far superior to the simple timber span used in pre-Roman Etruria.

They could also create a much more durable surface by the use of paving stones, made usually from the extremely hard grey basalt known as *selce*, and, apart from these technical advantages, were in a position to align the roads with little regard for pre-existing settlements. As a result, the Roman trunk-roads tend to take as direct a line as possible, often (like the southern section of the Via Aurelia) bypassing many of the towns.

The evolution of these long-distance roads is well defined in south Etruria and has been the subject of a number of studies, notably by Ashby (1927, 1929) and Ward Perkins (1957, 1962a). There are four roads of particular importance, all of which originate at the Milvian Bridge, on the north side of Rome. These roads comprised: (1) the Via Clodia, which headed north-westwards around the western edge of Lake Bracciano and thence up into central Etruria to Saturnia; (2) the Via Cassia, which went to Chiusi, Arezzo and Florence and then over the Apennines into north-east Italy; (3) the Via Amerina, a route that passed through Nepi, Falerii Novi and thence up into Umbria via Orte; and (4) the Via Flaminia, the major trunk-road to the north-east, with Rimini and the Adriatic coast as its ultimate objective. This arrangement of long-distance highways provided Rome with a network of communications which remained largely unchanged until the building of the autostrade in recent decades; yet the individual roads display considerable variation in layout, chronology and function and it is as well to discuss them separately.

The only highway with a firm date is the Via Flaminia, built by Gaius Flaminius in 220 B.C. (Ashby and Fell, 1921; Martinori, 1929; Ballance, 1951), not long after the conquest of the Ager Faliscus. The most striking feature about the road is its directness of line, laid out so as to avoid virtually all of the existing towns in the territory through which it ran. Immediately north of Rome, for example, it kept well to the east of Veii, first following a line along the prominent ridge that runs up to Castelnuovo di Porto and then joining the watershed that divides the Ager Faliscus from the Ager Capenas. Falerii Veteres was bypassed well to the east and the road crossed into Umbria at a bridge situated some way south of Otricoli. Thus, even though there was probably a ridgeway track along this line in pre-Roman times (Jones, 1962, 165), the Via Flaminia was clearly intended to serve much more than local traffic and was probably, as Wiseman (1970) and Harris (1971) have emphasized, envisaged principally as a military route, allowing rapid access into the Po Plain. Whether it was surfaced with *selce* at the time of its original construction is unclear (although the Via Appia had been paved as early as 293: Livy, 10, 47, 4), but there are now abundant surviving traces of both the kerbstones and the paving, varying in width between four and eight metres. There are also numerous examples of the bridges (Ballance, 1951), including an impressive viaduct across the Treia valley, to the east of Civita Castellana (Ashby and Fell, 1921, 158-60; Ballance, 1951, 86-8). Here the road was carried down into the valley by means of a massive embankment revetted with masonry and pierced by an arched passage or culvert, known as the Voltarella. The gradient is steep, about 1 in 8, but quite practicable for wheeled transport. Once on the river flood plain, a causeway took the road up to the bridge (most of which is destroyed) and across to a second great ramp, 10.8 metres wide, again faced with masonry. Here the gradient is less—about 1 in 12—and this gentle slope is maintained at the top of the valley by a cutting in the rock which brings the road out on to the plateau. Overall, the viaduct (which on the basis of the masonry is unlikely to be later than Augustus) is a magnificent illustration of the lengths to which the Roman engineers were prepared to go to provide an easily negotiated valley crossing.

Yet we should beware of assuming that all of the 'consular' roads were laid out with as little regard for pre-existing features as the Flaminia. Very often they incorporated substantial stretches of older roads, only relaying the surface and creating new bridges where necessary. One such road is the Via Clodia, whose destination—the countryside of central Etruria and especially the settlement at Saturnia—implies much more limited objectives than those of the other trunk-roads. In fact, large parts of its route seem to have existed long before it was rationalized as a Roman trunk-road. It branched from the Via Cassia at La Storta, nine Roman miles to the north of Rome, and for the first few kilometres followed the line of the old Etruscan route between Veii and Caere, around the head of the Galeria Valley (Ward Perkins, 1955; Hemphill, 1975). It then parted company from the earlier road to strike north-westwards toward Bracciano and shortly afterwards picked up the line of another pre-Roman route, which headed northwards into the hilly terrain of central Etruria. This road provided a link between Etruscan towns such as Blera, Norchia, Tuscania and Saturnia, all of which remained continuously inhabited through Roman times; however, unlike the Aurelia and Flaminia, the Roman Via Clodia was not diverted around these sites—instead, the surface was paved and proper bridges were constructed so that the road provided easy access to the city of Rome. It was intended therefore more as a service route than for rapid long-distance travel, much as its Etruscan predecessor had been.

Unfortunately, we can only guess at the date of the Roman layout of the Clodia and estimates have varied widely. It is likely that it came into use soon after the region was finally subdued in the early part of the third century; but the major reorganization may well be much later—possibly, as Harris (1971, 166-7) has suggested, coinciding with the foundation of the *colonia* at Saturnia in 183 B.C., its ultimate destination. Much better dated, however, is the road that was quite clearly intended to be the principal trunk-road to the north, the Via Cassia. Convincing arguments have been put forward (Harris, 1965; Wiseman, 1970) for a date of 154, when C. Cassius Longinus was censor, and this view has won general acceptance. The road has, however, a complex history. Its precursor appears to have been in part the Via Veientana, which formed one of the oldest routes between Veii and Rome (Ward Perkins, 1955), and in part the Etruscan road (Fig. 21) that left Veii through the north-west gate and then headed via Pisciacavallo and Baccano to Nepi and Sutri (Ward Perkins, 1957,

139–43; 1961, 60–1). Initially, therefore, traffic was channelled through Veii in much the same way as towns like Blera and Tuscania controlled passage along the Via Clodia. With the construction of the Cassia in the mid second century B.C., the strategy was completely altered. The new road was laid out with as total a disregard for existing urban centres as its neighbour, the Via Flaminia. Thus Veii was bypassed some distance to the west and it was not until Sutri, 40 kilometres to the north-west of the Milvian ridge over the Tiber, that the Cassia approached a town. Its line was in fact chosen with great skill. Despite the myriad streams that drain the slopes of the Monti Sabatini, it used only one bridge between Tomba di Nerone and Sutri, an economy of effort that betokens considerable care in setting out the route (although the engineers do appear to have drained the Baccano crater (Pl. Ia) to facilitate the crossing of the Monti Sabatini). At the same time, the line that was chosen is notable for its easy gradients and straightness of direction. Like the Flaminia its objectives lay in northern Italy and everything was done to ensure a rapid passage.

The construction of Flaminia and Cassia show unmistakably how, in the period between c. 220 and 150, the priorities swung away from local roads to a network of communications that was to bring all Italy within the orbit of Rome. The contrast is further heightened by another securely dated road, the Via Amerina (Frederiksen and Ward Perkins, 1957). Like the other trunk-roads, its history is complex. In its original form, it represented the main route between Veii and Nepi, following the same line as the pre-second-century course of the Via Cassia and only diverging from that route at the Baccano crater. Here the Amerina swung off to the right, traversing the numerous gorges which inhibit movement to the north by means of a series of massive cuttings and viaducts. This impressive stretch of road (Pl. VIIa) was almost certainly first laid out when Nepi became a Latin colony in the early fourth century, as an alternative to the difficult and indirect route via the central Ager Veientanus and Narce (Fig. 21). But the main period of construction of the Amerina undoubtedly belongs to the decades that followed the conquest of the Ager Faliscus in 241 B.C. The new stretch of road ran from Nepi through the northern Ager Faliscus to Orte and then into southern Umbria; thus, like the Via Clodia, it seems to have been designed as a service road for this newly conquered territory rather than as a long-distance line of communication. Its general date is not in doubt since it is orientated with extraordinary precision upon the axis of the street system of Falerii Novi and we may therefore assume that it must have been built at some time between c. 240 and 220 B.C. As such it must have been laid out about 150 years after the stretch to the south of Nepi and it is therefore interesting to see that there are considerable differences in technique. The newer section is for example much straighter in alignment than its southern counterpart, as if the initial survey was much more carefully done. The cuttings also show distinct differences, preference being given in the later road to long, straight trenches leading down to a high bridge. The crossing of two adjacent rivers, the Fosso Tre Ponti and the Rio Maggiore,

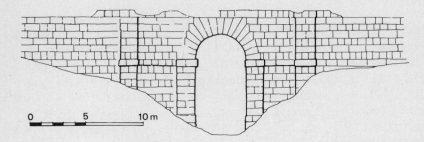

29 Republican bridge carrying the Via Amerina across the Fosso Tre Ponti, south of Falerii Novi. (Source: Frederiksen and Ward Perkins, 1957)

will illustrate the point. Both gorges were approached by wide straight cuttings whose length was sufficient to ensure a gentle gradient. Of the bridges, the better preserved is that over the Fosso Tre Ponti (Fig. 29; Pl. VIb), but both bridges seem to follow the same model and were presumably built to a single plan. The masonry technique was that of headers and stretchers laid without either mortar or cramps and dowels; a date in the third quarter of the third century is thus stylistically very plausible. There was a single arch, approached by two massive masonry abutments supported by buttresses. The height of the arch was over nine metres above stream level and the carriageway nearly eight metres across, a viaduct built to a truly impressive scale.

So far, therefore, we have distinguished two main groups of trunk-road, the Clodia and the Amerina serving more local needs, while the Cassia and Flaminia provided long-distance routes of communication and may initially have been laid out for specifically military purposes. In addition there also came into being a series of secondary roads, some of which are known to have been administered by the same *curator* who was responsible for trunk-roads like the Cassia, Clodia and Amerina (Frederiksen and Ward Perkins, 1957, 192). Amongst these secondary roads was the Via Annia (which may have linked Sutri and Falerii Novi) and the Via Ciminia. The latter was a paved country road which headed north-west from Sutri, to skirt the eastern edge of Lago di Vico (Duncan, 1958, 84–6). It presumably then followed a route over Monte Cimino and down into the Viterbese but its actual course has yet to be defined in detail. Even though it was a public road, run—at any rate in the second century A.D. (the date of the relevant inscriptions)—by a board of *curatores viarum,* it nevertheless was built on a much more modest scale than the main trunk-roads. Its width seems to have been only about three metres—just room for two vehicles to pass—and much of its course is marked not by cuttings but by the cheaper expedient of recessing the road into the hillside. Similarly, wide detours were made to avoid major natural obstacles and in places the gradients were extremely steep, with one short stretch which approaches 1 in 5. This road, while maintained at public expense, can never have been planned as a direct line of communication between major centres. It is best interpreted as a road designed to link town with country. As such it is but one of many paved Roman roads in south Etruria, laid out solely for local needs.

The purpose of these roads varied. One for example ran along the crest of the Monti Sabatini westwards to the Via Flaminia at Morlupo. Many sections of the Roman paving are still quite visible today and it is clear that it began at Monte Maggiore, a hill composed largely of *selce,* the basalt widely used for road paving. Enormous quarries cut into the side of this hill make it plain that the road was laid out in the first instance to transport the quarried blocks to the main road, although later it became the focus of a number of large farms and villas. Similarly, the *selce* deposits at Monte Aguzzo, in the Ager Veientanus, were also extensively exploited and, in consequence, a paved road was built to haul the heavy stone to the Via Flaminia (Ward Perkins, 1968, 111). Paved roads may also have served some of the larger *tufo* quarries, such as those at Grotta Oscura between the Flaminia and the Tiber Valley (Frank, 1924, 17–21), and would undoubtedly have facilitated the distribution of the tiles and pottery which was manufactured at numerous points in the Campagna. But it is equally clear that most of the paved roads were constructed to improve local communications and especially to transport the produce of the farming estates. As such, many of these roads represented little more than a modification of their Etruscan predecessors, where the improvements were restricted to the laying of stone paving, the building of simple bridges and on occasion the realignment of the road-cutting. This much is clear on the evidence of sites that flank the roads, which indicate that in many instances the route had been open long before the Roman period. Thus, in the Ager Capenas, the lateral communication between towns like Capena itself and Nazzano (both sites of pre-Roman origin) was improved though not substantially altered (Jones, 1962, 128), and the Via Tiberina was paved over its whole length to provide an all-weather route along the west bank of the Tiber (Jones, 1963, 135). Similarly, in both the Ager Veientanus and the Ager Faliscus, the pre-existing network continued to form the main basis for local communications, even though many of the old centres (which had formed the foci of the pre-Roman road system) were by now totally abandoned.

The date of the paving of these secondary roads is much more difficult to determine, especially as it is quite apparent that individual roads often went through several phases of repair and rebuilding. The Flaminia, for example, is known to have been extensively restored under Augustus in 27 B.C., while a section through the Via Cassia, recorded in 1966 between Tomba di Nerone and La Storta, also indicated progressive relaying and enlargement of the surface. In this case there appear to have been two phases of gravel metalling, before the cutting was enlarged and a more durable paving of regular *selce* blocks was laid down (Fig. 30). The paved surface can be shown to antedate a nearby Roman building which, from the pottery, seems to have been occupied during the first and second centuries

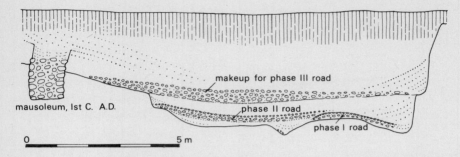

30 Section across the Via Cassia at Tomba di Nerone, showing three successive road
surfaces, predating an early Imperial mausoleum.

A.D. Similarly, where it has been possible to study sections across minor
roads, there have usually proved to be several resurfacings. At the Podere
S. Angelo, for example, on the route of a minor paved road between
Malborghetto and Sacrofano, there was a build-up of over two metres above
bedrock with at least three successive road levels (Ward Perkins, 1968,
126–7). The upper two were both paved with *selce* but the lowest consisted
of a hollow way, five metres wide, set into the bedrock. Drainage ditches
flanked the road surface and appear to have been recut at least once. The
form of the surface was not clear from the section but it may well have
consisted just of the bare rock, in the same manner as Etruscan roads.
Fortunately we can establish a *terminus post quem* for the first resurfacing,
since the make-up levels for the basalt paving included a good deal of
pottery dating to the second half of the first century A.D.; the paving must
therefore have been laid about A.D. 100 or later.

Another site, at the Vallelunga Autodrome, to the west of Campagnano,
gave much more information about the earliest road surface. This road
parted from the Via Amerina near the Baccano crater and took a northerly
direction towards a large group of rich villas. It must have been intended
to carry the farm produce down to the main road and thence to Rome. The
paved road (Pl. VIIIa; Fig. 31) was 2.30 metres wide and was carefully
constructed with good quality paving in *selce* and kerbstones along either
side. In addition there were markers made of larger stones along the
southern kerb, set exactly 20 Roman feet apart. These can be paralleled on
many of the trunk-roads including the Via Amerina, Clodia and Appia and
may have been intended to indicate distances.

In 1970, the opportunity came to lift a substantial stretch of the paving
and examine its foundations. After the removal of a thick layer of make-up,
an earlier road was exposed, whose surface consisted solely of the bedrock.
Scored in this surface were a series of deep ruts, representing at least three
sets of wheel tracks, between 2 and 2.20 metres across. It seems clear that
once the road surface had become too worn, then the simple expedient was
adopted of shifting the line a short distance to one side. In this way expensive
repair work was avoided and maintenance bills must have been minimal.

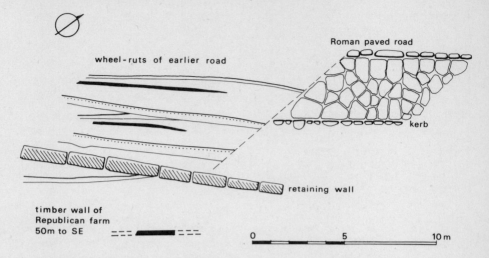

31 Plan of successive country roads and other features at Vallelunga in the southern Ager Faliscus.

Yet during the winter rains such roads must have been extremely difficult for heavy carts and it was presumably with this in mind that the decision was taken to pave the surface. Quite when this was done is conjectural, but the make-up did contain some Republican pottery and one sherd which may date to the first century A.D. It looks therefore as if the Vallelunga paved road may have been laid out about the same time as the Malborghetto route, described above. Exactly who may have financed these secondary roads is by no means always clear but in some cases it is certain that they were paid for privately by rich landowners. For example, there are a number of villas in south Etruria which have their own service drive, some of them of considerable length, like the *diverticulum* which connected the villa of S. Giovanni a Pollo (Fig. 37) with the town of Sutri, over two kilometres away (Duncan, 1958, 88–9). This must have been constructed by the affluent owner of this large villa, to bring the produce of a big estate to the town. Similarly, near the Bivio di Formello in the Ager Veientanus, we know of a small bridge, 1.58 metres wide, that was constructed in the first century A.D. by a private landowner to carry a minor road into a series of estates north of the Fosso del Forco (Guzzo, 1970). One masonry arch and the abutments survived, built of dressed *tufo* blocks without mortar. But the important discovery was that the keystone of the arch bore on both sides an inscription, which tells how T. Humanius Stabilio built the bridge *in privato trasientibus*—'at his own expense for those who crossed it' (Pl. VIIIb).

This discovery shows very explicitly how the more influential landowners were prepared to invest resources in the improvement of local communications. Their objective was to facilitate the passage of goods to and from the towns, especially Rome, and in this respect it is interesting to note that

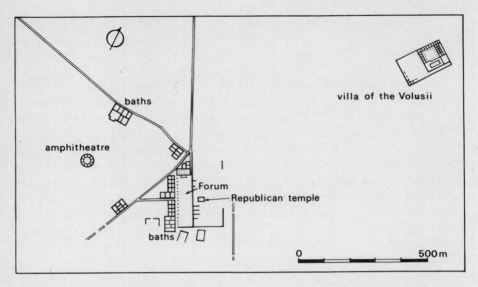

32 Schematic plan of Lucus Feroniae. (Sources: Schmiedt, 1970; Bartoccini, 1963; Autostrade, 1968)

the few minor roads to which we can assign approximate dates do correspond chronologically, as we shall see, with the period of maximum rural prosperity. Never had the countryside been so thickly populated as in the first and early second centuries A.D., a sure incentive for the improvement of communications. Yet it is important to realize that the great majority of the country roads remained either unpaved or only roughly metalled with gravel. They were the equivalent to today's 'strade bianche', the network of country tracks that has grown up almost on an *ad hoc* basis to serve the rural community. The disadvantage of such tracks is the extreme difficulty of passage during the winter months when deep erosion gullies constantly form in the surface of the road. But they were a cheap expedient, especially in an area where much of the engineering had already been done in Etruscan times and maintenance was not particularly expensive. Consequently the unpaved road was in Roman times and remains today the most commonly used form of country road.

The towns and road-stations

The corollary of the development of the trunk-road system was a steady drift down to the main highways, where a series of small wayside stations began to grow up. Many of these were sited at junctions between main and secondary roads and must often have been the result of spontaneous growth. Others, such as Forum Cassii (S. Maria di Forcassi, near Vetralla), were dispersed along the major highways at fairly regular intervals and may have been built up under specific Roman stimulus to provide services for official travellers. Both have their counterpart in the roadside stations of present-day Italy, where contemporary wayside development is often directly superimposed upon a layout of classical buildings. At the same time, there was a network of larger towns which acted as local market centres as well as foci for industrial and commercial life. These larger towns were, as we have seen, by no means as numerous as in the pre-Roman period. Only a small proportion of the Etruscan and Faliscan nucleated centres were actively fostered and many seem to have been deliberately abandoned. There were however two new foundations, the north Faliscan town of Falerii Novi (Fig. 28), whose main features have been summarized above and, in the southern Ager Capenas, the site of Lucas Feroniae (Fig. 32). This important settlement was identified only as recently as 1953, ending many years of speculation about its location. It lay on the edge of the Tiber Valley on a shelf of travertine, just to the north of the *casale* of Scorano. It setting is immediately reminiscent of the terrain of Falerii Novi, with many miles of level plain extending in all directions around the town. Local communi- cations—enhanced by the nearness of the Tiber—can have presented no difficulty and there was a direct route to Rome along the Via Tiberina. The site itself is now completely deserted and, up to the time of its discovery, almost totally buried beneath a thin layer of topsoil. Now twenty years of excavation have laid bare a good deal of the forum complex, together with the remains of temples, streets, houses and also a small amphitheatre. But the real importance of the site stems from its religious associations. Feronia was an Italic goddess who, as inscriptions show (Jones, 1962, 192), was widely venerated across central Italy. Every year a festival was held at Lucus Feroniae and was attended by numerous devotees, amongst them Etruscans, Sabines, Latins and Faliscans (Strabo, 5, 2, 9; Livy, I, 30). In addition the *fanum* also afforded the opportunity for a good deal of commercial interchange, aided no doubt by the town's position at a natural crossroads between the territories to the east and west of the Tiber. The temple appears to have been located at the north end of the forum (Bartocinni, 1963). Here there was a raised podium, retaining traces of a large temple. This was flanked by two pillars, both bearing the name of the goddess. More recent excavations have also brought to light numerous dedications made by the devotees (Moretti and Battaglia, 1975), as well as many fine votive offerings; it is clear that the cult was subscribed to by a diverse congregation, many of whom appear to have been freedmen and slaves.

One aspect of the cult which was revealed by the more recent excavations is an emphasis upon healing. This has emerged from the discovery of a deposit of votive objects just to the north of the temple (Moretti and Battaglia, 1975, 110–54). The ex-votos are made of cream terracotta and are accurate and often life-size representations of parts of the human body—heads, feet, hands, legs, genitals and even some internal organs, such as uteri. Such finds are by no means uncommon. During the period between c. 350 and 150 B.C. there grew up many sanctuaries, both in urban and rural contexts, that specialized in curing various sorts of illness, and it was customary (as in many parts of Europe today) to supplicate the deity by offering a clay model of the afflicted part. There is no doubt too that many sanctuaries did offer some form of medical treatment, most probably a course of bathing in sacred pools, fed by the sort of sulphurous spring that is so widespread in the volcanic region of Italy. Pliny (*Nat. Hist.* 31) in fact lists the wide variety of cures that could be achieved in this way, while, nearer at hand, we have the popular (and efficacious) contemporary examples of Bath or Lourdes. A great many of the Republican sanctuary sites are now known and some, like Lucas Feroniae, have yielded large samples of votive objects. Unfortunately few sites have been treated to the numerical analysis that they deserve but, where figures are available, these do indicate an element of medical specialization. At the Campetti sanctuary at Veii, for example, the sample was dominated by ex-votos representing the genital organs (Torelli and Pohl, 1973) which, as Dr Calvin Wells has suggested (Potter, 1979), may well indicate a high proportion of sexually transmitted diseases—as one might expect in an urban environment. At Ponte di Nona (Fig. 34), a sanctuary site forming the nucleus of a small road-station on the Via Prenestina, 15 kilometres east of Rome, the picture is quite different. The ex-votos form an enormous deposit of over 8000 recognizable pieces consisting very largely of limb fragments, especially feet and hands (Fig. 33). These are precisely the parts of the body that one might expect to be damaged in a rural environment where much of the population was engaged in farming—and, as Ward Perkins and Kahane (1972) have shown, Ponte di Nona was indeed the centre of an area that was largely peopled by smallholders. Whether there was any definite specialization in the Lucus Feroniae sanctuary is a matter that must await full publication of the finds; but in the meantime we can note that this site is but one—albeit very celebrated—centre for a healing cult that achieved exceptional popularity during the period of the early to mid Republic

Certainly the temple of Feronia became very prosperous for, in 211 B.C., Hannibal thought it worth his while to cross the Tiber at Eretum and plunder the shrine (Livy, 26, 2). Some traces of this destruction have been identified archaeologically (Moretti and Battaglia, 1975, 111) and there seems to have been a major reconstruction of the layout of the town some time afterwards. The most probable context is the foundation of a *colonia*—the *colonia Iulia Felix Lucoferoniensis*—sometime in the later first century B.C. The exact date is disputed (Harris, 1971, 308–9) but it is likely to have been under Augustus, when there was a deliberate attempt to foster some of the older urban centres. Amongst these was Veii, which was created *municipium Augustum Veiens* (*CIL*, XI, 3797), and became very prosperous in the succeeding Julio-Claudian era (Ward Perkins, 1961, 57). Yet we cannot see this as an isolated phenomenon. Following his victories at Philippi and Actium, Augustus had a great many veterans to settle and his response was to create a large number of *coloniae* and to reallocate a certain amount of land. As such it was a policy which followed fairly naturally

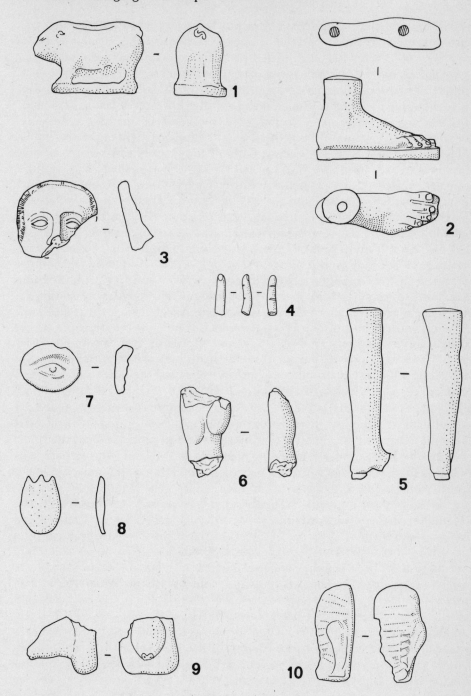

33 Votive terracottas of *c*. 250–150 B.C. from the sanctuary at Ponte di Nona. With the exception of 1, 3 and 5, all are modelled approximately at lifesize. (1) Pig; (2) foot; (3) face mask; (4) finger; (5) leg; (6) hand; (7) eye; (8) tongue; (9) male genitals; (10) uterus.

from the grants of colonial status made under Sulla, Caesar and the *triumvirs*—in 46 B.C., for example, Caesar's agents were engaged in a survey of the territories of Veii and Capena with land resettlement in mind (Cicero, *ad Fam*. 9, 17, 1)—but it was the Augustan settlement that seems to have had most impact in south Etruria (Harris, 1971, 303–18). This much is clear both from the large quantity of Julio-Claudian building-dedications found at towns like Lucus Feroniae, Veii and Caere, and, more explicitly, from the very considerable number of public buildings that were put up in this period. The urban centre at Lucus Feroniae provides a good illustration (Fig. 32).

The forum was laid out in the form of a long rectangle, about 30 metres broad and over 200 metres in length. A portico with Tuscan columns flanked its west side, behind which was a long row of small *tabernae* or bars, each with a marble-topped counter containing one or more wine jars. The back of each bar was made up of two or more rooms, the living quarters of the proprietor and his family; these were constructed in *opus reticulatum*, a technique commonly used between *c*. 50 B.C. and A.D. 50. Half-way along this side of the forum there was a wide paved avenue with, at the corner, the remains of a *schola*, whose floors were elegantly paved with rectangular pieces of coloured marble. Then there were more bars and, at the south-west end, a large bath-house with black and white mosaic floors of early Imperial date. The east side, on the other hand, was rather differently laid out. It was demarcated by a high wall built of *opus reticulatum* with, behind, the remains of more small buildings and the altar and footings of a Republican temple, constructed with large masonry blocks. This was presumably the original temple to the goddess Feronia, whose shrine was retained when the town was laid out in its present form. Indeed something of the plan of the small Republican houses that clustered round the temple has recently been uncovered in a long trench excavated beside the west portico (Moretti and Battaglia, 1975). The main focus of the Augustan forum lay, however, at the north end where there was an imposing aisled basilica, built on a high podium of large limestone blocks. Approached by a wide flight of stairs, in front of which was an altar, this basilican complex incorporated a number of different structures, amongst them an *aerarium*, where the funds, records and military standards of the *colonia* were kept, and a small apsidal shrine to the Emperor Augustus. Although much of the forum in its present form was undoubtedly constructed during his reign, this is one of two public works which can be securely dated by the evidence of epigraphy.

The second is the town's aqueduct, the Aqua Augusta (Bartoccini, 1963; Jones, 1962, 197–201), identifiable from an inscription which describes the carrying out of extensive repairs. The water was distributed through the town by a complex system of conduits and pipes and also discharged into a large storage tank situated on the east side of the forum. The supply originated two kilometres to the west of the town from a small but perennial river, the Fosso Gramiccia. Here there are traces of two dams, one a V-shaped structure, pierced by a spillway, and the other a much less massive wall, built diagonally across the stream. The V-shaped dam carried an arrangement of twin pipes, whereas the simpler wall held only one outlet, and it is a fair presumption, therefore, that the decision was made to increase the quantity of water supplying the town—possibly in conjunction with the repairs mentioned in the inscription. This arrangement would have supplied about three-quarters of a million gallons a day, a modest quantity by comparison with even the smallest of Rome's aqueducts but a figure that is closely comparable to the water requirements of many small Italian towns.

The other excavated structures at Lucus Feroniae fit fairly well into the conventional picture of the Roman town, with remains of houses flanking the streets, public baths, a public lavatory situated close to the north-east corner of the forum and a small, nearly circular amphitheatre, measuring 34.10 × 32.30 metres. Most of these buildings belong to the first century A.D. and, together with the epigraphic record, provide clear testimony of the prosperity that characterizes this century both in the towns and countryside of south Etruria. That this prosperity also continued into the early second century is evident from an inscription which describes Trajan as 'restitutor coloniae'. It was found in the Augusteum at the north end of the forum (Moretti and Battaglia, 1975, 96) and, if linked with the description of repairs to the aqueduct, suggests a programme of rebuilding down into the 120s or 130s. Thereafter, the town went into decline: the epigraphic record thins out quite considerably during the second century and, while we lack the detailed evidence in published form, it is clear that the settlement was all but defunct by the fifth to sixth centuries—a story that is repeated at many of the Roman towns, especially those constructed, like Lucus Feroniae, on low-lying ground.

The history of Roman Veii is also rather similar. Destined to obscurity when bypassed by the main trunk-roads (it was noted in antiquity only for the dreadful quality of its wine: Martial, 1, 103, 9), Veii appears to have enjoyed just a brief period of prosperity in the days of the early Empire. This followed the grant of municipal status under Augustus, datable from an inscription (*CIL*, xi, 3797) to before 1 B.C. There are a number of imperial dedications belonging to the Julio-Claudian period, but the volume of such records then drops sharply, the latest being a single inscription in honour of Constantius I, datable to between A.D. 293 and 305 (*CIL*, xi, 3796): significantly it is also the latest datable inscription of any sort from the site, and we can probably envisage a slow decline of the town during the mid to late Empire. Archaeologically, our knowledge of the layout and history of the town is meagre. Such excavation as has been carried out belongs almost entirely to the nineteenth century and the record of this work is at best scanty. Nevertheless, it is clear that the focus of the town was directly superimposed upon the principal area of Etruscan and early Republican occupation, in the north-east part of the main plateau (Fig. 14). Today there is nothing to be seen in this area except for heavily ploughed scatters of rubble and pottery; but a combination of old excavation reports and surface observation suggests a nucleus some 700 metres in length, with the forum situated close to the old Etruscan crossroads (Ward Perkins, 1961, 57–71). Nearby was a theatre and, to judge from inscriptions, temples both to Mars and to Augustus. The houses spread out along the roads in a form of ribbon development, while other buildings—presumably suburban villas—were scattered over large parts of the plateau, most of which must have been cultivated with market gardens. It was a type of town—apparently without any formal layout—that is still familiar today, especially in parts of southern Italy, and, in its irregular street plan, clearly betrays its long Etruscan ancestry.

Similarly, at Sutri (Duncan, 1958, 66–73), the form of the Roman town was considerably influenced by the irregular topography of the spur that the Etruscan founders chose for their site (Fig. 22, Pl. XIa). There was no real possibility of superimposing a regular grid of streets upon such awkward ground and, though we lack direct evidence, we can probably assume that the town developed in a very loosely planned way. The one public building that is directly attested in the archaeological record is the amphitheatre, which was inserted into the end of a low ridge to the south of the town. It is remarkable both for its fine preservation and for its method of construction, for almost the entire structure was cut out of the rock. Only the two entrances contain any quantity of walling, in each case consisting largely of brick. Unfortunately, we cannot establish the period of the building with any certainty, since no inscription or closely dated architectural feature has been recovered from the site. But the commonly held view that the amphitheatre is likely to have been built shortly after Sutri's elevation to the status of a *colonia* in the late first centure B.C. is a reasonable conjecture, given the emphasis upon the construction of public works at that time. Similarly, the town's main cemetery, which lay close to the site of the amphitheatre, seems also to have come into being about this period. The graves (Duncan, 1958, 113) flanked the west side of the Via Cassia for a length of over 140 metres and, in the manner of Etruscan chamber tombs, were cut into the cliff, in the form of niches or rooms. Several had ornamental facades, including pilasters and elaborate pediments and, in one case, relief designs of a patera and jug. Such tombs, lining the main approaches to Sutri, can only have been the burials of the more wealthy and influential members of the community.

Much of Sutri's prosperity must have derived from its position upon the principal trunk-road up into central Etruria; it was the first town on the line of the Via Cassia after Rome itself and would have served a good deal of the transit traffic. Nepi enjoyed a similarly well placed position on the Via Amerina, and must also have been a wealthy town. In fact, the *Liber Coloniarum* (217, 15–16), refers to the settlement as a *colonia* but this attribution is generally thought to be incorrect (Wiseman, 1970). However, there is an inscription from the site that describes Nepi as a *municipium* (*CIL,* XI 3214), a high rank that is entirely consistent with what we know of the Roman town. The finds are not numerous for there is a heavy overlay of medieval and modern structures, but the volume of building inscriptions, tombstones and altars (many of which are still preserved in the porticoes of the cathedral and town hall at Nepi) is nevertheless quite sufficient to attest to its prosperity. As at Sutri, the local topography—a tongue-like spur of land, flanked by deep gorges (Fig. 13)—must have shaped the way in which the town developed, and its layout also probably owed a great deal to that of the Faliscan settlement that had existed on the site since at least the eighth century B.C. There is unlikely to have been any real attempt to superimpose the regular grid of *insulae* found at Falerii Novi and many other Roman towns, although there must have been a forum and basilica; these probably lay on the more open ground at the west end of the town where the Via Amerina passed through the settlement. Yet, whereas towns like Falerii Novi fell into decline in the later centuries of the Imperial period, Nepi appears to have become increasingly important. In the sixth century, for example, it is described by Procopius as a fortress (φρούριον: *Bell. Goth.* 4, 35), which was situated directly on one of the main routes used by the barbarian tribes in the attacks upon Rome. Its strategic significance was evidently considerable, a rôle that it continued to maintain down into the early Middle Ages (Bullough, 1965). The combination of a strong position and good communications with Rome must have been important factors in ensuring the survival of town life.

In fact, Nepi and Sutri stand apart from the Roman towns of south Etruria in their survival into the medieval period; the rest, although often prosperous market centres in early Imperial times, seem in almost every case to have slowly fallen into decay during the later centuries of the Empire. The only other possible exception is Nazzano, a settlement in the northern Ager Capenas which is likely to have ranked as a *civitas*, perhaps the *civitas Sepernatium* (Jones, 1963, 107–10). Like Sutri and Nepi, Nazzano is a hilltop site occupied since Etruscan times down to the present day. We cannot prove continuity of occupation but the probability is high, especially since the pre-Roman and Classical remains are abundantly represented in the vicinity of the town. Amongst these is a circular temple of Imperial date, which lay close to the present-day church of S. Antimo, and many dedications to Diana, Magna Mater and Bona Dea. There are also altars which were set up to Septimius Severus and other emperors of the third century A.D. Closely dated finds of the late Roman and early Middle Ages are otherwise lacking, but the superimposition of a medieval town upon the Roman settlement suggests a degree of continuity that is lacking at most comparable Classical sites to the north of Rome.

Yet, the overall number of Roman towns in south Etruria was by no means high, especially when compared with the proliferation of nucleated settlements that characterized the later Etruscan period. Including Capena and Nazzano (neither of which can have been especially large) we know only of seven towns within the 2000 square kilometres to the north of Rome. This can be explained in two ways: first, by the presence of a large rural population; second, by a marked growth in roadside settlements. Both are phenomena that are extremely familiar today and in part can be seen as testimony to a steep rise in the size of the population; but they are also a measure of the impact that the creation of efficient communications had upon rural life.

The road-stations were in many cases the product of a drift to major crossroads where basic services were needed by the traveller. The distribution was governed to some extent by a process of natural selection so that they were spaced out at regular intervals along the major trunk-roads; they were in effect overnight stopping places where horses could be changed and accommodation provided at the *mansio*. Their names, as listed in the road itineraries, often reflect this function: thus, travelling up the Via Flaminia from Rome, one reached first *Ad Rubras,* where the Tiberina and Flaminia diverge, and then, after 20 Roman miles, *Ad Vicesimum* (= *Ad XX*) (Ashby and Fell, 1921); or, along the Via Cassia, there were road-stations at Tomba di Nerone (*Ad V*); La Storta (*Ad IX*), where the Clodia and Cassia diverged, and *Ad Baccanas*, at the junction between the Amerina and Cassia. Unfortunately, we know all too little about the layout of these settlements, since none has been excavated to any great extent. Yet the surface finds leave no doubt about their overall history: that they began to develop during the late Republic and, like most of the towns, were at their most prosperous during the first two centuries A.D. Then they too began to decline, so that very few have yielded many artifacts that date much later than *c.* A.D. 400.

Careiae is a case in point. This was a small road-station that grew up beside the Via Clodia some five kilometres to the north-west of the junction with the Via Cassia (Ward Perkins, 1955, 63–4). The name is attested both by Frontinus (*De Aqu.* 71) and in road-books like the Antonine Itinerary (300, 2), the Peutinger Table (5, 4) and the Ravenna Cosmography (274, 8). Whilst the standing remains are confined to a cistern and the core of a tomb, the surface traces imply a continuous build-up of houses and other structures on either side of the road, extending over a distance of nearly half a kilometre. Tuscan and Corinthian capitals, statues, a wide range of imported marbles and large quantities of painted plaster and mosaic tesserae show that many of these buildings were architecturally quite pretentious and at least one complex, some 200 metres distant from the road, had a large bath-house; it may have been the *mansio*. The surface finds also give a good idea of the history of the site. The pottery series begins with black glaze sherds of late Republican date, but the bulk of the material dates to early Imperial times. There are no Red Slip-ware vessels later than the fourth century and, significantly, there is also a large coin hoard, which has been buried—perhaps for security—in the mid third century A.D. All the available evidence implies, therefore, that the main *floruit* of *Careiae* belonged to the period between *c.* 100 B.C. and A.D. 250.

Much the same is also true of another road-station with a large surface collection, Aquaviva. This lay at the junction between a small country road and the Via Flaminia, some four kilometres to the south-east of Civita

Castellana. The principal nucleus lay on the Flaminia ridge where traces
of at least a dozen substantial buildings could be identified in ploughed
ground. Almost every one had mosaic floors, painted plaster and marble
decoration and in some instances the debris extended over areas as large as
40 × 40 metres. Unlike *Careiae*, however, the buildings appeared to have
been much more spread out, with substantial gaps without building debris
between the remains of each house. In addition, there was also a huge
circular mausoleum, where part of a large inscription, probably dating to
the mid to first century A.D., was recovered in 1968 (Pl. Xa). It read:

> QVOT EGO DIV LABORAVI
> LOCVM QVAISIVI VBI REQVIESCERE
> ET TIBI

This may be translated as: 'As long as I toiled I sought a place to rest; for
you as well.' Presumably this was the tomb of a man of some affluence who
had retired to a country house built on the edge of this wayside village; 'for
you' must refer to his wife. The remains of this house, close by the
mausoleum, were in fact quite obvious, its location being marked by an
enormous quantity of building debris, covering over 6000 square metres;
this included such exotic architectural traces as glass tesserae, objects that
are common only in the richest buildings. The house itself yielded pottery
extending in date from the late Republican period down into the fourth
century A.D., but it is one of the few sites in the Aquaviva complex to yield
such a complete range; of the other buildings, all produced finds of early
Imperial times but only one had fourth-century sherds and none disclosed
any later pottery. We can hardly doubt that, like *Careiae*, it was the period
between the first century B.C. and the second century A.D. that saw the
heyday of Aquaviva.

The absence of any identifiable trace of a systematic layout of the road-
stations is a consistent feature of these sites; they evidently developed
piecemeal, as often as not by a process of ribbon development. Yet it would
be a mistake to see them as entirely the product of a drift of the rural
population down to the main roads. Just as La Storta, a contemporary road-
station on the Via Cassia, owes its origin to the church built in memory of
the vision of S. Ignatius Loyola in 1537, so some of the wayside settlements
of Classical times grew up as religious or medicinal foci. At Ponte Nepesino,
for example, a Roman bridge that spans the Fosso Cerreto just to the south
of Nepi, the sulphur springs became the centre of a substantial thermal
establishment. The buildings (the so-called 'Terme dei Gracchi') lay on the
flat meadows beside the Roman bridge and, to judge from the few surviving
remains, were elegant and substantial (Frederiksen and Ward Perkins,
1957, 87); no doubt, they drew upon the same springs that are today
marketed as *aqua minerale di Nepi* and which rise a short distance to the
east of the Roman buildings. Some traces have also been identified of what
may have been a small temple, reminding us that such thermal establish-

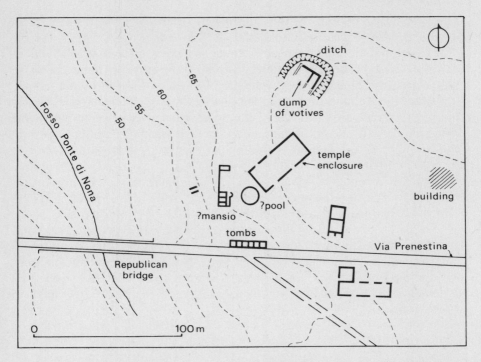

34 Plan of the sanctuary and road-station at Ponte di Nona, *Ad Nonas*. (Source: Quilici, 1974)

ments, and the cures that they offered, were normally linked with specific deities.

At Ponte di Nona, on the Via Prenestina, something of the plan of one of these sites has become clear through aerial photography and excavation (Quilici, 1974). The settlement was called *Ad Nonum* (*Ad IX*), a reference to its distance from Rome, and is well known for its finely preserved bridge, probably built in the first century B.C. We have already referred to votive terracottas recovered from the site in the course of recent excavations by the British School at Rome (Potter, 1979). These consisted in the main of life-size terracottas representing parts of the human body, which were offered by the afflicted either in supplication or in gratitude to a healing deity, perhaps Asclepius. The temple (all of which, together with much of the rest of the site, has been destroyed by *pozzolana* quarrying) lay close to the line of the Via Prenestina (Fig. 34). It was surrounded by a wall, demarcating the sacred area, while near by were a circular bathing pool and a building that has been identified as a *mansio*. Evidently there was an extensive complex of structures associated with the healing cult which, to judge from the votive terracottas, pottery and coins, was in vogue between *c*. 250 and 150 B.C. The later history of the site is more obscure but there are traces both of mausolea lining the main road and of comfortably appointed houses of Imperial date. Perhaps, as the cult centre went into decline, the settlement became a more conventional road-station, frequented by travellers and the local rural population. The latest finds disclosed by recent excavations included sherds of the fifth century A.D., which are probably to be associated with a period of vine growing in the area formerly occupied by the temple.

Neither the Republican temple complex at Ponte di Nona nor the Roman buildings that succeeded it show any evidence of overall planning in the layout of the site. Some of the houses fronted on to the main road but, significantly, the orientation of the temple bore no relationship to the line of the Via Prenestina. Everything suggests a process of *ad hoc* evolution that reached its apogee in late Republican and early Imperial times, to be followed by gradual depopulation. Thus, road-stations like Ponte di Nona followed a pattern of growth and decline that closely matched that of the great majority of the towns; they were a comparatively short-lived phenomenon that depended very largely upon the maintenance of the trunk-roads and, particularly, of free passage along these. Not surprisingly, as conditions deteriorated in the later centuries of the Empire, they were among the first settlements to be abandoned, a process that we shall examine in detail in the next chapter.

The countryside

One of the features that has emerged with extraordinary consistency from surface surveys in various regions of Italy is the very high density of rural settlement in the Roman period. The countryside, whether in the river valleys of Apulia and the Abruzzi, the coastal flats bordering the Tyrrhenian Sea or the hilly terrain of Etruria, seems to have supported a very large farming population, which brought all but the most marginal land into cultivation. Density figures of several sites per square kilometre, all of them apparently occupied in the same period, have now been recorded from many parts of the Italian peninsula, often in geographically quite remote districts: they imply both a fast-increasing population and a powerful incentive to invest in agriculture, with the result that the scale of rural development reached an unprecedented level. Unfortunately we are not yet in a position to make the comparative study from region to region that will eventually be possible. An enormous body of new data is presently being collected, the current surveys including detailed work in such diverse areas as the Ager Cosanus, the Monte Cassino area and the Biferno Valley. At the same time, survey work is being combined with excavation of a number of rural sites, such as the superbly preserved country house at Sette Finestre near Cosa, a group of rather smaller villas at Tor Angelo near the Via Gabina to the east of Rome, or the farming complex at Monte Irsi in Apulia (Small, 1977). When all these data are published, we shall be much less reliant upon such studies as Carrington's (1931) analysis of the *villae rusticae* in the Naples area, a region where only part of the picture is presently

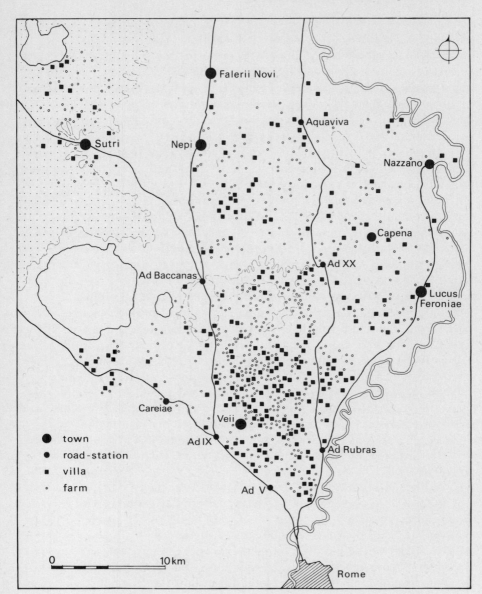

35 South Etruria Survey: villas and farms of *c.* A.D. 100.

available and may in any case be distorted by an exceptionally high percentage of rich country houses.

In the area to the north of Rome the body of evidence is now comparatively full, so much so that for many parts of this region we can draw detailed maps showing the location of what must be almost every farm and villa. Moreover, the quantities of surface finds are normally so great as to give a very good idea of both the date and the history of these sites, as well as some indication as to the extent and nature of the buildings. This is important in the sense that there appear to be distinct and well defined differences of rank between these sites. At the lowest end of the scale are small scatters of tile and pottery, rarely covering more than a few hundred square metres; many are likely to represent the remains of the huts and shacks (Pl. IIIb) that are still widely found in the Campagna (Close-Brooks and Gibson, 1966). In the Ager Faliscus, these accounted for 35 per cent of the total number of rural sites, and, as today, may in many cases have been used by shepherds wintering in the lowland with their flocks. Others probably consisted of subsidiary buildings on large estates, while some of the more extensive scatters may well represent the ploughed-out and denuded remains of more substantial sites. Next, rather higher up the social scale, we find what are most plausibly interpreted as the remains of small farms. These normally have several quite distinct characteristics. In terms of size, their area rarely exceeds 2000 square metres, and tends to average between 1000 and 1400 square metres. Within this nucleus the well preserved site will normally yield large quantities of building rubble, especially blocks of *tufo*, as well as some painted wall plaster, *opus spicatum* bricks from floors laid in a herringbone pattern, a few fragments of white Italian marble and, quite frequently, the tesserae from black and white mosaic floors. These components derive, therefore, from modest but fairly comfortable farmhouses, which, if the distribution patterns are in any way meaningful (Fig. 35), seem to have controlled their own small estates. Not surprisingly, they constitute the most common rank of site with, in the Ager Faliscus, a total of 84 examples, amounting to 43 per cent of the sample.

Still higher in rank than these farms are sites that, for sake of convenience, we may describe as villas. In antiquity it was clearly recognized that a distinction could be drawn between the *villa, casa* and *tugurium* (Varro, *RR* 2, 10, 6; Columella, *RR* 12, 15, 1) and it is likely that our ranking scheme, based on archaeological criteria, has similar validity. The remains of the villas stand out not only because of their much larger size—the average scatter of debris is *c.* 3500 square metres—but also for the much greater luxury of the building components. It is not unusual, for example, to find the hypocaust tiles and water-storage systems for a bath-house, while the remains of column drums and mouldings show that the house was often quite elaborately laid out with porticoes and peristyles. The internal fittings were also much more elegant, with multi-coloured painted plaster, a variety of marble veneers, mainly imported from the east Mediterranean, and sometimes stucco decoration. The mosaics seem, on the basis of the variety of the tesserae, to have been altogether much more complex, and finds of glass tesserae from wall and vault mosaics are not uncommon in the largest sites. The overall impression, therefore, is of a rich country house which in many cases was equipped in an especially luxurious way, presumably to accommodate the owner and his family on their occasional visit to the countryside.

The remains of high-ranking villas are by no means uncommon in the Campagna (Fig. 35). In the Ager Faliscus, for example, there are at least 44 sites which account for 22 per cent of the sample. Further north, in the Sutri region, the number diminishes, there being less than 30 within the area surveyed by Duncan (1958), under 13 per cent of the total number of Roman sites. By contrast, in the Ager Veientanus, the proportion is much higher. Ward Perkins (1968, 156) lists as many as 86 examples, which implies that in most parts of this area at least one site in three belongs in this category. The overall pattern, therefore, seems to be one of a considerable density of rich villas—one for every two square kilometres is a widely represented statistic—with, at the same time, a much greater concentration in the immediate environs of Rome. Land close to the capital city was no doubt as much at a premium as it is today and in both periods it was the affluent who snapped up and developed the best property. Yet it would be a mistake to envisage the growth of the rich estates as a rapid process. The great majority of the prosperous villa sites had, to judge from surface remains, a very long history indeed. Many started life as pre-Roman farms, whilst others originated as part of the land resettlement schemes that seem often to have followed the Roman conquest of a region. The Villa Sambuco, a recently excavated site near to S. Giovenale in the Tolfa Hills, may well prove to be typical of many of these early farms (Ostenberg, 1962). This was a small rectangular house, built of masonry, but measuring only 23 × 17 metres. It was set in good farmland, and its ground floor appears to have been laid out primarily as storage space for the produce of the estate, mainly comprising, one supposes, oil, wine and grain. A staircase led to an upper storey which was presumably designed as living quarters for the farmer. The date of construction appears to have been in the late second century B.C., a period when the rural population was rising sharply.

In Campania there were of course by this time some simple courtyard houses, laid out upon lines that were to become widely adopted as a standard plan in the Imperial period; but it is to be doubted that such houses were at all common before the first century A.D. in south Etruria. Wherever Republican farm sites without an overlay of later Roman material have been identified, they normally appear to have been quite small in size and, like the Villa Sambuco, of modest architectural pretensions. Indeed, many of the farmhouses may well have been built partly or wholly in timber. At Vallelunga, in the south-western Ager Faliscus, for example, part of just such a building was identified in the course of renovation to a motor-racing track (Fig. 31). The house was 13 metres in width and had been constructed with exterior walls of timber, resting on a masonry base. In addition there was one internal partition, made entirely of wood, dividing the house into two rooms. These had rock floors, which were covered with a thin layer of refuse that included a good many sherds of the second and first centuries B.C. Vallelunga appears therefore to have been contemporary with the Villa Sambuco and may well have been similarly planned.

Rather later in date but equally unpretentious is a site excavated by Barri

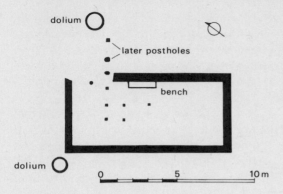

36 Plan of a small farmhouse of *c.* 50 B.C.-A.D. 30 at Monte Forco in the Ager Capenas. (Source: Jones, 1963)

Jones (1963, 147–58) at Monte Forco in the Ager Capenas (Fig. 36). The farm was one of six, strung out at regular intervals of 150 to 250 metres down a narrow elongated ridge, a short distance to the east of the Via Flaminia. None of these sites appears to have been of any great size, and, if occupied all at the same time (as the surface finds imply), they must have formed a series of smallholdings with individual estates of about 5 to 10 *iugera* (12,500 to 25,000 square metres). The farm at Monte Forco consisted of a simple rectangular building measuring 10.95 × 5.15 metres externally. It had a single doorway and no internal partitions. Animals and people may well have lived side by side. Outside was a farmyard with at least two storage jars (*dolia*), set into the ground and used probably for water storage. The building itself was constructed in *opus reticulatum*, a technique popular in the late Republican to early Imperial period where small blocks of tuff (or in some cases basalt) were set in a diamond pattern. At Monte Forco, this reticulate was combined with the use of masonry quoins, suggesting an Augustan date for the building. This is supported by the pottery from the construction levels, which included a few sherds of black glaze and some *terra sigillata*, the group as a whole probably falling between *c.* 50 BC. and A.D. 30. In fact there is a very plausible historical context in which to set this and other nearby farms. In 46 B.C., as Cicero tells us (*Ad Fam.* 9, 17, 2), Caesar's agents were engaged in a land survey of the territories of Veii and Capena. They had in mind the resettlement of veterans, and the creation of a *colonia* at Lucus Feroniae may, as we have seen, been one of the consequences. Such farms as Monte Forco, modest though they were, could well have been a result of such a land survey, with a systematic allocation of plots in previously undeveloped areas; certainly there is nothing in the archaeological record from Monte Forco to contradict such a conclusion.

What was the subsequent history of this site? Unfortunately the excavated area was small but there is a sufficient quantity of finds to show that occupation persisted down into Imperial times, probably terminating in the second century. The floor level was raised at least twice, the latest surviving level being associated with a series of post-holes, which implies a major alteration in function: probably the building was converted into a wooden barn. If so, it may represent the incorporation of the farm into the land of a larger estate, a process which, as we shall see, became increasingly common from mid-Imperial times.

The importance of the excavations at the Villa Sambuco, Vallelunga and Monte Forco is that they show us something of the more common classes of rural building to be found in the Roman Campagna in Republican times. Much of the population must have lived in small farms such as these, exploiting all but the most marginal land. Numerically, the figures for Republican settlement are in fact extremely impressive: they are set out below with, for comparison, the number of rural sites occupied in period IV, the fifth to fourth centuries B.C.

	Period IV	Period V
Ager Faliscus	104	142
Ager Veientanus	127	242
Ager Capenas	22	90
Sutrium area	1	32
Hemphill	32	63
Craven	59	66

It should, of course, be borne in mind that period V covers as much as 300 years and that a site may well have been occupied for only a part of that time: the actual number of farms occupied at any one moment would thus be much less than these statistics imply. Nevertheless it would be hard to deny the overall significance of the distribution map (Fig. 27) with its implication of a dense concentration of smallholdings. What of course the map does not tell us is the way in which the land was owned—several smallholdings could easily have belonged to a single estate—but only a detailed chronological breakdown of the Republican pottery finds and a great deal more excavation could fill out this aspect of the Republican landscape. Yet it is worth emphasizing that there is little in the archaeological record to show the existence of the great slave-run *latifundia* seen by Tiberius Gracchus in his celebrated journey through Etruria (Plutarch, *TG* 8). This is not an observation based just on the lack of identifiable estate centres; rather it is implicit both in the regular distribution of the farms and in the broken, dissected terrain of south Etruria—a landscape much better suited to small landholdings than to very large agricultural units.

What, then, was the economy of these farms? As yet we still lack the samples of animal bones and seeds that will afford some positive evidence; equally we must be cautious in assuming that the picture of agrarian life discussed by the Roman agronomists (White, 1970) can be applied wholesale to south Etruria. Yet it is likely that the mixed economy of the present day, with its particular emphasis upon vine and olive cultivation, was equally prevalent in the Classical Campagna. Vine trenches of early Imperial date have been identified by excavation at Santa Cornelia, just to the north of Veii, and have also been noted at a number of other sites. At a villa site at Monte Canino in the Ager Capenas a press was excavated (Pallottino, 1937b), and fragments of other presses (presumably both for wine and oil) have also been recorded as surface finds from several sites. Similarly, grain mills, made of a hard leucitic lava, commonly occur in surface contexts and imply that a good deal of the land was given over to cereal cultivation. However, we know little of the overall balance of the economy. We can assume the raising of sheep, goat, cattle and pig played as important a part in Classical times as documentary and archaeological evidence imply for the early Middle Ages (Duchesne, 1886; Barker, 1973); but the ratio between the cultivation of cereals and other sown crops as opposed to vines and olives remains unclear. Indeed, the whole question of the origins of arboriculture in the Rome region is still virtually unstudied. At Narce, a site with domestic occupation down into the seventh century B.C., there were no traces in the plant record of either vines or olives (Jarman, 1976) while, at Rome, vine pips appear only in period IV, dated by Gjerstad (1966, 342) to 625–575 B.C. It would in fact be surprising had vines and olives (Vallet, 1962) not been cultivated before this date (as they unquestionably were elsewhere in Italy), but it may be that their introduction to the Campagna did not take place on a large scale until mid-Etruscan times.

Certainly, by the late Republican period, the larger *villae rusticae* in areas like the Bay of Naples were often equipped with sophisticated arrangements for the pressing and storage of oil and wine. At Francolise near Capua, for example, Dr Molly Cotton investigated two such sites, which, although nearly a kilometre apart, appear to have been complementary in character (Blanckenhagen, Cotton and Ward-Perkins, 1965). One, San Rocco, was essentially a comfortable residence while the other, Posto, was laid out as the working centre of an estate. Posto appears to have been marginally the earlier of the two sites, probably founded between 120 and 80 B.C., while the first phase of San Rocco should date to *c.* 50 B.C.: no doubt the profits of the early farm were invested in the construction of the owner's residence.

The functional purpose of the Posto villa is very apparent both from its setting on low ground well suited to olive growing, and from the buildings and their fittings. The villa was laid out around an open court, flanked by rooms on three sides and with a boundary wall on the fourth. A set of fairly spartan residence rooms, presumably for the bailiff and his family, took up much of the north wing, while the east and west ranges consisted entirely of farm buildings. Along the west side was an open-sided lean-to shed, with a row of wooden columns down the farmyard side. This was no doubt used partly as a byre, and also as a storage area for farm equipment and vehicles. To the east were other buildings in both stone and timber, some of these perhaps for slaves and others perhaps as drying and storage rooms for the crops, as advocated by the Roman agronomists. But the most distinctive agricultural fittings were several cement-lined vats, used in the separation of olive oil. These lay near to the residence rooms and will have been used to hold the various qualities of oil—for unguents, cooking and as a fuel for lamps—that derived from different pressings. In addition, there were also large *dolia*, set into the ground, and perhaps used, as Varro (I, 13, 6) describes, for the fermentation of wine.

The functional character of the Posto building becomes especially clear when compared with the main residential complex at San Rocco. Here the villa was constructed in an inconvenient but attractive setting towards the top of Monte Telefono, with commanding views towards both the mountains and the sea. Whilst the overall plan is once again that of a courtyard villa, the great majority of the rooms were designed as reception areas or private accommodation, the few working rooms being relegated to the back part of the complex, on a lower terrace. Mosaic pavements and walls with painted plaster leave no doubt of the affluence of the owners, who presumably controlled most of the surrounding terrain, including the estate centre at Posto. Later both villas saw some structural modification, the San Rocco villa becoming initially even more luxurious and then (probably in the mid first century A.D.) incorporating some oil-separation vats into one wing of the residential area. At Posto, too, the property was improved with a rebuild of the residential area and, in the first century A.D., the construction of a small bath-house. Either the bailiff was by this time in a position to invest money of his own in the improvement of the living quarters or it may be that the estate was divided up so that Posto became an owner's residence. Despite these structural modifications, however, its basic function remained that of a working farm which, while lavish in comparison with sites like Monte Forco, was probably not untypical of the Campanian countryside.

In south Etruria, on the other hand, we still lack villa sites that have been studied and published with commensurate detail, even though, as we have seen, they certainly existed. Indeed, in many respects the larger villas of the Campagna probably did not differ greatly in their layout and decor from their Campanian counterparts. However, it should be clearly stated that our picture of these sites still relies very heavily upon the results of partial excavation, combined with surface observations, and will undoubtedly undergo a radical transformation as more work is done. In the Ager Capenas, for example, there are still only two rural sites for which we have any usable sort of plan, although neither villa has yielded a detailed history. One lay on Monte Canino (Fig. 37), some five kilometres south-east of Castelnuovo di Porto. Excavated by Pallottino in 1934 (Pallottino, 1937b; Jones, 1962, 162–3), it revealed three main periods of construction. The earliest feature consisted of a wall in *tufo* blocks which ran across most of the site; it was associated with late Republican black glaze pottery and is likely to have belonged to a substantial *villa rustica*; but there are no further details of its plan. In the early Imperial period this was replaced by a large house, lavishly decorated with stucco and a considerable variety of marbles, many of them imported. The known part of the villa measured nearly 70 metres square and was built in *opus reticulatum*. It was laid out with a

37 Comparative plans of three villas: Giardino, Ager Capenas (Source: Jones, 1962); S. Giovanni a Pollo, near Sutri (Source: Duncan, 1958); and Monte Canino near Castelnuovo di Porto (Source: Pallottino, 1937a).

range of large residential rooms and two side wings, probably flanking an open court. In the south-west wing were the remains of a wooden press, underlining the functional aspect of this part of the house: this room may well have been used for the production and storage of wine and oil. Further to the south-east of this complex there appear to have been other structures, perhaps a farmyard with barns and sheds resembling the plan of the Posto villa. Clearly this was a large and important villa, well sited to take advantage of the nearby Via Tiberina. However, its subsequent history remains obscure. The finds suggest that it remained in occupation into late Imperial times but at some subsequent stage it was converted into a cemetery area. The focus of the burials lay a short distance to the north-east (Fig. 37) where a rectangular building with an *ambulacrum*, a colonnaded portico, was constructed. Its date is not clear but the form of some of the column capitals indicates that construction work was going on in the eighth

IXa *Above* Roman cistern at Grotta Vecchiarelli. (Photo: *BSR*)

IXb *Right* Le Mura di Santo Stefano. (Photo: *BSR*)

Xa *Above* Inscription from a mausoleum at the road-station of Aquaviva.

Xb *Left* Early medieval church at Santa Rufina on the Via di Boccea. (Photo: *BSR*)

XIa *Right* Aerial photograph of Sutri and the area to the south-east. (Photo: *BSR*)

XIb *Below* Faleria, a typical medieval promontory town.

XII *Overleaf* The fifteenth-century monastery at Santa Maria del Sorbo which overlies a medieval settlement. (Photo: *BSR*)

century and it may be that we have a rare example of continuity of use into the early Middle Ages. Indeed the site has plausibly been identified with a church of S. Cristina, mentioned in a document of 794 (Tomassetti, 1913, 286), which, if correct, would confer special interest upon the site.

Monte Canino is, however, a comparatively small site. Another well preserved country house in the Capena area, at Giardino (Fig. 37) lay on a long spur beneath the town of S. Oreste, overshadowed by the southern end of Monte Soracte. The site consists of three main terraces stepped down the hillside and measuring overall c. 200 × 70 metres (Jones, 1962, 183–5). The main residential complex lay on the upper terrace, where there still survive the remains of mosaic pavements and a hypocaust, probably laid out round a court. This range of buildings was separated from the middle terrace by a huge cement-lined cistern, 63.5 metres in length and 4.90 metres in width. The exceptional size of this chamber necessitated the use of some internal reinforcement, for which ten brick arches were employed; but, surprisingly, even so massive a cistern was deemed insufficient for the needs of the villa and a series of supplementary storage rooms was constructed, extending down the whole length of the south range of the middle terrace. Just what prompted such exceptional measures must remain unclear until the site is properly studied: but the key may lie in its geological setting. The Giardino site lies on a spur of limestone, outcropping to the south of Monte Soracte; in limestone areas, unlike those of *tufo*, water cannot be obtained by deep drilling, and thus in the summer months the country in the lowlands tends to become dry and barren. The provision of water both for domestic needs and, more especially, for the stock, must therefore have been a matter of great importance and could well explain these large cisterns. Unfortunately we do not know where the farm buildings lay. The most likely area is the large expanse of the lower terrace, but only retaining walls are presently visible and the area has never been excavated. Nevertheless it would have been a convenient place for the farmyard, barns, byres and other agricultural buildings and has not yielded any evidence for more exotic features, such as tessellated floors or marble inlays.

The date of the Giardino villa has yet to be established by excavation although the style of the masonry and the surface finds indicate that it may well have been built in the first century A.D., with some modifications (including the building of a further cistern) in the second century. As such it belongs to a large number of villas that were laid out on a fairly lavish scale in the early Imperial period. At S. Giovanni a Pollo (Fig. 37), for example, comfortably within striking distance of Sutri, there survive the remains of just such a villa (Duncan, 1958, 105–6). It was presumably owned by an affluent citizen of Sutri, who put in a paved road, two kilometres in length, between his estate and the town. The principal building comprised a courtyard house measuring 41 × 56 metres; but there were also subsidiary buildings, including a bath-house. All the available evidence points to a comfortable country residence, with painted wall-plaster, mosaic floors and columns with Doric and Ionic capitals.

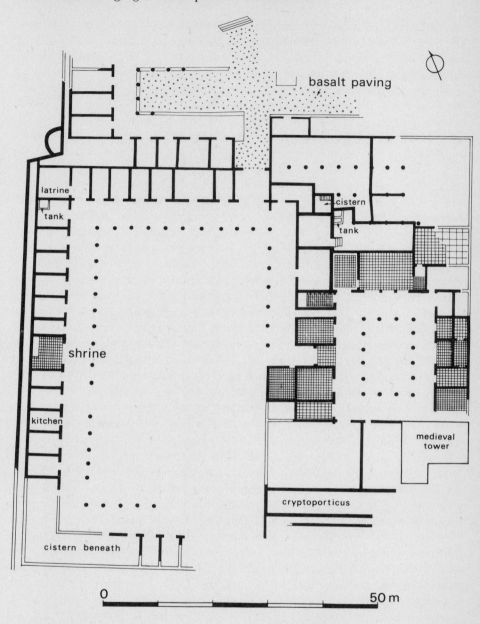

basalt paving

latrine

tank

cistern

tank

shrine

kitchen

medieval
tower

cryptoporticus

cistern beneath

0   50 m

38 Plan of the villa of the Volusii, on the outskirts of Lucus Feroniae. (Source: *Autostrade,* 1968)

The best-documented site in the region lay on the floor of the Tiber Valley, a short distance to the north-east of the town of Lucus Feroniae (Fig. 32). This suburban villa was first identified during the building of the Autostrada del Sole in 1962 and was then excavated and magnificently conserved (Fig. 38). Although still only summarily published (Autostrade, 1968), it is a site of exceptional interest since we know that it was owned for a time by a noted senatorial family of the early Imperial period, the Volusii Saturnini. Two members of the family are to be associated with the villa: Quintus Volusius Saturninus, who was a consul in 56 A.D. under Nero, and his son, Lucius, a consul in 87. Both made dedications in the household shrine where the inscriptions still survived intact, providing a rare chance of linking a building with a known Roman family. Furthermore, the villa itself is also finely preserved and a good deal of its layout has been made visible. The site was an extensive one, occupying a rectangular platform which measured 120 × 180 metres. There seem to have been buildings over much of this area but most of the excavation has been directed at the main residential complex, at the north end. This showed that the villa was first laid out towards the end of the Republican period and then was substantially enlarged by the Volusii during the first century A.D. The original nucleus consisted of a series of spacious and elegant rooms, grouped around a colonnaded atrium. Here were both reception areas and private rooms, most of which were provided with magnificent black and white or polychrome mosaic floors, many of them of exceptional quality. Nearby were open and colonnaded areas of garden, as well as a *cryptoporticus* leading down to other rooms to the south. The essential features of this plan remained unchanged throughout the history of the villa (which appears to have extended at least into the third century A.D.). But in the first century A.D. there was a major enlargement of the building. This took the form of an enormous open court, surrounded by a portico and three ranges of rooms, which was added on to the west side of the residential area. At the same time an entrance was added on to the north end and a further court, paved with *selce* blocks, constructed along this side. This work we can attribute to the Volusii whose household shrine was located in the middle of the west wing of the new court and was magnificently paved with a circular black and white mosaic of subtle and intricate design. The reasons for this extension seem to have been twofold. In the first place, it is clear that the servants' quarters were completely remodelled since many of the rooms have mills and ovens and were evidently intended as a kitchen area. Large cisterns were also installed at the south-west corner, implying that there may also have been a new bath-house. Thus, taken together, there were substantial improvements to the domestic amenities. But the second main innovation is perhaps of more far-reaching importance. The excavation along the north wing of the villa showed that most of the new rooms in this area were connected with agricultural activity, such as storage of produce and equipment. This also explains the heavy-duty *selce* paving in the new courtyard area. It is clear, therefore, that the Volusii not only intended to improve the comfort and decor of their country house but also wanted to foster the estate on which the villa stood. As such, it is a significant reminder of the dual purpose of these elegant villas which represented not only a rural retreat but also a good investment in farming.

	Total P.V. sites (Republican)	% abandoned before P.VI	Total P.VI sites (c. 30 B.C.–A.D. 100)	% new sites P.VI	% abandoned before P.VII	Total P.VII sites (2nd cent. A.D.)	% new sites P.VII
Ager Veientanus	242	11%	327	32%	20%	307	15%
Eretum area	53	28%	57	37%	17.5%	56	12.5%
Ager Faliscus	142	32%	207	39%	33%	199	37%
Ager Capenas	90	50%	100	55%	36%	124	49%
Sutrium area	32	67%	50	76%	44%	67	60%
Craven	66	32%	70	22%	6%	71	8%
Hemphill	63	29%	71	32%	27%	57	15%

Note: Period VII sites (2nd century A.D.) include all sites with Red Slip wares although in practice some of these could well be much later in the Roman period.

Table 5

The scale of investment in country estates at this time is hard to evaluate in any detail without much more excavation, but the data from the surface survey do provide some sort of insight into the main trends. The relevant information is set out in Table 5, together with the percentages of abandonment and new settlement. It would be a mistake to regard these figures, with their appearance of precision, as anything more than a general guide. Not only are we comparing periods of different length, but percentages of abandonment and new settlement are obviously subject to wide margins of error when calculated from surface data. But we can on the other hand probably regard the overall trends as expressed by these figures as a reasonable approximation to the truth, for the sample is large and remarkably consistent from area to area.

What conclusions can we draw, therefore, from these data? The first and most important inference is that rural settlement reaches a peak in almost all parts of the Campagna in the first century A.D., when density figures of between two and three sites per square kilometre are by no means uncommon. Thus the building of sites like the Giardino villa and the enlargement of the Volusii villa at Lucus Feroniae would appear to be part of a trend that is widely represented through south Etruria. Secondly there are some interesting regional differences between areas that lie close to Rome and those in more remote districts. Thus in Sutrium and the northern parts of the Ager Capenas it is not until the second century that the more marginal land was brought into cultivation, presumably because these remoter areas were deemed much less desirable (a pattern that is being repeated in the rural expansion of the present day). Closer to Rome, on the other hand, even the more inaccessible parts had mostly come into occupation by the mid to late first century A.D. At the same time there also seem to have been marked differences in the population turnover. Near to Rome the percentage of sites that represent either new foundations or sites being abandoned remains comparatively low: once founded, a farm tended to stay in occupation, even though the owner may have changed. Further north, the picture is rather different. In the Sutri area, for example, no less than 67 per cent of the Republican sites appear to have gone out of use at the end of the first century B.C., while an even greater proportion, 76 per cent, of the early Imperial farms represent new foundations. These figures are of course very approximate and need verification by excavation; but the sample is such that we can be sure that there is a strong element of truth in them. Indeed, the character of the sites themselves provides some confirmation: as one might expect, it is usually the low-ranking sites, the house of a smallholder, which tend to weight the statistics. The picture of the small farm that rapidly goes out of business is sufficiently familiar from the present day to call for no further comment.

By about A.D. 100, therefore, the countryside of south Etruria was being farmed on a scale that was quite unprecedented. There were numerous rich villas, and many more small farms, built on a modest scale and controlling fairly minor areas of land. Many of these were to fail, but a few prospered,

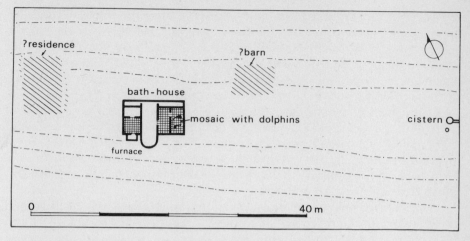

?residence

?barn

bath-house

mosaic with dolphins

cistern

furnace

0   40 m

39 The villa at Crocicchie on the Via Clodia. The contours are schematic.

like the farmer who owned a smallholding close to the Via Clodia at Crocicchie. This site, built on a narrow ridge overlooking the road, consisted of three principal buildings (Fig. 39). Two are known only as surface scatters, one measuring 10 × 6 metres, the other 6 × 4 metres. The larger scatter included a sufficient quantity of *opus reticulatum* blocks and *terra sigillata* to show that this was the site of a small farmhouse of the first century A.D., probably not dissimilar from that at Monte Forco (Fig. 36). The other scatter may well indicate the position of a barn or byre, while a short distance along the ridge was a complex of plaster-lined underground cisterns. It is evident, however, that this farmer (or a subsequent owner) did prosper, for between the two buildings was a well preserved small bath-house. Architecturally this was an extremely simple structure. It was laid out in a linear pattern with just an apsidal *caldarium* to provide some architectural variety. The five rooms included an undressing room (*apodyterium*)—decorated appropriately with a mosaic bearing two lively dolphins—and three heated chambers. There must also have been a cold plunge, probably at the north-west corner of the building. Both the style of the brick masonry and of the mosaic are consistent with a third-century date so it is clear that the farm had been in existence for a hundred years or more before the owner could afford even this modest structure. In fact the site does not seem to have remained in occupation much longer for there is no fourth-century material in the sherds found at Crocicchie: but by this time, as we shall see, other pressures were coming to bear and the reasons for its final abandonment may not be entirely economic. The site is on the other hand an extremely useful reminder that, even in mid to late Imperial times, not all farmers in the Campagna were accommodated in large estates. The smallholder has down to the present day fulfilled an important role in the Campagna, partly because much of the terrain is best suited to this type of farming; certainly in both Classical and modern times it is the small farm that far outnumbers the large estate.

Farms were, however, by no means the only sites to be found in the Roman landscape of south Etruria. A few sites have been tentatively identified as rural sanctuaries (e.g. Frederiksen and Ward Perkins, 1957, 76) and there are strong literary and epigraphic reasons for supposing the presence of others. Mount Soracte, for example, was associated with Apollo Soranus, to whom there was a shrine high on the summit of the mountain (Pliny, *Nat. Hist.* 7, 19), presided over by special priests, the Hirpi (Jones, 1963, 125–6). Similarly, on one of the highest hilltops in the Ager Veientanus, Monte Musino, there may well have been the sanctuary to Hercules Musinus described by Pliny (*Nat. Hist.* 2, 211), although this is a supposition derived from the evidence of the place-name rather than on archaeological grounds and has never been verified (Ward Perkins, 1968, 44). We in fact know very little about the overall distribution and nature of these sanctuaries, many of which may well prove (like Monte Musino and Monte Soracte) to lie beneath medieval sites. Tombs and cemeteries, on the other hand, are much more easily identified, if only because many of the mausolea were constructed with extraordinary durability. The concrete cores of these monuments, usually robbed of their marble sheaths, are one of the commonest sights along the line of the major Roman roads and they are not infrequently found in more rural areas. A number of rich cemeteries have also been identified, often situated near to a group of villas, and there are records of several rock-cut catacombs and other underground tombs (e.g. Jones, 1962, 178). These sanctuaries, cemeteries and mausolea were evidently an important feature of the Classical landscape and merit more systematic excavation and sustained study than they have presently received.

Another equally interesting element in the landscape were the sites that grew up through exploitation of the mineral resources of the region. *Tufo* blocks were undoubtedly quarried very widely, although mainly for local purposes: the villa at S. Giovanni a Pollo, for example, took its building-stone from a source only 100 metres away (Duncan, 1958, 106). But some quarries served much wider markets, most notably those at Grotta Oscura, which exploited the hard beds of rock between the Via Flaminia and Via Tiberina, and shipped the blocks to Rome along the Tiber. *Selce* (basalt) was also extracted on a large scale, there being quarries at Galeria by the Via Clodia, near Monterosi on the Via Cassia, Monte Aguzzo in the Ager Veientanus and at Monte Maggiore, a hill in the Sabatini range dividing the Ager Veientanus and Ager Faliscus. Paved haul-roads (presumably constructed by the quarry owners) were built to link the Monte Aguzzo and Monte Maggiore quarries with the Via Flaminia and both sites became the focus for groups of richly appointed country houses; indeed, those at Monte Maggiore are so numerous as to suggest the existence of a small settlement, resembling in size and layout the plan of a road-station. Evidently the mining of *selce* was a profitable business with a market that included public contracts for the maintenance of the highways as well as a good deal of business in the private sector, with the paving of roads and other building work. In fact the scale of the demand seems to have been fairly continuous throughout the Roman period, for none of the associated sites show much evidence of decline before the fourth and fifth centuries, and it is fair to assume that the quarries were operative until this time. Probably they supplied much more than the local markets, a good deal of the basalt going to Rome and further afield.

The other major mineral resource of the area, the deposits of clay, was, on the other hand, exploited almost entirely for local use. The biggest commercial enterprise was the Tiber Valley brickyards which eventually came under Imperial control; but, as a study of the brickstamps for the Ager Veientanus has shown (Ward Perkins, 1968, 159), even this mass-production industry had only a limited marketing area. The reason is fairly obvious. Bricks and tiles are heavy and therefore expensive to distribute and it was generally much easier to exploit local beds of clay and thus cut down upon production costs. The only other requirements were firewood and water, both of which were readily available in the Campagna; consequently it was logical and cheap to set up local production centres to provide for the vastly expanding market of Republican and Imperial times. Such sites are on the whole easy to recognize; they are usually marked by large quantities of wasters, together with baked clay fragments from the dome of the kilns. In the Sutri area, for example, Duncan (1958, 98) identified two such sites, placed near to outcrops of clay and only a short distance from the town. They presumably supplied both the *colonia* and many of the suburban villas, although neither kiln site was in fact very large or long-lived.

Similarly, there were also local potteries, exploiting the same clays to make both kitchen and table wares of quite good quality. Duncan (1964, 87) located two of these sites in the vicinity of Sutri and carried out a small-scale excavation upon one of them. This disclosed part of a small workshop, 11 metres in width, and constructed with walls of concrete and rubble. In one angle of the building was a rudimentary rectangular updraught kiln, made up of clay, tile and *tufo* fragments. In front was a shallow stoking room and round this an enormous quantity of wasters. The range of the vessels is of considerable interest for they included not only a series of jugs, bowls and jars for kitchen purposes but also a number of thin beakers and cups, many of them with colour washes. These finer vessels were evidently intended to be marketed as tableware and are a product of surprising quality for so small a workshop. However, the kiln seems to have been operative only for a decade or so, probably between *c.* A.D. 60 and 70, and it may well have been the advent of African Red Slip-wares upon the market (Hayes, 1972) that caused it to go out of business. Nevertheless, the site clearly underlines the importance of such workshops in the local economy and they must in fact have been quite common. For example, at Prima Porta there was a site of similar size and date, producing poor quality imitations of *terra sigillata* and at San Biagio, on the plateau to the south-east of Nepi, there was a quite large area of production, with kiln debris that covers over 1,000 square metres. Here the owners decided to concentrate upon the manufacture of coarse-wares, for all the wasters belong to grey-ware lids and jars; in the event it was a wise decision for the pottery industry expanded and seems to have remained in production until well into the Imperial period.

These pottery and kiln sites provide therefore a tantalizing glimpse of the economic structure of the period: essentially a small-scale service industry, directed mainly at a local market. With the exception of the *selce* quarries, whose stone may have been sold outside the region, there was comparatively little major industry and most of the main investment must have been placed in agricultural estates, producing food for the markets of Rome. It is a picture which is again in many respects strikingly similar to that of the present day.

6
From Roman to medieval:
A.D. 300–1300

In the Classical period it was a dispersed pattern of settlement that characterized the landscape of south Etruria. A very high proportion of the population lived on villa estates and farms, which spread into all but the most remote parts of the Campagna. A number of villages also grew up, especially around the more important crossroads, but towns flourished only where they could play a rôle as a local administrative and service centre. There is thus an impressive sense of design in the pattern of settlement at this time, made more readily apparent by a comprehensive network of highways and secondary roads that conferred accessibility upon almost all parts of the countryside.

In the Middle Ages all this was to change. The process began as a slow decline of rural life, combined with a gradual running-down of many of the urban centres. Before long this had turned into a migration of major proportions, probably linked with a sharp fall in the size of the population, that left all but a handful of the rural estates deserted and untended. At the same time, many of the towns—especially those situated on the trunk-roads and thus vulnerable to attack—were slowly depopulated and ultimately abandoned. In their place there emerged a quite different model of settlement which very clearly reflects the uncertainties of the period. Its basis was the village or small town, impregnably situated either on hilltops or, more commonly, at the tip of a promontory or spur. The natural strength of such positions was further enhanced by artificial defences, usually a combination of ditches, walls and towers, so that many of these sites became in effect massive fortresses. Moreover, there was a conscious choice of locations that were remote from the main roads and preferably hidden and inaccessible; many of the medieval villages were tucked away on low spurs jutting into river valleys so that they were all but invisible from the surrounding plateau. Security and protection are thus the hallmarks of these sites and were to remain so throughout the Middle Ages.

The extraordinary antithesis that the Roman and medieval landscapes represent can at first sight be readily explained. The collapse of the western Roman Empire had been accompanied by a series of drastic military reverses, including in A.D. 410 the sack of Rome itself by the Visigoths under Alaric; at the same time the processes of central government began rapidly to decay. In 476 the last western emperor was deposed and the order and stability that the *pax Romana* had imposed was finally extinguished. In the centuries that followed, Italy was to see in full measure the consequences of the tribal migrations beyond the Alps, with at first movements of Visigoths and Ostragoths and then Lombards and Franks. Rome, her territories eroded and at times under siege, became a shrinking city. There were times when old public monuments were despoiled, many areas flooded, and plague was rife (Llewellyn, 1971, 195). Yet, governed by the Papacy, Rome also displayed an extraordinary resilience to the processes of change. It is well to remember, for example, the volume of new building that took place in the early medieval period (most notably the Lateran and St Peter's), and the efforts that were made by the Papacy to maintain and restore churches and monasteries. In the ninth century however the Papacy faced sustained and widespread attacks by the Moslems. In 846, Rome herself was looted by an Arab army and the surrounding countryside devastated. Early in the tenth century there were Arab bands occupying areas near to Sutri and, as Benedict (a monk who lived at S. Andrea on M. Soracte) records, there was prolonged fighting. 'For thirty years', he notes 'the Saracens ruled in the Roman countryside and the land was made a desert.' He goes on to describe battles like that between 'the Saracens and the citizens of Nepi and Sutri in the Baccano crater where many Saracens were killed and wounded' (Zucchetti, 1920, 157). Clearly the countryside round Rome was by now (if not before) a very insecure place in which to live, and it is not surprising to find that the great majority of open rural sites had effectively disappeared. Consequently the population of the Campagna had to look to their own defence, with the result that a new settlement pattern was created: that of the fortified village, the basic unit of the medieval period.

This historical picture, one of declining authority and increasing insecurity, would seem therefore to match perfectly the archaeological evidence for a widespread movement to found nucleated sites with strong defences. In reality, however, much of the detail is blurred and current interpretations controversial (Luttrell, 1974). In part this is due to a scarcity of documents that antedate the tenth century; but, equally, there are many ambiguities in the archaeological record, stemming principally from a paucity of excavation but also from deficiencies in our understanding of the development of pottery styles. Some critically sited excavations, combined with further research into the documentary record, can be expected to cast a great deal more light into this transitional period, and the hypotheses which we shall consider must consequently be regarded as provisional.

The late Roman period: A.D. 300–500

There has yet to be any full excavation of a late Roman site in south Etruria, and, consequently, we are still reliant upon surface evidence for our picture of this period. Fortunately, there is ample material with which to date the sites, in the form of African Red Slip-ware. This remained the principal ceramic tableware in central Italy down to about A.D. 600 (Hayes, 1972, 416), and most of the forms and some of the fabrics can now be

	Total no. of sites with Red Slip-ware	RP I (c. 80–320)	RP II (c. 350–450)	RP III (c. 450–625)
Ager Veientanus	316	307	92	46
Hemphill	60	57	10	6
Craven	71	?	?	?
Ager Eretanus	57	47	20	7
Sutrium	67	?	?	?
Ager Capenas	124	?	?	?
Ager Faliscus	199	see below		

Table 6

assigned quite close dates, as a result of Hayes' research in this subject. However, some of the surveys, particularly those of the Ager Capenas and the Sutrium region, took place before Hayes began his work on the pottery, and consequently we have as yet no detailed statistics for the later Roman sites in these areas. On the other hand there are figures for the Ager Veientanus (Ward Perkins, 1968; Hemphill, 1965) and the Eretum area on the other side of the Tiber (Ogilvie, 1965) as well as unpublished data from the Ager Faliscus, making a total of 549 sites altogether with a detailed breakdown (Table 6). With such a massive sample, therefore, we can be certain of a reasonably accurate indication of the main settlement trends during this period.

The tripartite scheme devised by John Hayes for his analysis of the red slip pottery (traditionally described as 'red polished ware' or 'RP'; Ward Perkins, 1968, 12–13) is based principally upon distinctions in fabrics. This has the advantage that most of the featureless body sherds can be assigned to a specific category, but excludes the precision that a full study of the forms would have provided. For that reason a more sophisticated analysis was attempted of some of the Red Slip-wares found in the Ager Faliscus survey, so that the data could be listed by century. The finds from only 116 of the 199 sites with Red Slip-wares were examined, but a simple percentage calculation provides an estimation of the likely total:

Ager Faliscus	2nd cent.	3rd cent.	4th cent.	5th–6th cents
No. of sites	95	67	31	22
% of sample	82%	58%	21%	19%
Estimated total	163	115	52	38

These detailed statistics for the Ager Falicus bear out the trend repeatedly observed both in neighbouring areas and in other parts of Italy (e.g. Dyson, 1977): that from the beginning of the third century the total number of sites in occupation began to fall dramatically. Thus, in the Faliscan region, nearly 40 per cent appear to have been abandoned by about A.D. 300 and

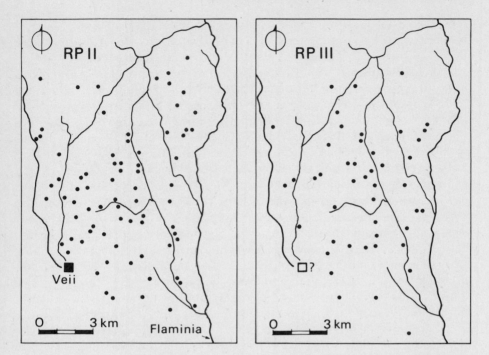

40 Ager Veientanus: distribution of sites with Red Slip-ware II (*c.* 350–450 A.D.) and III (*c.* 450–625 A.D.). (Source: Ward Perkins, 1968)

more than 50 per cent by the end of the fourth century. Nor was this phenomenon confined to the more outlying regions: near to Rome, for example, much the same pattern has been demonstrated both to the north (Fig. 40) and east of the city, so that in the Ager Veientanus 'of the 310 sites known to have been in occupation at the end of the second century, three-quarters had vanished a century later' (Ward Perkins, 1968, 152), and in the area of the Via Gabina the percentages are all but identical (Ward Perkins and Kahane, 1972, 117–19). Again, in the hilly country to the south of Lake Bracciano, Pamela Hemphill's survey (1975) demonstrated that the total number of sites in occupation in the fourth century was just about one-sixth that of the second century, representing an even faster rate of decline.

Such consistency of results must obviously be significant, especially when we bear in mind the histories of excavated villas like Francolise and Sette Finestre which (although not in our area) were also abandoned during the second century A.D. On the other hand, the sharp fall in the population of the countryside that these statistics imply must be balanced against the well proven trend for the enlargement of individual villas at the expense of their neighbours (White, 1970, 420). There must always have been a tendency for the more successful landowners to absorb nearby smallholdings into their own estates, with the effect upon the archaeological data of a gradual reduction in the total number of sites in occupation. In the Grottarossa area just to the north of Rome, for example, survey work has demonstrated an enormously regular layout of Republican sites, suggestive of land allotments made to army veterans. Of the sites, only a tiny proportion were maintained in occupation into the Imperial period, implying a process whereby some farmers bought out their neighbours in order to enlarge their holdings (Jones, 1963, 146). An exactly analogus situation in the Praeneste area is in fact described by Cicero (*de leg. agr.* 2, 28, 78), when land allotted to Sulla's veterans was quickly reconstituted into much larger estates. North of Rome we lack this sort of documentary evidence but there are other ways of measuring the trend, the most useful being a comparison of the ratio between villas and smallholdings.

We have already shown that a quite clear-cut distinction can be drawn between the remains of high- and low-ranking sites and to this we can now add the evidence of the Red Slip-wares. This suggests that the proportion of larger sites did in fact rise quite considerably in the later Roman period. Thus, in the Ager Veientanus, no less than 49 of 86 villas with evidence for second-century occupation also seem still to have been occupied in the fourth century, a proportion that is matched in adjacent regions like the Ager Faliscus. In contrast to this, the proportion of smallholdings falls quite dramatically with, in the Veientine area, a drop from 230 second-century sites to only 43 in *c.* A.D. 400. Clearly we can attribute some of this decline to the absorption of smallholdings by the owners of the larger estates. On the other hand it would be wrong to underestimate the rôle of the small farmer in the period between *c.* 300 and 500 A.D. In all areas for which we have detailed statistics, small farm sites continued to equal or surpass the number of large villas, showing that *latifundia* were by no means the sole agrarian unit in the countryside in late Roman times. Indeed, in most areas there is evidence for the foundation of several new smallholdings in the third to fifth centuries, suggesting that an investment in a modest rural property was still thought of as a practical proposition. At the same time, the growth of large estates and the survival of some of the small farmers can hardly have offset completely the effect of the decline in the total number of sites. This much becomes clear with a glance at the distribution maps for the late Roman period (Fig. 41); even allowing for their many deficiencies, it is still quite obvious that cultivation must have lapsed over quite considerable areas. In the hilly and difficult terrain that divides the Veientine and Faliscan regions, for example, or in the tangled countryside to the south-west of Lake Bracciano, the disappearance of sites with late Roman pottery is so pronounced as to imply more or less complete desertion of the areas. Either the land was made over to pasture or, more likely, it was allowed to revert to the scrub and woodland that it still often bears today.

We can therefore infer from our data that there was a steady decline in the number of rural sites from early in the third century A.D. To some extent this was a product of the absorption of smaller units by some of the

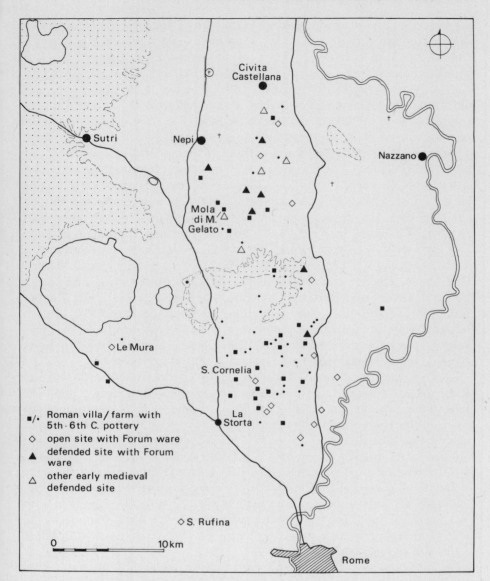

Roman villa / farm with
■ / • 5th - 6th C. pottery

◇ open site with Forum ware

▲ defended site with Forum
ware

△ other early medieval
defended site

41 South Etruria Survey: the early Middle Ages.

larger estates, but that cannot, on the other hand, wholly explain the scale
of the decline. Certainly, some land went out of cultivation but, in addition,
we have to conclude that the overall size of the rural population must have
fallen. The temptation, of course, is to assume that there was a migration
from the countryside into the towns and villages but, on examination, this
hypothesis does not seem to stand up. The evidence is not very satisfactory,

being derived mainly from surface data; but it does have the merit of consistency. Thus, if we take the Roman towns and road-stations of south Etruria, we find that the majority of the sites—Veii, Lucus Feroniae, Capena, Falerii Novi, *Ad VI*, Careiae, *Ad Baccanas, Ad Gallinas, Ad Vicesimum* and Aquaviva—initially enter a period of decline during the mid Empire and do not appear to have maintained their urban status much, if at all, beyond the end of the fourth century. The only exceptions would seem to be Nepi, Sutri and possibly Nazzano, together with the road-station of *Ad Nonas* (La Storta) which is cited as the *burgo Nono* in documents of the eleventh century (Wickham, 1978), and must therefore have survived as a settlement. For the rest the archaeological record is apparently unambiguous. The pottery sequence generally continues into the fourth century and then dwindles away, with few or no sherds of the fifth and sixth centuries. The dated inscriptions also demonstrate much the same pattern: if we consider Veii, for example, the latest known dedication is to Constantius I, made between A.D. 293 and 305 (*CIL* xi, i, 3796). Similarly, both Falerii Novi and Lucus Feroniae (where the epigraphic collection is also large) show a dearth of mid-Imperial inscriptions and an absence of late Roman examples. Indeed, the major excavations currently in progress at Lucus Feroniae have yet to yield evidence of any important building that post-dates the second century and it seems clear, therefore, that substantial parts of this town had been abandoned by *c*. A.D. 400, if not before.

Even so, we must be cautious in assuming too extensive a depopulation of the urban centres. At Falerii Novi, for example, there was a monastic settlement on the site for much of the early Middle Ages (Silvestrelli, 1970) and it is therefore hard to imagine, despite a paucity of very late Roman pottery, that all vestiges of urban life had disappeared as early as A.D. 400. Similarly, at Capena, at least one of the Roman buildings was maintained into the Middle Ages (Tomassetti, 1913, 306) and must also imply some prolongation of town life, although again there is no other direct evidence. The fact is that without extensive excavation, directed specifically at examining the latest levels in these town sites, we are not yet in a position to do more than conjecture about the scale and nature of the urban decline in the late Roman period.

Certainly the picture is a complex one with strong variations from region to region. At Tuscania, for example, a Viterbese town some 30 kilometres to the north-west of our region, excavations upon the main acropolis in 1974 (Potter and Gianfrotta, 1979) demonstrated that the Roman houses flanking a small paved street had been totally abandoned by the late fourth century and that the street itself had also fallen into disuse. The site then remained empty until the eighth century when a new road was constructed, together with substantial post-built houses that can be associated with the Lombard occupation of the site. At the coastal town of Luni (*Luna*) close by the Apuan Alps of north-west Italy, the picture is on the other hand rather different. The site was initially founded as a Republican *colonia* and prospered during Roman times as a maritime outlet for the Carrara (or

Luna) marble that was quarried near by. The town was a Byzantine stronghold until A.D. 640, when it fell to the Lombards, and it remained an important administrative centre until the eighth or ninth centuries. Extensive excavations have now been in progress on this site for several years and, apart from disclosing a good deal of the Classical plan, have also begun to cast light upon the archaeology of the late Roman–early medieval transition (Ward-Perkins, B., 1978). It has emerged that the forum was stripped of much of its marble paving at some point in the late Roman period, and that by about A.D. 500 wooden houses with beaten clay floors were being constructed over its eastern side. At the same time scattered inhumation burials began to appear over many parts of the Classical town, indicating that there were derelict building plots available for these interments within the walls. The long-established law prohibiting all but extra-mural burial must also have lapsed and, while the excavators are at pains to point out that the present sample is far too small for any firm conclusions, it is nevertheless quite clear that there had been quite fundamental changes in the urban way of life by this time. Even so the town appears to have remained prosperous, for it continued to import foreign goods, amongst them African Red Slip-ware, glass lamps from Syria, and wine and oil in various types of amphorae.

This fascinating glimpse of some form of town life persisting into the early Dark Ages at Luni cannot yet be matched in south Etruria; but, on the other hand, if we here read the meagre body of available evidence aright it will in fact be paralleled at very few sites. Everything points to a level of depopulation that is as marked in the towns as it is in the countryside. Precisely what factors lie behind this is a matter that is well beyond the scope of this book; undoubtedly they are complex and various (Jones, 1964, 762; 1966b). Malaria, for example, has often been adduced as an element, and was certainly endemic in the Campagna (Celle, 1933). Moreover, its effects must have been exacerbated by the flooding that, as we showed in Chapter 2, became increasingly prevalent in low-lying areas from the third century A.D. Settlement in both valley bottoms and the coastal flats was certainly affected very badly by this deterioration of conditions (arguably the product of climatic fluctuation) and it is tempting to see the abandonment of sites like Lucus Feroniae as a consequence of these environmental changes. Indeed, in the early Middle Ages, parts of Rome itself were continually troubled by flood waters and the ill-health that these induced (Llewellyn, 1971, 195). Thus in 590, Gregory of Tours (*HF* 10, 1) was told that

in November of the previous year the waters of the Tiber had overflowed Rome in such a flood that the ancient buildings had been destroyed and the granaries of the Church wrecked, containing some thousands of bushels of wheat, which had been lost. There then followed a plague called *inguinaria*: it broke out in the middle of January and first of all attacked Pope Pelagius, who quickly died of it; and after his death there was a great mortality among the people.

Just how pervasive plagues such as these may have been is difficult to assess; but there does seem little doubt that the population must have fallen quite considerably (Boak, 1955). Indeed, if we extend this argument, it would seem that a demographic decline is one of the principal keys to the interpretation of our data for this period; just as we postulated a massive increase in the size of the population during the first millennium B.C., so we can best explain the pattern of settlement decline in the mid to late Roman period by a comparable fall. The precise features that initiated this trend must remain obscure but its measurable effect is clearly spelt out in the decay of the towns and the gradual abandonment of many of the country estates. The long-term consequences of this trend we shall examine in subsequent sections.

The papal *domuscultae*: A.D. 500–800

The centuries that follow A.D. 500 become in archaeological terms increasingly elusive. This is in part a comment upon the decline in the quality of life (as Llewellyn implies in titling his history of the period *Rome in the Dark Ages*); but it is also a reflection of the ignorance about the varieties and development of artifacts, particularly local pottery styles, which stems principally from a lack of excavations. This situation is of course already in the process of change and, as medieval archaeology gathers momentum, we can anticipate something of a data explosion over the next few years. Meanwhile we can hope to offer only a very provisional picture, based on the results of a sparse number of excavations (some not yet fully published), a considerable body of surface evidence, and a certain amount of documentary material.

We may begin by outlining what we know of the main pottery sequence. The latest Roman tablewares, African Red Slipped products, continued to reach central Italy down to about A.D. 600 (Hayes, 1972, 416) and then appear to terminate fairly abruptly. Presumably the market outlets were sufficiently disorganized by this time to render unprofitable such commercial enterprise, and it may well be that supplies had steadily dwindled during the sixth century, so that our distribution maps show only the sites of those affluent enough to purchase the wares.

Whatever the truth of the matter, however, it is the case that from the early seventh century, we lose the benefit of closely datable wares, a situation which prevails until the introduction of the first widespread medieval product, the so-called Forum ware. This pottery, which is distinctive for its thick green glaze and barbotine decoration, occurs typically as a jug or pitcher, with a spout and single strap handle (Whitehouse, 1965; Mazzucato, 1968a, 1972). The largest known group was found in the forum of Rome in 1900 and, since this included some wasters, it has been generally assumed that Rome was its main centre of manufacture. The chronology of Forum ware is, on the other hand, very much more controversial and cannot be regarded as clearly established. The main fixed point comes from Santa

Cornelia, a site that we shall discuss in detail below, where typical sherds occurred both in early ninth-century levels and in deposits that pre-dated *c*. A.D. 780. Similarly, at the church of Santa Rufina, north-west of Rome, Forum ware vessels were sealed by a mosaic floor dated on stylistic grounds to about A.D. 750; thus, the two sites would seem to show that the ware was certainly in production in the late eighth century. Where it originated is, however, not at all clear; it may, as Whitehouse (1965, 1967) thinks, have been introduced from the Byzantine world in the second half of the eighth century; or it could have appeared somewhat earlier. But we still lack the stratified groups of seventh- and early eighth-century material with which to establish an answer.

For the same reason we are unable to identify any other distinctive or common ceramic forms for this transitional period: we have in fact a typological gap of more than 150 years. The only known ware that may span this gap is a series of jugs in a pale buff fabric, decorated with bands of combing not unlike that on Villanovan pottery. 'Combed ware' has been noted in late Roman deposits in north Africa and has been found in association with Forum ware at Santa Cornelia, Santa Rufina and Mazzano Romano (Potter, 1972, 142); it also occurs in seventh-century Lombard graves at Fiesole near Florence (Hessen, 1966, 1968) and has been recognized in late Roman and early medieval layers at a Roman villa near Potenza. This is far short of adequate evidence but there is now hope that combed ware may prove to be a useful type-fossil for the period. For the rest, we have to recognize that there is still a good deal of pioneer work to be done in the identification of the early medieval type series (especially the origin of the baggy coarse-ware pots which, by the end of the eighth century, had become standard kitchenware) and must modify our conclusions accordingly.

Turning to the settlement evidence, we may begin by examining the pattern of rural sites, and the degree to which the Classical system of farming survived into the early Middle Ages. The issue has recently been subject to some controversy (Whitehouse, D., 1973; Luttrell, 1974; Wickham, 1978), arising partly from difficulties in reconciling the historical and archaeological data, but also from the chronological deficiencies outlined above. Thus, on the one hand, is the view persuasively advanced by Ward Perkins that 'the Classical estates survived at least as late as the closing years of the eighth century' (Ward Perkins, 1962a, 401) and that it was only then that the reversion to nucleated sites in defended positions began: 'with the collapse of papal authority in the later ninth century A.D., it was no longer safe to live in the old villas and farms of the open countryside, and one by one these were abandoned in favour of the nearest easily fortifiable site' (Ward Perkins, 1972, 878). Others have argued, on the other hand, that the migration from a dispersed system of farming into the promontory and hill villages started at a much earlier date. Jones (1974), for example, sees the trend beginning as far back as the third century A.D. and others have suggested that it was well under way from early in the

Middle Ages, certainly before the end of the eighth century (Whitehouse, D., 1973; Potter, 1975).

Much of this debate has centred round the archaeological material collected in the course of the South Etruria Survey: but recently there has been an important contribution by a historian, Pierre Toubert (1973), who has made an exhaustive study of the other areas of Lazio, especially the well documented Sabine region to the east and north-east of Rome. Toubert's principal conclusion provides a novel twist to the debate. The reversion to nucleated settlement, he argues, belonged principally to the tenth or eleventh centuries when the rural population was grouped into villages (*castra* or *castella*), many of which were fortified, by the lords or *domini*. This process of *incastellamento* was, however, not the result of pervasive insecurity (it post-dates the major threat, that of the Arab attacks), but a deliberately implemented act of colonization in newly acquired territory, where the *domini* were specifically concerned to create a firm hold over the inhabitants. In this way they could tie the people to the land and make an effective exploitation of their holdings. This model has, on the whole, found widespread acceptance. It is well documented (if only because it was mainly the great monastic houses like Subiaco and Farfa that were responsible for the reorganization of the land), and the villages are securely dated. Moreover, the subsequent history of many of the *castellae* also supports the argument: at least 80 were largely abandoned by A.D. 1200, clearly revealing the artificial element in their foundation. These sites were not the natural choice of the local populace but were selected more for political (and principally strategic) reasons that from the dictates of common sense.

Toubert's model for Lazio east and south of Rome is of crucial importance in that it provides a clearly defined sequence for the change in settlement patterns, combined with some sound dating evidence. In south Etruria, however, the absence of any great monastic houses means that our documentary record for this period is meagre and we have to rely more on archaeological evidence. Nor can we assume that Toubert's model is in any way closely applicable to the situation west of the Tiber; in fact, as we shall see, there is good reason to suppose both that the two regions evolved in a rather different way and that the pattern within south Etruria was much less consistent from area to area.

The one feature that all areas share in common is the demonstrable existence of the Classical pattern of farming during the fifth and sixth centuries. The Veientine (Ward Perkins, 1968) and Faliscan areas include between them nearly 70 sites with material of this period, clearly proving that parts of the region still remained under cultivation (Figs. 40, 41). The main blanks in the distribution map lie in areas of marginal land, like the Sorbo crater in the north-west Ager Veientanus and, most strikingly, along the main highways. We know that the Via Flaminia played an important rôle in the Gothic wars of 535–52 and that the Via Amerina also remained a much used route until the late Middle Ages (Bullough, 1965, 1968), and there can be no doubt that this traffic discouraged the would-be wayside settler. Most villa and farm owners preferred to leave a wide margin between their estates and the highways in this tumultuous period.

After A.D. 600, as we have seen, we lose the benefit of the closely datable African Red Slip-wares and, consequently, have no detailed knowledge of the settlement pattern during the next 150 years. Not until the introduction of Forum ware can we once again pick up something of the main threads. Fortunately we have also the benefit of some crucial documentary evidence, recorded in the *Liber Pontificalis* (Duchesne, 1886, 501–2, 506–7); it refers to the creation of four estates or *domuscultae*, one of which, known as Capracorum, lay in the heart of the survey area:

The same most holy Pope [Hadrian I] created and founded four papal estates, of which one is called Capracorum, in the territory of Veii, about 15 miles out of Rome. Of this estate, the original farm of Capracorum together with several other farms adjoining it, was his own property, inherited from his family; and to it he added a number of other estates, giving just compensation for each to the persons from whom he bought them. This *domusculta* of Capracorum, with its *massae* [lands], *fundi* [farms], *casales* [farm buildings], vineyards, olive groves, watermills and all else appertaining to it, be established under apostolic privilege and with the sanction of solemn penalties, that it should for all time continue to be applied to the use of our brothers in Christ, the poor; and that the wheat and barley grown each year in its fields should be carefully collected and stored apart in the granary of our holy church. The wine, too, and the vegetables grown each year in the domains and fields of the aforesaid *domusculta*, should similarly be diligently collected and stored separately in the storehouse of our holy church. And of the pigs which should each year be fattened in the *casales* in the said *domusculta*, one hundred head should be slaughtered and stored in the same storehouse.

The founder of Capracorum, Hadrian I, was Pope between 772 and 795, and it was probably about 780 that he created the *domusculta*. As Partner (1966) has shown, it was but one of a series of such estates which ringed the city of Rome, in an attempt to solve the very real food shortages that had afflicted the city since before the days of Gregory the Great. Hadrian, as the passage quoted above makes clear, was in fact responsible for laying our four of these *domuscultae* (amongst them the extensive estate of Galeria, which stretched north-west of Rome towards the Via Clodia), consolidating the pioneer work of his Greek predecessor, Pope Zacharias (741–52). That they were successful for only a short time was no fault of their authors. Not long after Hadrian's death, there began the first Arab raids and, as these intensified during the first half of the ninth century, so the *domuscultae* became increasingly vulnerable. A celebrated inscription (Tomassetti, 1913, 109) describes how men from Capracorum worked on the Leonine Wall around St Peter's after the Arab attack of 846, by which time the *domuscultae* must have been firmly on the decline. Moreover, they were also unpopular amongst the Roman nobles, who contrived to damage the estates by fire in 816 (Llewellyn, 1971, 252), and were continually looking to recover land that they claimed to have lost to the church. In combination, these pressures

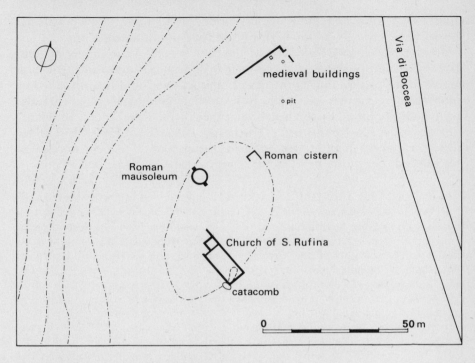

42 Plan of the excavated structures at Santa Rufina.

were too great upon the *domuscultae* and, although they were still yielding some revenue in the early tenth century, they can hardly have been functioning on any scale (Partner, 1966, 76).

Even though the *domuscultae* proved to be short-lived, they nevertheless represent an important phase in the transition between the disintegration of the dispersed system of farming and the formation of the nucleated villages. Subsequently we shall try to estimate the degree to which the Classical estates had gone out of use by the time the *domuscultae* were being founded; but first, we must consider the results of recent excavations upon two sites of this period, Santa Rufina and Santa Cornelia. Unfortunately, neither site has yet been published in more than an interim way and our description and conclusions must be correspondingly provisional.

We shall deal first with the smaller of the two, Santa Rufina, which was an ecclesiastical site that lay some ten kilometres to the north-west of Rome, close to the Via di Boccea (Fig. 41). Here the landscape takes the form of a series of gentle ridges, divided by shallow stream valleys, the typical setting for a Classical villa or farm. In fact, the excavation by Lady Wheeler disclosed precisely that: a scatter of debris from nearby farm buildings, founded in the Republican period and occupied well into Imperial times (Fig. 42). In addition, there were the remains of a large and imposing circular mausoleum, conspicuously positioned on the crest of the ridge

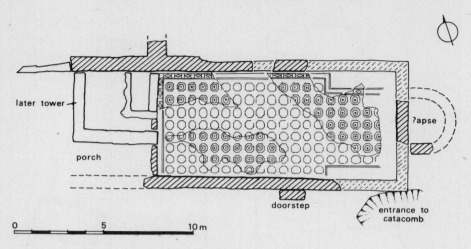

43 The early medieval church at Santa Rufina.

overlooking the road; it was presumably set up for the family that owned
the villa estate. Just how long the villa remained in occupation is unclear
but there is a good deal of late Roman material on the site and it may well
have been maintained as the centre of a farming estate into the early Middle
Ages. At this time there was an important change of function. Some time
towards the middle of the eighth century, a small chapel, dedicated to St
Rufina, was constructed close by the Roman mausoleum. The chapel (Fig.
43; Pl. Xb), which was laid out over a catacomb cut into the *tufo*, consisted
of a small rectangular stone nave, measuring only 13 × 5.90 metres
internally. This room, which was approximately orientated east–west, was
floored with a roughly made mosaic, where the dominant motif comprised
eight rows of small concentric rectangles, drawn in green and red porphyry.
On stylistic grounds, the floor should probably date to about A.D. 750, an
attribution that is corroborated by several sherds of Forum ware that were
found beneath it. To the west there was originally an antechamber, but this
had been subsequently modified into a rectangular structure, measuring
3.20 × 3.50 metres internally, perhaps the foundations of small bell-tower;
we can probably associate this partial rebuild of the chapel with the
construction of other, apparently domestic, buildings a little further along
the ridge.

The importance of the site of Santa Rufina lies in the fact that it can be
directly correlated with a church described in the *Liber Pontificalis*. According to this account (Duchesne, 1886, 508), Hadrian I renovated a church
dedicated to two sisters, Rufina and Secunda, who had been martyred under
Valerian and Gallienus. Subsequently the building was embellished by Leo
IV and, after being damaged by Moslem raiders in the second half of the
ninth century, was further restored in 906. Tomassetti (1910, 487–91)
convincingly argues on the evidence of the still current place-name of Santa
Rufina that the church described in the *Liber Pontificalis* was to be found

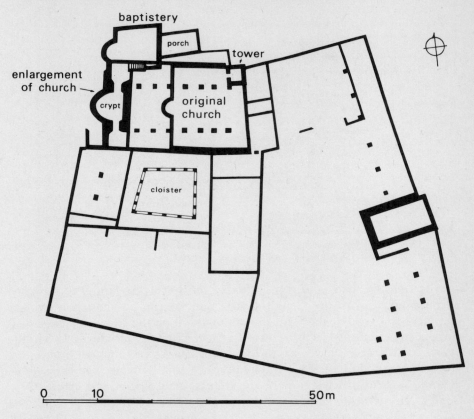

baptistery

porch

tower

enlargement
of church

crypt

original
church

cloister

0   10   50m

44 Schematic plan of the early medieval complex at Santa Cornelia, near Veii.

in this area, and it is now clear from the recent excavations that he was right. Certainly it may be taken to typify a rural complex of the mid eighth century, built in the open countryside upon one of the old villa estates, very much in the manner of Classical times.

Much the same is true of another recently excavated site, that of Santa Cornelia, with the important difference that here we seem to be dealing with the remains of one of the actual estate centres of the *domusculta*, that of Capracorum (Ward Perkins, 1968, 163–4). The buildings lay near to the modern Casale Santa Cornelia, on a low hill in lightly dissected countryside, some three kilometres to the north of Veii (Fig. 41). This open setting is identical to that of the numerous Roman villas to be found in the area, and for a long time this is exactly what the surface traces were taken to represent. In 1961, however, excavations were begun on the site by Charles Daniels and soon showed it to consist of a substantial early medieval complex, belonging to the period of the *domuscultae*. As at Santa Rufina there had initially been a Roman villa near by (Ward Perkins, 1968, 97) with material of the early Imperial period, and some of the vine trenches and pits associated with this early phase in the occupation of the site were identified beneath the buildings of the *domusculta*. But the principal remains were entirely medieval in date, representing a complicated sequence of superimposed buildings, spanning the eighth to twelfth centuries (Fig. 44). They divide into two main phases.

In the first period there were two ecclesiastical buildings, placed at the north-west corner of an irregularly laid out courtyard, bounded by a stone wall; the limits of this court are not known with any precision but do not appear to have measured more than 65 × 75 metres, well within the limits of the larger Roman villas in the area. The main church was a simple rectangular basilican building, divided into three aisles. It was no longer than the chapel at Santa Rufina, 13.5 metres, but was much broader, being 14.5 metres in width. There was an apex at the west end and a small tower (probably constructed in a secondary phase) at the north-east corner. Close by was a second building which served as a baptistery. Like the main church it consisted of a simple rectangular structure, 7.50 × 7 metres, with a single apse at the west end; but there was also a long porch to the east, probably added, as was the campanile, at a later period.

The ecclesiastical buildings provide a sharp contrast with the other structures of the complex. These consisted of a range of lean-to sheds, constructed with the end of the courtyard as the back wall and with a series of wooden posts, resting on stone bases, forming an open front. In addition there were barns and other rooms, built principally in stone, so that the whole arrangement is strongly reminiscent of the layout of a Roman farm, such as the Posto villa at Francolise (Blanckenhagen, Cotton and Ward Perkins, 1965). This then was the working area of the estate centre which, if correctly identified as Capracorum, should represent the granary, store-house and administrative offices of the *domusculta* founded by Hadrian in *c*. A.D. 780.

The identification and dating hinges mainly on historical rather than on archaeological evidence, particularly the association of the modern place-name, Santa Cornelia, with Capracorum in the documentary references to the site. Thus we are told how Pope Hadrian, when establishing a church at Capracorum, ordered that the remains of four martyrs, amongst them Saint Cornelius, should be transferred there (Duchesne, 1886, 506–7), thus establishing an early link between the saint and Capracorum. By 1021 there are references to *S. Cornelii in Crapario*, an association that is perpetuated in documents of the next two centuries. A combination of place-name and historical evidence would seem therefore to exclude most doubt that this was the original centre of Hadrian's estate. There is, moreover, some confirmation from documents of 1041 and later, collected by Tomassetti (1913, 109–12), which describe the site as a *monasterium*. This conversion to monastic status can in fact be readily related to the buildings of the last phase at Santa Cornelia, datable to early in the eleventh century (Ward Perkins, 1968, 164). The excavations revealed not only a drastic remodelling of the old basilican church at this time but also the construction of an extensive complex of monastic buildings in the south-west part of the court adjoining the church. The latter included two large halls, divided by a small cloister, together with the remains of several other rooms. The church, whilst incorporating much of its precursor, was substantially enlarged towards the west by the addition of a crypt, a raised presbytery and an arrangement of one major and two smaller apses. At the same time a porch was added to the façade, whose columns, portico arches and doorway were found collapsed in front of the building. There were also modifications to the farm buildings, indicating that the monks continued to maintain some of the surrounding land in a state of cultivation.

The identification of this monastic complex can probably be said to provide ultimate confirmation that the excavated site of Santa Cornelia was in fact the Capracorum of the *Liber Pontificalis*; the correlation between documentary and archaeological data is too close to leave much doubt. What, however, we do not know is the degree to which the *domuscultae* represented an attempt to revive a system of farming that had all but collapsed by the late eighth century. Both the layout and the open setting of the early *domusculta* buildings at Santa Cornelia are (like Santa Rufina) highly reminiscent of the classical villas of the Campagna; but the overall total of villas in this region that have yielded archaeological evidence of continuous occupation into the eighth century (i.e. late African Red Slip pottery and sherds of Forum ware and contemporary material) is very small (Potter, 1975). In fact, in the Ager Faliscus, as we shall see, there is reason to think that the medieval nucleated village had already begun to replace the Classical villa site as the model of settlement—a trend which, if correctly interpreted, would undoubtedly go some way towards explaining why the *domuscultae* were deemed necessary.

Nearer to Rome, on the other hand, the pattern may well have been different. Just as in Toubert's area east and south of the Tiber (Toubert, 1973), most of the nucleated villages have yet to yield evidence of a period of foundation earlier than the ninth century. Similarly, as Wickham (1978) has recently emphasized, the documentary record for early medieval land organization in the Ager Veientanus implies that the classical estates (*fundi*) remained the basic agrarian pattern for most of the later first millennium. The break with the old structure of land use came later, probably in the tenth century, by which time the medieval villages were certainly coming into existence, a conclusion which finds further support from the very recent excavations in September 1977, at Le Mura di Santo Stefano. This is the site of a finely preserved three-storey building (Pl. IXb), part of an extensive villa complex served by its own approach road from the Via Clodia. Like Santa Rufina and Santa Cornelia it lies in open rolling countryside, unprotected by any natural feature. The present excavations took place on the shelf of flat ground just to the north of the standing remains. They revealed part of a church, together with a number of tombs and some associated structures (Fig. 45). As the successive apses show, at least three phases of building are represented, all apparently belonging to the late Roman to early medieval period. In fact, the plan of the church is so directly

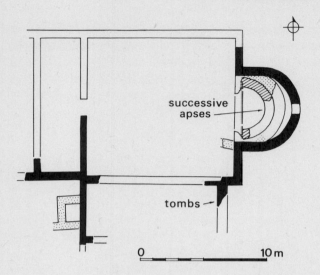

successive
apses

tombs

0   10 m

45 The early medieval church at Le Mura di Santo Stefano, near Anguillara.

comparable with that of the first phase at Santa Cornelia, that it is likely that both were constructed at about the same time. If so, Le Mura could well be one of the villa estates that did remain in occupation through into the early Middle Ages.

Thus, despite the fact that early medieval material has been recognized from only seven Roman sites within the Veientine area (Potter, 1975, 228), we should probably accept the evidence of the *Liber Pontificalis* as being literally correct: that when Hadrian I acquired *fundi*, *casales* and *massae* for the *domuscultae* of Capracorum, there were estates and farms that perpetuated the classical structure of agrarian life. Only in more northern areas of the region does the pattern seem to vary, for reasons that we shall advance below.

The medieval village: its characteristics and origin

The fortified village was as characteristic a feature of the medieval landscape as the villa was of the Roman countryside. To the north of Rome (Fig. 46) there are the remains of more than 100 such sites, often conspicuous by their *rocca* or castle stronghold, their towers and the number and size of their churches. Many, of course, are still inhabited, forming the *centro vecchio* of towns that have expanded outwards from their medieval nucleus; but many more now lie deserted and remote, with ruins densely overgrown by *macchia* and trees. The sites lining the Treia Valley might be taken as typical, with fortified villages occupying almost every major spur and promontory of its course, some 20 kilometres long, to the Tiber; they range from existing towns and villages, like Civita Castellana, Calcata and

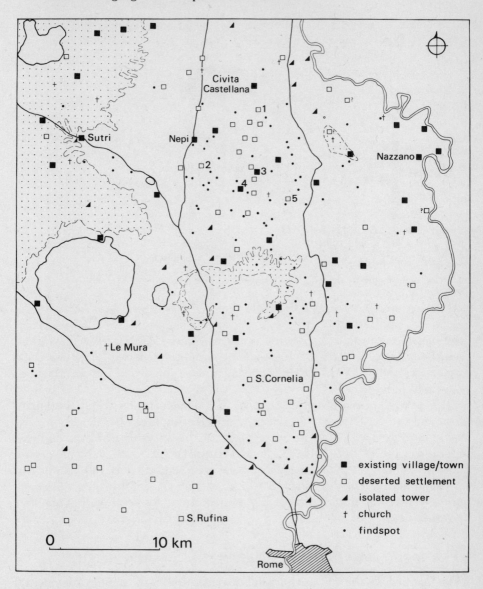

46 South Etruria Survey: medieval sites. (1) Castel Paterno; (2) Castel Porciano; (3) Calcata; (4) Mazzano Romano; (5) Torre Busson.

Mazzano, to abandoned but imposing ruins like Castel Paterno (where the Emperor Otto III was to die on 23 January 1002), Agnese, Santa Maria di Calcata and Castellaccio.

Of these, the village of Calcata (Pl. XV) illustrates to perfection the qualities sought by the medieval settlers in choosing a site. Perched on a narrow pedestal of rock, less than 100 metres in width, the village can be approached only by means of a narrow ridge joining the pedestal with the side of the valley; all other sides are protected by the sheer vertical cliffs that are so prominent a feature of the volcanic terrain. At the same time, the top of the pedestal lies well below the level of the surrounding countryside, so that the settlement is visible only when one comes right to the edge of the valley—a characteristic that recurs so frequently that it must have been deliberate, just as true hilltop positions were more often than not rejected. Two other features are striking about Calcata. One is the enormous number of caves which honeycomb the cliffs round the settlement, providing simple but comfortable houses, byres for stalling mules and cattle, and storage space for local produce, especially wine. The other is the castle, whose gatehouse forms the main entrance into the village and whose walls now consist of a circuit of tall houses extending virtually without a break round the entire perimeter of the rock pedestal. Even though the village was extensively rebuilt in the post-medieval period, there is little doubt that it retains essentially the same layout as its medieval precursor and probably appears little different.

The manner in which a village such as Calcata may have evolved is only gradually becoming apparent as more excavation is undertaken. To date, the most comprehensively investigated site in south Etruria lies a short distance to the west of Calcata (Fig. 46), at Castel Porciano (Mallett and Whitehouse, 1967). This village, which has been deserted since the early sixteenth century, lay on a spur formed by the confluence of three streams. As at Calcata, its access is restricted to a narrow path of rock which widens into a small plateau, measuring 150 × 45 metres (Fig. 47). Its natural defences were therefore strong and could readily be made impregnable by the construction of walls and a ditch. In fact there appear to have been two main lines of fortification: first a substantial ditch cut across the narrowest point of the ridge, about 100 metres to the south of the settlement, and then a masonry tower, fronted by a second ditch, which protected the main entrance into the village and enfiladed the only easy approaches to the site. The settlement itself (Fig. 48) turned out to have evolved in several distinct phases, in each of which the buildings became increasingly substantial and elaborate. The original nucleus consisted of a rectangular mound, some 25 metres square, placed centrally within the plateau. It was protected on at least two sides by a rock-cut ditch, nearly three metres in width, and contained a small tower, with sides of 3.75 metres, built of good quality *tufo* masonry. Such towers are a recurrent feature on all the medieval sites of south Etruria and often form part of the principal residence: but so far there is no evidence to show that they were being constructed before the eleventh century, a date that would suit the masonry style of the Porciano example perfectly well. On the other hand, both the documents and the pottery imply a rather older date for the foundation of the site. Like many of the villages in the Ager Faliscus, Porciano is first listed as a *fundus* (farm) belonging to the *domusculta* of Capracorum (Tomassetti, 1913, 111) and this date is corroborated by the discovery of four pieces of Forum ware on

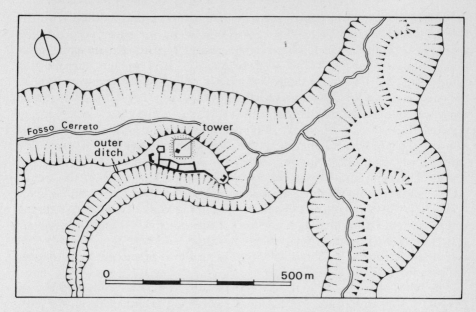

47 The topographic setting of Castel Porciano. (Source: Mallett and Whitehouse, 1967)

the site (identified since the report on the excavation was written) as well as 69 fragments of sparse-glaze ware, a common lead-glazed fabric in vogue between the ninth and early thirteenth centuries (Whitehouse, 1967, 53–5).

On both archaeological and historical grounds, therefore, we can conclude that the first period at Porciano ought to extend back to the eighth century, if not before. At this time, as work at sites like Tuscania is now showing (Potter and Gianfrotta, 1979), many buildings were being constructed in wood and it is quite possible that the masonry tower at Porciano was preceded by a timber one, which awaits identification by excavation. There may also have been other timber structures on the plateau, for traces of such buildings have been identified by excavation at the comparable site of Belmonte (Stiesdal, 1962). However, it is also clear that many of the people must have lived in caves, cut into the upper part of the cliffs surrounding the plateau. As at most medieval sites in the volcanic terrain, there are numerous examples of such caves at Porciano, often arranged in three or four successive levels. That some were used to stall animals is clear from the presence of tethering holes, mangers and troughs; but others were equally certainly human habitations, since they are provided with beds, windows and niches and, in one case at Porciano, a central column, decorated with a crudely carved capital. None of the caves is securely dated but the manner in which some had been inserted into the side of the central enclosure argues that they may well have been built from the earliest phases in the occupation of the site.

Before long, the settlement began to expand over much of the plateau. The ditch round the central mound was partially back-filled and a number

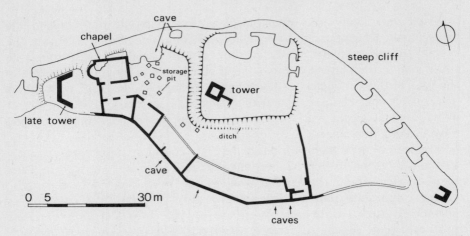

48 Detailed plan of Castel Porciano. (Source: Mallett and Whitehouse, 1967)

of deep storage pits were dug into the rock in the area to the south. These pits, which have a flask-shaped profile and a square mouth, rebated for a lid, are again a very common feature of the medieval sites. An eighth-century example has been excavated at Tuscania (Potter and Gianfrotta, 1979) as well as many others of later medieval and Renaissance date (Ward Perkins *et al.*, 1973). They were used for storage purposes, especially for grain, and in some instances as cesspits, and then, once their usefulness had ended, were normally back-filled with refuse. At Porciano the pits proved to be disappointingly sparse in rubbish (most was tipped over the cliff), but those at Tuscania have yielded enormous groups of pottery, small objects, bones and seeds, providing an invaluable sample of medieval rubbish. Thus we know from the animal bones, for example, that the traditional emphasis of the economy did not alter in the Middle Ages, the percentages being dominated by sheep and goats, as in prehistoric deposits in the region (Barker, 1973).

This expansion in the settlement at Porciano cannot be dated closely but is likely to belong to the twelfth or thirteenth centuries. Mallett believes that a rough perimeter wall may also have been constructed at this time and infers the presence of several stone buildings. But the major change came in the period between *c.* 1275 and 1350, when the documents indicate that the settlement had passed into the hands of the great Roman Hospital of Santo Spirito (Mallet and Whitehouse, 1967, 116). The earliest record listing Porciano among the holdings of the hospital dates to 1295 and includes a reference to the church of St Andrea; this can be identified with the remains of a small chapel measuring only 9 × 7.6 metres, built between the central mound and the entrance to the south. Apart from a single apse at the west end, the only features of note are traces of a screen wall and the *tufo* footings for an altar; it was apparently a very simple building, with a tiled roof, a superstructure of wood and a floor of bare rock. It was nevertheless demonstrably later than one of the storage pits and belongs to a period when many other stone buildings were being put up. Thus, to this same phase, we can assign an extension of the main residence, within the central mound, and the construction of a solid perimeter wall lining the south side of the plateau, the part most vulnerable to longbow shot. Along the back of this perimeter wall was a row of stone houses, each with rooms about seven metres square; their arrangement is reminiscent of the circuit of houses at Calcata and many other villages in the region, which must have evolved in a similar way.

The scale of these modifications to the layout of the settlement is especially striking, so much so that Mallett suggests that 'with the passage into the hands of the hospital, the settlement might have been converted from a loose village community into a seigneurial castle of a type more common in northern Europe' (Mallett and Whitehouse, 1967, 146). Certainly Porciano can never have supported a large population and, even by the fourteenth century, this was beginning to decline. The latest buildings consist of two three-sided towers, placed at each end of the plateau. The walls are especially thick—over a metre—and they may well have been constructed in response to the introduction of siege cannon, known in the papal states from the mid fourteenth century, the approximate period of the masonry used in the towers. But their use must have been very short-lived, for there is no mention of Porciano in the list of those paying salt tax in the mid fourteenth century (Tomassetti, 1897), and by 1467 (the latest medieval reference to the site) it is referred to as a *tenementum* rather than a *castrum*. The pottery tells the same story, one of decline from some time in the fourteenth century and of a complete cessation of occupation by about 1520: once Porciano had ceased to be the focus for the local populace it soon, like many of its neighbours, dwindled in importance and was gradually deserted.

We have described Porciano in some detail because in many respects it can be said to typify the medieval village of the Campagna and, at the same time, it represents one of the most thoroughly studied. The variation between these sites is principally one of scale. Thus the tower, a feature common to nearly every known medieval site (Lawrence, 1964) ranged from the very simple structures to be found at Porciano to large and elegant versions, like the black and white banded example, provided with internal rooms and a privy, at Pietra Pertusa in the Ager Veientanus (Stiesdal, 1962). S. Maria di Calcata, a deserted promontory site opposite the village of Calcata, provides another fine instance (Pl. XIVb). The tower stands isolated on a low knoll towards the end of a spur, protected by a rock-cut ditch and a stone wall. The base of the tower is massively built, with walls 1.60 metres thick and overall dimensions of 12 × 9 metres. Inside, the ground floor room has an elegant vaulted ceiling and there were at least two storeys above. Nearby are caves of identical type to those at Porciano and traces of storage pits with square rebated mouths. The overall layout therefore is that of another small stronghold, planned entirely with defensive consid-erations in mind but in this instance provided with a comparatively com-fortable main residence. But, as at Porciano, S. Maria also became

XIII The 1974 ex-
cavations at Colle San
Pietro, Tuscania.

XIVa *Opposite top* The
medieval tower and
casale at Torre Busson.
(Photo: *BSR*)

XIVb *Opposite bottom*
Santa Maria di Calcata.

XV *Above* The village of
Calcata.

XVIa *Left* Medieval pack-bridge below Castel Sant'Elia. (Photo: *BSR*)

XVIb *Below* Post-medieval posting station at Osteria di Stabia, on the Via Flaminia.

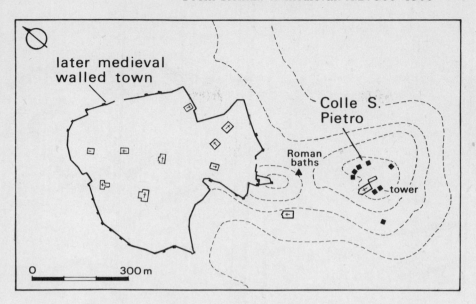

49 General plan of Tuscania.

increasingly obsolete in the later Middle Ages, and although a monastery was built on the open ground in front of the castle in the fourteenth century, the village was already by this time well on the way to total desertion.

The Faliscan area in the Middle Ages seems in fact to have formed something of a frontier between the territory of Rome and the powerful cities of the Viterbese to the north. This is without doubt the principal explanation for the extraordinary concentration of small fortresses and defended villages to be found in the area. There were also of course larger agglomerations, such as Civita Castellana, Nepi and Sutri, but so far we know little of the medieval layout of the towns. Our best studied example in south Etruria comes in fact from the site of Tuscania, a town (Fig. 49) situated in undulating volcanic countryside on the northern edge of the Viterbese basin, some 30 kilometres to the north-west of the South Etruria Survey region. In February 1971, the Tuscania region was badly damaged by a localized but severe earthquake: many buildings collapsed and the town of Tuscania was evacuated. Following the disaster, a programme of restoration was put in hand, combined with a certain amount of excavation (Ward Perkins *et al.*, 1972, 1973), directed primarily at an exploration of parts of the old walled town. The surprising feature that emerged from this work was that the *centro medioevale* of present-day Tuscania was not occupied on any significant scale before the thirteenth century and that its main development belonged to the period of the mural defences, the fourteenth and fifteenth centuries. The early medieval nucleus (as well as the urban centre of the Etruscan and Roman town) clearly lay elsewhere, the obvious candidate being an isolated flat-topped hill, Colle San Pietro,

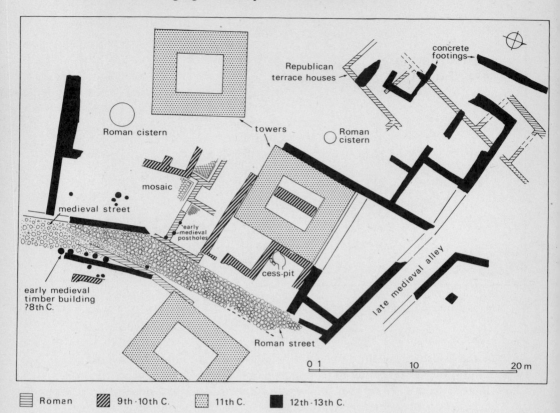

Roman | 9th-10th C. | 11th C. | 12th-13th C.

50 Selective plan of the Roman and medieval buildings on Colle San Pietro, Tuscania.

which lies to the south-east of the present-day town. The hill takes its name from a magnificent Romanesque basilica, San Pietro, which, with the nearby church of S. Maria Maggiore, a number of towers (Pringle, 1974) and other ecclesiastical buildings, forms an entirely separate medieval nucleus. In 1974, work of restoration upon one of the towers near to San Pietro brought to light a Roman cistern and mosaic floors; then, as further clearance proceeded, a whole complex of buildings was revealed, some late Etruscan, some Roman (including a paved street) and many of them of early medieval date (Fig. 50; Pl. XIII). This discovery of the early nucleus of the town was followed first by a systematic record of the exposed remains (Potter and Gianfrotta, 1979) and currently by proper excavation of the adjacent area; as a result it is now clear that there is a succession of structures upon the site that is at present unique for south Etruria.

Occupation on the site began early in the first millennium B.C. and carried on almost unbroken down to the later Middle Ages when the present-day centre began to develop. For most of this time the buildings flanked a narrow street that climbed the northern slopes of Colle San Pietro, heading towards the crest of the hill. In the Imperial period this street, paved with blocks of basalt, was lined with small town houses, comfortably provided with mosaic floors; but, towards A.D. 400, this area of the acropolis was abandoned and a layer of humus began to accumulate over the street. The area remained disused for over 300 years, although there must have been some sort of community during this period, since Tuscania sent bishops to the Roman Councils of both 595 and 649 (Silvestrelli, 1970, 839); but in the eighth century the site was once again reoccupied. The first step was to resurface the street on an alignment that diverged slightly from that of its Roman predecessor. Then, wooden houses were put up on either side of the road, one, with a frontage of at least nine metres, being constructed with a series of massive individual post-holes, while another converted a Roman house by setting timber uprights into the old wall foundations. Near by was a rock-cut storage pit, filled with domestic refuse: there were many nearly intact coarse-ware jars and a very large quantity of bones, consisting mainly of chicken but also including the skeleton of an ill-fated cat. Subsequently, these timber houses were rebuilt in stone, Roman material, and then in a good quality ashlar, well cut and regularly coursed. The buildings also became more elaborate, the later houses consisting of numerous small rooms, grouped round an open court which, in one case, contained the cesspit for a garderobe. The fill of this pit provided the principal dating evidence for the structures of this period, the sherds including numerous pieces of buff-ware jars, painted with red bands (Whitehouse, 1969); the assemblage as a whole can best be ascribed to the ninth and tenth centuries. By this time the basilica of San Pietro had been built near by (Raspi Serra, 1971, 171–5) and ecclesiastical influence was becoming increasingly prevalent. This manifests itself very explicitly in the eleventh century when the summit of Colle San Pietro was ringed with towers, enclosing the church buildings in a protective curtain. Three of these towers lay within the excavated area, one still standing and the other two surviving only at foundation level. The domestic buildings that had previously occupied the site were swept away and replaced by the massive foundations of these towers, sunk to a depth of at least six metres. Their walls were over two metres thick and the outside dimensions averaged 8.20 × 9.20 metres. The standing tower, although subsequently modified by the addition of arrow slits and concrete floors, was constructed with one room below ground level, and at least two above: the ground floor room had a barrel vault, a door to the north and a window to the west; presumably such towers served as residences as well as for military purposes.

The stamp of ecclesiastical authority that the building of this defensive curtain implies did not last for long. Within a short period of its construction, domestic houses once again began to grow up round the towers. One substantial *palazzo* with massive concrete foundations was terraced into the hill slopes to the north-west and another was built immediately to the north, leaving only a narrow alley-way between them and the tower. Other houses also appeared to the south so that by the thirteenth century the hillside must have been converted into a typical medieval town quarter with narrow streets, domestic buildings and the towers all cheek by jowl. By this time, however, the town had already begun to expand across the valley towards the north. The Rivellino ridge was now under development, a commercial quarter was beginning to flourish by the River Marta, and houses were appearing upon the accessible plateau area where the present town is sited. As the process of drift accelerated, so Colle San Pietro became increasingly deserted. The pottery record is one of sharp decline from *c.* 1300 onwards until almost complete abandonment by the early fifteenth century. About this time two of the three towers within the excavated area were demolished to foundation level (almost certainly to provide masonry for the new mural defences), and the usable stone was stripped from the private houses. Only the church buildings and six towers were left standing, while the remaining area gradually reverted to arable and pasture.

The detailed picture to emerge from the investigation of a small area of Colle San Pietro underlines the importance that urban archaeology has for the medieval period; as further work proceeds we can expect to build up a much better idea of the manner in which towns like Tuscania may have evolved. Already we can demonstrate a striking contrast between the settlements of the larger communities and the remains of small seigneurial castles like Porciano, emphasizing that the medieval nucleated sites played quite different rôles, according to their size and strategic importance. Much depended upon the factors that governed their original foundation and it is to this question that we must now turn.

Our primary source of evidence is the multitude of documents housed in the archives of the great monastic houses and elsewhere, many of which contain detailed references to the medieval settlements of south Etruria. What is particularly interesting in the present context is the date of the first reference to these sites, since this provides a secure fixed point for the emergence of the medieval landscape. In fact the dates cluster in a remarkable way, forming a distinct chronological horizon. Thus, if we take some of the towns and villages of south Etruria that are still inhabited, we find that Mazzano is first referred to in 945, Calcata in 974 and Stabia (present-day Faleria) in 998; Isola Farnese and Formello in 1003 and 1013 respectively; and Campagnano di Roma in 1076. The deserted sites follow an identical pattern: Pietra Pertusa, for example, first appears in 974, Sorbo and Torre Busson in 996 and Castel Paterno in 1002. We can be quite positive therefore that the pattern of nucleated settlements had been firmly established throughout south Etruria by the end of the eleventh century and mostly rather earlier.

When we look at the pattern in detail, however, some rather interesting variations emerge. In the Ager Veientanus the Classical *fundus* seems from documentary evidence to have remained the basis of land organization down to the end of the ninth century (perpetuated no doubt by the *domusculta* of Capracorum) and only then does a new pattern emerge, based principally on the larger medieval villages of Isola Farnese, Formello and Sacrofano. Wickham (1978), who has made a careful study of the documentary material, has therefore inferred that the transition from a dispersed to a

nucleated pattern of settlement took place in the tenth century, corroborating
the conclusion reached by Ward Perkins (1968, 165) on archaeological
grounds, discussed above. In the Ager Faliscus, on the other hand, the
picture does seem to be significantly different. Most conspicuous is the fact
that the medieval nucleated settlements demonstrate a much closer relationship with the late Roman sites than in any of the areas near to Rome
(Fig. 41). The point is most graphically made by the reoccupation of the
natural acropolis of Falerii Veteres, now called Civita Castellana, and the
corresponding desertion of Falerii Novi. We cannot prove a direct migration
from Falerii Novi to Civita Castellana but, given the historical association
between the two sites, it would seem extremely plausible. Indeed, the
documentary record makes it clear that Civita Castellana was already an
important centre by the ninth century (Silvestrelli, 1970), implying that the
process of drift had begun a good deal before. Similarly, in the countryside
of the Ager Faliscus, we can also detect a close relationship between villas
occupied into the late Roman period and the medieval village sites. Castel
Paterno provides an excellent example. The castle lies at the head of a long
narrow ridge which extends southwards to the upland area round Faleria.
In early Imperial times the ridge was farmed by at least five small estates,
but these gradually declined in the late Empire, so that by the fifth century
A.D. there was just one large villa, situated some 250 metres from the end
of the ridge. It is easy to imagine, therefore, that in the troubled period of
the sixth to seventh centuries the occupants of the villa decided to abandon
these unprotected buildings and move to the much safer position afforded
by the terminal spur of the Paterno promontory. If so, it was a process that
was probably duplicated all over the Ager Faliscus (and in adjoining areas),
since almost every medieval village lies close to the remains of a late Roman
villa or farm, in what appears to be a meaningful juxtaposition. To cite but
one other example, the defended village of Porciano represents the logical
retreat for the inhabitants of a large villa, occupied into the sixth century
A.D., at Casale L'Umiltà, which lies on exposed ground within sight of the
Via Amerina and only a few hundred metres from Porciano.

When then did this process of migration begin? Despite the lack of any
comparative excavation upon a contiguous villa and village, there do seem
to be several pointers. First, a detailed study of the surface collections made
on the sites of the late Roman villas failed to yield any evidence for
continuous occupation into the *domusculta* period of the eighth and ninth
centuries. Forum ware was identified on only two Roman sites, both of
them very low ranking and without any other pottery that post-dated the
end of the fourth century (Potter, 1975, 227). In contrast, Forum ware and
contemporary ceramic types turned out to be comparatively well represented
upon the medieval village sites (unlike the Ager Veientanus), implying that
the migration may well have begun by the eighth century and possibly
earlier. For example, at a secluded promontory site called Pizzo, two
kilometres to the south of Mazzano Romano, there were large quantities
of Forum ware, sparse glaze sherds and numerous pieces of buff pottery

decorated with combing; the assemblage should date to between the eighth and twelfth centuries and may begin rather earlier. Still visible on the site are rock-cut caves resembling those at Porciano, a rectangular tower, and a defensive wall in poor quality masonry of early medieval type. A short distance to the south, on a shelf of low ground by Monte Cinghiale, are the remains of a villa which, on surface evidence, was continuously occupied from Republican times down to the late fifth or early sixth century; it could well have been abandoned in favour of the better protected site of Pizzo.

In the Ager Faliscus, all the indications point, therefore, to a process of migration from the villas to the fortified positions typical of the medieval villages between the sixth and eighth centuries. In 1971, the opportunity arose to test this hypothesis by excavating a site with a comparatively full documentary record, the still-inhabited town of Mazzano Romano. Mazzano is a typical promontory settlement, where the nucleus of the village was established upon a low spur, jutting into the gorge of the River Treia. It is first referred to in a document of A.D. 945, when it was given by Prince Alberic to the monastery of St Gregory on the Coelian Hill in Rome; here it is described as a castle (*castellum*) with houses and buildings (*casis et edificiis*). The excavations (Potter, 1972) took place within of the town. Despite the very small size of the area that was examined, this investigation disclosed the remains of an older church, datable to before the thirteenth century, as well as of two earlier periods of building. Both the older structures were built of stone and their foundation trenches contained no material later than Forum ware. In fact there were no less than 21 sherds of Forum ware, a significantly high proportion which must imply that occupation began well before the date of the first documentary reference.

By piecing together the evidence from Mazzano, Porciano, Pizzo and other sites in the countryside to the north of the Monti Sabatini it is clear, therefore, that the medieval nucleated sites were certainly coming into existence by the eighth century and may very possibly have been settled even earlier, by the population of the late Roman villas shifting ground to more secure positions. In this respect the documentary records that refer to the eighth and ninth centuries are very interesting. Tomassetti (1913, 109–12) provides a list of the estates (*fundi*) which fell within the territory of the *domusculta* of Capracorum: it is clear from the evidence of the place-names that the total estate extended as far north as Nepi, and included within its area many of the medieval sites that we have been discussing. Thus Tomassetti lists amongst the properties of the *domusculta* the *fundi* of Campanius (= Campagnano di Roma), Calcata, Mazanus (possibly an erroneous inclusion), Stabia (= Faleria), Porcianus and Roncilianus, all of which can be identified with existing or deserted medieval settlements. It looks, then, as if these are the names of the late Roman villas and farms that are situated close to the fortified villages—names which were transferred with the migration to the promontory sites. Indeed it may well be that the northern estates of the *domusculta* of Capracorum were being farmed not from the Roman villas but from the incipient medieval villages.

One site is of particular interest in this context. It lies in the valley of the River Treia, some three kilometres to the south-west of Mazzano Romano, at the Mola di Monte Gelato. The 'Mola' comprises two mill-towers of post-medieval date, which served Mazzano until very recent times; but the valley itself has been a focus of occupation for a much longer period. There was a small Faliscan site on the bluff to the south side of the river, while in Republican times a large Roman villa was built on a shelf of flat ground near the bottom of the valley. The surface collections of pottery take occupation down to the fifth century A.D., and early medieval buildings are indicated both by a marble slab, decorated with interlace, and a spiral colonnette, the probable period of a chapel with associated burials *a cappuccina*, excavated in the nineteenth century and discussed by Tomassetti (1882, 147). Overlooking this villa and the whole valley is a medieval castle, Il Castellaccio, which is perched on a low hill to the south of the Mola. Although now densely buried in undergrowth, a rectangular tower, 4.9 × 5.9 metres, can still be seen, together with cave habitations and a rock-cut ditch that encircles three sides of the hill. It is presumably the successor to the villa complex in the valley bottom.

So far as we know, the Mola di Monte Gelato does not occur as a place-name in any of the older medieval documents, and it could well therefore be a candidate for one of the many unidentified settlements that are listed. But Tomassetti, in discussing the site, has developed the interesting and important theory that this may have been the *Castrum Capracorum* that in a papal bull of 1053 was granted to the chapter of St Peter's. In the bull, *Castrum Capracorum* is described as being 27 miles from Rome, and is quite clearly distinguished from the original Capracorum, by now the monastery of S. Cornelia, which was itself granted to the monastery of S. Stefano Maggiore. In later bulls, *Castrum Capracorum* is linked with a church of St John, which apparently lay on the River Treia and had gone out of use by 1128 (Partner, 1966, 75–6). It looks, then, as though the estate centre of the *domusculta* of Capracorum may have been moved north to the Mola di Monte Gelato in the late ninth or tenth centuries, and is to be identified with the castle of Il Castellaccio, while the chapel in the valley bottom is that of St John. If so, it confers a special historical importance upon this site, underlining the conclusion that the medieval settlements in this region gradually emerged out of the structure of late Roman settlement.

Nearer to Rome and in the areas of Lazio east and south of the Tiber the pattern was, on the other hand, quite different. Here, as Toubert (1973) and Wickham (1978) have shown, the medieval villages represent a sharp break with the pre-existing agrarian structure, where the Roman *fundus* and its associated land divisions were almost totally ignored. The tenth century saw the imposition of a quite novel system which had little to do with a move towards security; it was essentially an act of colonization which, while leading to the same end result—the occupation of fortified sites—was the product of completely different factors, an important reminder of the dangers of generalization.

Aftermath: from medieval to modern

The decline of the medieval landscape is vividly attested by an enormous number of abandoned villages and castles. Of a total of nearly 100 nucleated sites occupied during the Middle Ages, more than 60 now lie deserted and in ruins. Even with those that do survive, the civic focus has often shifted away from the old centre to areas which are altogether more accessible and provide room for expansion. Faleria is a good example (Pl. XIb). This is a village with a documentary record that extends back to at least 998. Its medieval nucleus, consisting of a medley of houses and small streets, lay at the tip of a long spur, which juts out into a steep-sided ravine. A massive castle built half-way along the spur guards the main approaches and effectively isolates the settlement from the open countryside beyond the valley. Now, however, the medieval buildings are empty and decayed, the castle mainly abandoned, and the centre of the town shifted on to the open plateau beyond the promontory. Before long, all the medieval part of Faleria will become completely derelict and overgrown and may well be demolished. A rather similar pattern can be traced at many other existing towns and villages. Rignano and Castelnuovo di Porto, where the drift has been towards the main trunk-road of the Via Flaminia, provide two good examples. Equally at Calcata (Pl. XV) a completely new urban centre is gradually being constructed on nearby plateau land while the old town (some of whose houses have collapsed into the valley in recent years) rapidly decays. Only where outside investment has paid for restoration of the old buildings, as at Mazzano Romano or Isola Farnese, has the process of desertion been stemmed—although how permanently is a matter of conjecture.

Whilst the abandonment of the old centres of existing towns is largely a phenomenon of the last dozen years or so, the decay of the more remote medieval settlements began much earlier—in some cases as far back as the thirteenth century. This is not the place to examine this process in detail, for much of the historical data still remain to be thoroughly sifted; but it is clear that the bulk of the now deserted sites were being steadily depopulated between c. 1350 and 1550. The precise factors that lay behind this decline have yet to be properly worked out, but one element that is attested archaeologically is the growth of new foci, often situated close to the main roads. At Monterosi, for example, the old hilltop citadel was abandoned in favour of a new site beside the Via Cassia, which seems to have been first

168

settled in the fifteenth century. It probably coincided with the opening of a more direct route to Viterbo, the Via Cimina, about 1450. At the same time, posting stations with an inn, stables and a chapel were also growing up—often close by their classical precursors. At Baccano, for example, the fifteenth-century road-station lies only a short distance to the south of Roman *ad Baccanas*, just as Osteria di Stabia (Pl. XVIb) was built almost on top of Roman Aquaviva. As in Classical times, the main roads were beginning to carry a much greater volume of traffic and slowly the facilities for travellers were developed.

Another analogy with the classical landscape can be found in the creation of a number of new farming estates, whose centres consisted of massively built houses, described as *casali*. A few of these *casali* developed out of the more accessible medieval villages: Torre Busson (Pl. XIVa), where the estate buildings date from the fifteenth century, is a good example. But many more were newly established in the open countryside and, even though they often incorporated towers and other defensive features in their design, they are nevertheless a clear indication of a changing strategy in the cultivation of the Campagna. Whilst we should not exaggerate the pace of this change, the *casali* of this period appear therefore to mark the beginning of a new phase in the landscape history of the area. By the eighteenth century when, to judge from building inscriptions, there was a great deal of renovation and building in the towns and villages, quite large parts of the Campagna must have been farmed from open sites. Some Roman nobles were constructing summer retreats, such as Cardinal Chigi's mansion, the Villa Versaglia near Formello, and many small farms were being built. The impression from the material remains is of a gradual expansion in the population of the countryside, followed by the drastic upsurge that has characterized the present century. Even so, there are many features of the medieval landscape that proved surprisingly durable. The road system, for example, an extraordinary network of rock-cut lanes and tracks that proliferated round almost every settlement, continued to form the basis of local communications until very recent years. Similarly many of the medieval bridges, like the magnificent example crossing the stream below Castel Sant'Elia (Pl. XVIa), continued in use with little or no modification. The material remains of the post-medieval period underline the impression gained from much of the archaeological evidence of older phases: that the pace of change in this region was almost always gradual and conservative.

Bibliography

AJA   American Journal of Archaeology
ASR   Archivio della Società Romana di Storia Patria
BAR   British Archaeological Reports
BPI   Bullettino di Paletnologia Italiana
CIE   Corpus Inscriptionum Etruscarum
CIL   Corpus Inscriptionum Latinarum
JRS   Journal of Roman Studies
MAAR   Memoirs of the American Academy at Rome
Med. Arch.   Medieval Archaeology
Not. Scav.   Notizie degli scavi di antichità
PBSR   Papers of the British School at Rome
PPS   Proceedings of the Prehistoric Society

Acanfora, M. O., 1962–3. Gli scavi di Valle Ottara presso Cittaducale. *BPI* **71–2**, 73–154.

Adamesteanu, D., 1973a. Le suddivisioni di terra nel Metapontino. *In* Finley, M. I., (Ed.), *Problèmes de la terre en Grèce ancienne*, Civilisations et Sociétés 33, 49–61. Paris.

Adamesteanu, D., 1973b. *Metaponto*. Naples.

Agache, R., 1970. *Détection aerienne de vestiges protohistoriques, gallo-romains et médiévaux dans le bassin de la Somme et ses abords*. Amiens.

Alvarez, W., 1972. The Treia valley north of Rome: volcanic stratigraphy, topographic evolution and geological influence on human settlement. *Geologica Romana* **11**, 153–76.

Alvarez, W., 1973. The ancient course of the Tiber river near Rome: an introduction to the middle Pleistocene volcanic stratigraphy of Central Italy. *Bulletin of the Geological Society of America* **84**, 749–58.

Andrèn, A., 1940. *Architectural terracottas from Etrusco-Italic temples*. Skrifter utgivna av Svenska Institutet i Rom 6.

Anon, 1954–5. Formello. *BPI* **9**, 324–5.

Ashby, T., 1907. The Classical topography of the Roman Campagna—III (The Via Latina). *PBSR* **4**, 1–160.

Ashby, T., 1927. *The Roman Campagna in Classical Times* (1970 reprint). Tonbridge.

Ashby, T., 1929. La rete stradale romana nell'Etruria meridionale. *Studi Etruschi* **3**, 171–85.

Ashby, T. and Fell. R. A. L., 1921. The Via Flaminia. *JRS* **11**, 125–90.

Autostrade, 1968. Villa romana di 'Lucus Feroniae' scoperta durante i lavori per la costruzione dell'Autostrada del Sole. *Autostrade* **10** (8), 1–62.

Ballance, M. H., 1951. The Roman bridges of the Via Flaminia. *PBSR* **19**, 78–117.

Barfield, L. H., 1971. *Northern Italy before Rome*. London.

Barker, G. W. W., 1972. The conditions of cultural and economic growth in the Bronze Age of Central Italy. *PPS* **38**, 170–208.

Barker, G. W. W., 1973. The economy of medieval Tuscania: the archaeological evidence. *PBSR* **41**, 155–77.

Barker, G. W. W., 1975. Prehistoric territories and economies in Central Italy. *In* Higgs, E. S., (Ed.), *Palaeoeconomy*, 111–75. Cambridge.

Barker, G. W. W., 1976a. Animal husbandry at Narce. *In* Potter, 1976a, 295–307.

Barker, G. W. W., 1976b. *The archaeology of early man in Molise, southern Italy*. Campobasso, Superintendency of Antiquities for Molise.

Barker, G. W. W., 1977. The archaeology of Samnite settlement in Molise. *Antiquity* **51**, 20–4.

Bartoccini, R., 1963. Il rifornimento idrico della colonia Julia Felix Lucus Feroniae. *Autostrade* **7–8**, 1–16.

Biancofiore, F., 1967. *Civiltà Micenea nell'Italia meridionale*. Incunabula Graeca 22, Rome.

Bietti Sestieri, A. M., 1973. The metal industry of continental Italy, thirteenth to the eleventh century B.C., and its connections with the Aegean. *PPS* **39**, 383–424.

Bizzari, M., 1966. *La Necropoli di Crocifisso del Tufo in Orvieto*. Museo 'Claudio Faina'. Florence.

Blake, H. M., 1978. Medieval pottery: technical innovation or economic change. *In* Blake, Potter and Whitehouse, (Eds.), 1978.

Blake, H. M., Potter, T. W., Whitehouse, D. B., (Eds.), 1978. Papers in Italian Archaeology I: the Lancaster Seminar. *BAR* Supplementary Series.

Blake, M. E., 1947. *Ancient Roman construction in Italy from the prehistoric period to Augustus*. Washington D.C.

Blanc, A. C., 1955. Giacimento del paleolitico superiore ad *Equus hydruntinus* e sovrapposti livelli con ceramica neolitica e dell'età del bronzo, nella cava di travertino di Palidoro (Roma). *Quarternaria* **2**, 308–9.

Blanc, A. C., 1958. Torre in Pietra, Saccopastore e Monte Circeo. La cronologia dei giacimenti e la paleogeografia quarternaria del Lazio. *Boll. Soc. Geol. Ital.* **8** (4–5), 196–214.

Blanckenhagen, P. von, Cotton, M. A., and Ward Perkins, J. B., 1965. Two Roman villas at Francolise, prov. Caserta. *PBSR* **33**, 55–69.

Boak, A. E. R., 1955. *Manpower shortage and the fall of the Roman Empire in the west*. Jerome lectures, Ann Arbor.

Boëthius, A. *et al.*, 1962. *Etruscan Culture, Land and People*. Malmö and New York.

Boëthius, A. and Ward Perkins, J. B., 1970. *Etruscan and Roman Architecture*. Penguin History of Architecture. Harmondsworth.

Bonatti, E., 1963. Stratigrafia pollinica dei sedimenti post-glaciale di Baccano, lago craterico del Lazio. *Atti della Soc. Toscana di Scienze naturali* **40**, 40–8.

Bonatti, E., 1970. Pollen sequence in the lake sediments. *In* Hutchinson, G. E., (Ed.), *Ianula—an account of the history and development of the Lago di Monterosi, Latium, Italy*. Transactions of the American Philosophical Society **40** (4), 26–31.

Boni, G., 1903. Roma—Foro Romano—Sepolcreto del septimontium preromuleo. *Not. Scav.*, 75–427.

Bono, del G. L., 1971. Tolfa-Allumiere: miniere antiche e moderne. *Geo-Archaeologia* 1, 18–26.

Bradford, J. S. P., 1947. Etruria from the air. *Antiquity* 21, 74–83.

Bradford, J. S. P., 1957. *Ancient Landscapes*. London.

Bronson, R. and Uggeri, G., 1970. Isola del Giglio, isola di Giannutri, Monte Argentario, Laguna di Orbetello. *Studi Etruschi* 37, 210–14.

Brunt, P. A., 1971. *Italian Manpower, 225 B.C.–A.D. 14*. Oxford.

Brusadin Laplace, D., 1964. Le necropoli protostoriche del Sasso di Furbara. I—La necropoli ai Puntoni. *BPI* 73, 143–86.

Bullough, D. A., 1965. La Via Flaminia nella storia dell'Umbria (600–1100). *In Aspetti dell'Umbria dall'inizio del secolo VIII alla fine del secolo XI. Atti del terzo Convegno di Studi Umbri*. Perugia.

Bullough, D. A., 1968. *Italy and her Invaders*. Nottingham.

Butzer, K. W., 1974. Accelerated soil erosion: a problem of man-land relationships. *In* Manners, I. R. and Mikesell, M. W., (Eds), *Perspectives on Environment*, 57–77. Washington D.C.

Carrington, R. C., 1931. Studies in the Campanian villae rusticae. *JRS* 21, 110–30.

Castagnoli, F., 1974. La 'carta archeologica d'Italia' e gli studi di topografia antica. *In Ricognizione archeologica e documentazione cartografica. Quaderni dell'Istituto di topografia antica della Università di Roma* 6, 7–17.

Celle, A., 1933. *A History of Malaria in the Roman Campagna*. London.

Cherkauer, D., 1976. The stratigraphy and chronology of the River Treia alluvial deposits. *In* Potter, 1976a, 106–20.

Chiaro, del M. A., 1957. *The Genucilia Group: a class of Etruscan Red Figured plates*. University of California Publications in Classical Archaeology 3. Berkeley.

Chisholm, M., 1968. *Rural Settlement and Land Use*. London.

Close-Brooks, J., 1965. Proposta per una suddivisione in fasi. *Not. Scav.*, 53–64.

Close-Brooks, J., 1968. Considerazioni sulla cronologia delle facies arcaiche dell'Etruria. *Studi Etruschi* 35, 323–9.

Close-Brooks, J. and Gibson, S., 1966. A round hut near Rome. *PPS* 32, 349–52.

Colini, G. A., 1919. Veii—Scavi nell'area della città e delle necropoli. *Not. Scav.*, 3–12.

Collins, D., 1978. The Palaeolithic of Italy in its European context. *In* Blake, Potter and Whitehouse, (Eds.), 1978.

Colonna, G., 1974. Preistoria e protostoria di Roma e del Lazio. *In Popoli e civiltà dell'Italia antica* 2, 275–346.

Craven, K., 1838. *Excursions in the Abruzzi*, Vol. 1. London.

Crawford, O. G. S., 1924. *Air Survey and Archaeology*. Ordinance Survey Professional Papers 7. Southampton.

D'Agostino, B., 1974. La civiltà del ferro dell'Italia meridionale e nella Sicilia. *In Popoli e civiltà dell'Italia antica* 2, 11–91.

Davidson, D., 1976 (with Renfrew, C. and Tasker, C.). Erosion and prehistory in Melos: a preliminary note. *Journal of Archaeological Science* 3, 219–27.

Delano-Smith, C., 1978. Coastal sedimentation, lagoons and ports. *In* Blake, Potter and Whitehouse, (Eds.), 1978.

Dennis, G., 1848. *Cities and Cemeteries of Etruria*. London.

Drago, C., 1953. Lo scavo di Torre Castelluccia (Pulsano). *BPI* **8** (5), 155–61.

Duchesne, L. (Ed.), 1886. *Liber Pontificalis*, Vol. 1. Paris and Rome.

Duncan, G. C., 1958. Sutri (Sutrium). *PBSR* **26**, 63–134.

Duncan, G. C., 1964. A Roman pottery near Sutri. *PBSR* **32**, 38–88.

Duncan, G. C., 1965. Roman Republican pottery from the vicinity of Sutri. *PBSR* **33**, 134–76.

Dyson, S. L., 1979. Rilevamento topografico-archeologico nell'agro Cosano (prov. di Grosseto) da Wesleyan University e l'Accademia American, 1974–6. *Not. Scav.*, forthcoming.

Fenelli, M., La Regina, A., Mazzolani, M., Torelli, M., 1975. *Lavinium*, Vol. 2. Instituto di topografia antica dell'Università di Roma.

Fox, Sir Cyril, 1923. *The Archaeology of the Cambridge Region*. Cambridge.

Fox, Sir Cyril, 1932. *The Personality of Britain*. Cardiff.

Fraccaro, P., 1919. Di alcuni antichissimi lavori idraulici di Roma e della Campagna. *Boll. della Reale Società Geografica Italiana* **3–4**, 186–215.

Frank, A. H. E., 1969. Pollen stratigraphy of the Lake of Vico (Central Italy). *Palaeogeography, Palaeoclimatology, Palaeoecology* **6** (1), 67–85.

Frank, T., 1924. *Roman buildings of the Republic*. Papers and Monographs of the American Academy in Rome, 3.

Frederiksen, M. W., and Ward Perkins, J. B., 1957. The ancient road systems of the central and northern Ager Faliscus. *PBSR* **25**, 67–208.

Gell, Sir William, 1834–46. *The Topography of Rome and its vicinity*. London.

Giacomelli, G., 1963. *La Lingua Falisca*. Florence.

Gierow, P. G., 1966. *The Iron Age cultures of Latium*. Skrifter utgivna av Svenska Institutet i Rom 24, part 1.

Giglioli, G. Q., 1924. Vignanello—Nuovi scavi nella città e nella necropoli. *Not. Scav.*, 179–263.

Gjerstad, E., 1966. *Early Rome IV*. Skrifter utgivna av Svenska Institutet i Rom 17, part 4.

Guiliani, C. F. and Quilici, L., 1964. *La Via Caere-Pyrgi*. Quaderni dell'Istituto di topografia antica dell'Università di Roma, 1.

Guzzo, P. G., 1970. Sacrofano—ponte romana in località Fontana Nuova. *Not. Scav.*, 330–44.

Hanell, K., 1962. The acropolis [of San Giovenale]. *In* Boëthius *et al.*, 1962, 289–312.

Harris, W. V., 1965. The Via Cassia and the Via Triana Nova between Bolsena and Chiusi. *PBSR* **33**, 113–33.

Harris, W. V., 1971. *Rome in Etruria and Umbria*. Oxford.

Hayes, J. W., 1972. *Late Roman Pottery*. British School at Rome. London.

Hellstrom, P., 1975. *Luni sul Mignone. The zone of the large Iron Age building*. Skrifter utgivna av Svenska Institutet i Rom, 4th series, **27** (2), 2.

Hemphill, P., 1975. The Cassia-Clodia survey. *PBSR* **43**, 118–72.

Hencken, H., 1968. *Tarquinia, Villanovans and early Etruscans*. American School of Prehistoric Research, Peabody Museum, Harvard, 23.

Hessen, von O., 1966. *Die Langobardenzeitlichen Grabfunde aus Fiesole bei Florenz*. Munich.

Hessen, von O., 1968. *Die Langobardische Keramik aus Italien*. Deutches Archäologisches Institut Rom. Wiesbaden.

Heurgon, J., 1964. *Daily Life of the Etruscans*. London.

Heurgon, J., 1973. *The Rise of Rome to 264 B.C.* London.

Hutchinson, E., (Ed.), 1970. *Ianula: an account of the history and development of the Lago di Monterosi, Latium, Italy.* Transactions of the American Philosophical Society **40** (4).

Incardona, A., 1969. Le nuove ricerche nelle cavernette e nei ripari dell'Agro Falisco. *Atti della Soc. Toscana di Scienze naturali* **76** (1), 101–28.

Jarman, H. N., 1976. The plant remains. *In* Potter, 1976a, 308–10.

Jones, A. H. M., 1964. *The Later Roman Empire.* Oxford.

Jones, G. D. B., 1960. Veii: the Valchetta Baths. *PBSR* **26**, 63–134.

Jones, G. D. B., 1962. Capena and the Ager Capenas, Part I. *PBSR* **30**, 116–207.

Jones, G. D. B., 1963. Capena and the Ager Capenas, Part II. *PBSR* **31**, 100–58.

Jones, P. J., 1966a. Italy. *In* Postan, M. M., (Ed.), *The Cambridge Economic History of Europe*, Vol. 1, 340–431. Cambridge.

Jones, P. J., 1966b. L'Italia agraria nell'alto medioevo. *Settimane di studio del Centro Italiano di studi sull'alto medioevo, Spoleto* **13**, 57–92, 236–41.

Jones, P., 1974. La storia economica: dalle caduta dell'Impero romano al secolo XIV. *Storia d'Italia* Vol. 2, part 2. Turin.

Judson, S., 1963a. Erosion and deposition of Italian stream valleys during historic time. *Science* **140** (3569), 898–9.

Judson, S., 1963b. Stream change during historic time in east-central Sicily. *AJA* **67**, 287–9.

Judson, S. and Kahane, A., 1963. Underground drainageways in southern Etruria and northern Latium. *PBSR* **31**, 74–99.

Lamb, H. H., 1966. *The Changing Climate.* London.

Lamboglia, N., 1950. Per una classificazione preliminare della ceramica campana. *Atti del I Congresso internazionale di studi Liguri*, 139–206. Bordighera.

Lanciani, R., 1909. *Wanderings in the Roman Campagna.* Boston.

Lawrence, A. W., 1964. Early medieval fortifications near Rome. *PBSR* **32**, 89–122.

Llewellyn, P., 1971. *Rome in the Dark Ages.* London.

Lo Porto, F. G., 1963. Leporano (Taranto)—La stazione protostorica di Porta Perone. *Not. Scav.*, 280–380.

Lugli, G., 1962. *Carta archeologica del territorio di Roma.* Florence.

Luttrell, A. T., 1974. La Campagna a nord di Roma: archeologia e storia medievale. *Colloquio Internazionale di Archeologia Medievale: Palermo 1974.*

Mallett, M. and Whitehouse, D. B., 1967. Castel Porciano: an abandoned medieval village of the Roman Campagna. *PBSR* **35**, 113–46.

Martinori, E., 1929. *Via Flaminia.* Rome.

Martinori, E., 1930. *Via Cassia.* Rome.

Mattias, P. and Ventriglia, U., 1970. La regione vulcanica dei Monti Sabatini e Cimini. *Memorie della Soc. Geologica Italiana* **9**, 331–84.

Mazzucato, O., 1968a. *La raccolta di ceramiche del Museo di Roma.* Rome.

Mazzucato, O., 1968b. Ceramica medioevale romana: la produzione attorno al mille. *Palatino* 4th series, **12**, 147–55.

Mazzucato, O., 1972. *La ceramica a vetrina pesante.* Rome.

Meiggs, R., 1973. *Roman Ostia.* 2nd edition. Oxford.

Morel, J.-P., 1965. *Céramique à vernis noir du Forum Romain et du Palatin.* Mélanges d'archéologie et d'histoire de l'Ecole française de Rome, Supplément 3.

Moretti, A. M. S. and Battaglia, G. B., 1975. Materiali archeologici scoperti a Lucus Feroniae. *In* Moretti, M., (Ed.), *Nuove scoperte e acquisizioni nell'Etruria meridionale*, 93–175. Rome.

Müller-Karpe, H., 1959. *Beiträge zur Chronologie der Urnenfelderzeit nördlich und südlich der Alpen.* Römische Germanische Forschungen 22.

Murray-Threipland, L., 1963. Excavations by the North-West Gate of Veii, 1957–8: Part II. The Pottery. *PBSR* **31**, 33–73.

Murray-Threipland, L. and Torelli, M., 1970. A semi-subterranean Etruscan building in the Casale Pian Roseto (Veii) area. *PBSR* **38**, 62–121.

Nibby, A., 1837. *Analisi storico-topografico-antiquaria della Carta del dintorni di Roma.* Rome.

Nissen, H., 1883–1902. *Italische Landeskunde.*

Ogilvie, R. M., 1965. Eretum. *PBSR* **33**, 70–112.

Ostenberg, C.-E., 1962. Villa Sambuco. *In* Boëthius *et al.*, 1962, 313–20.

Ostenberg, C.-E., 1967. *Luni sul Mignone e problemi della preistoria d'Italia.* Skrifter utgivna av Svenska Institutet i Rome 4, 25.

Ostenberg, C.-E., 1975. *Case Etrusche di Acquarossa.* Comitato per le attività archeologiche nella tuscia. Rome.

Pallottino, M., 1937a. Tarquinia. *Monumenti Antichi* **36**, part 1.

Pallottino, M., 1937b. Capena—resti di costruzioni romane e medioevali in località 'Montecanino'. *Not. Scav.*, 7–28.

Pallottino, M., 1939. Sulle facies arcaiche dell'Etruria. *Studi Etruschi* **13**, 85–128.

Pareti, L., 1947. *La tomba Regolini-Galassi del Museo Gregoriano Etrusco e la civiltà nell'Italia centrale nel sec. VII a.c.* Rome.

Paribeni, R., 1906. Necropoli del territorio Capenate. *Monumenti Antichi* **16**, 277–490.

Partner, P., 1966. Notes on the lands of the Roman church in the early Middle Ages. *PBSR* **34**, 68–78.

Pasqui, A., 1903a. Civita Castellana—nuove scoperte di antichità dentro l'abitato. *Not. Scav.*, 453–9.

Pasqui, A., 1903b. Fabbrica di Roma—nuove scoperte dentro alla città di S. Maria di Falleri e attorno alla sua necropoli. *Not. Scav.*, 14–19.

Pasqui, A. and Cozza, A., 1894 (with Barnabei, F. and Gamurrini, G. F.). Antichità del territorio Falisco esposte nel Museo Nazionale Romano a Valle Guilia. *Monumenti Antichi* **4**.

Peroni, R., 1959. Per una definizione dell'aspetto culturale 'subappenninico' come fare cronologica a sè stante. *Atti della Accademia Nazionale dei Lincei, Memorie*, Ser. 8 (9), 3–253.

Peroni, R., 1960. Allumiere—Scavo di tombe in località 'La Pozza'. *Not. Scav.*, 341–62.

Peroni, R., 1962–3. La Romita di Asciano (Pisa)—riparo sotta roccia utilizzato dall' età neolitica alla barbarica. *BPI* **71–2**, 251–372.

Peroni, R., 1965. Significato degli scavi nel deposito a ceramiche di Palidoro. *Quaternaria* **7**, 309–11.

Phillips, C. W., 1970. *The Fenland in Roman Times.* Royal Geographical Society Research Memoir, 5. London.

Piggott, S., 1965. *Ancient Europe.* Edinburgh.

Potter, T. W., 1972. Excavations in the medieval centre of Mazzano Romano. *PBSR* **40**, 135–45.

Potter, T. W., 1975. Ricenti ricerche in Etruria meridionale: problemi della transizione dal tardo antico all'alto medievo. *Archeologia Medievale* **2**, 215–36.

Potter, T. W., 1976a. *A Faliscan town in South Etruria. Excavations at Narce 1966–71*. British School at Rome. London.

Potter, T. W., 1976b. Valleys and settlement: some new evidence. *World Archaeology* **8** (2), 207–19.

Potter, T. W., 1978. Population hiatus and continuity: the case of the South Etruria survey. *In* Blake, Potter and Whitehouse, (Eds.), 1978, 99–116.

Potter, T. W., 1979. Una stipe votiva repubblicana da Ponte di Nona vicino Roma. *Not. Scav.*, forthcoming.

Potter, T. W. and Gianfrotta, P., 1979. Scavi a Tuscania. *Archeologia Medievale*, forthcoming.

Pringle, D., 1974. A group of medieval towers in Tuscania. *PBSR* **42**, 179–223.

Puglisi, S. M., 1951. Gli abitatori primitivi del Palatino attraverso le testimonianze archeologiche e le nuove stratigrafiche sul Germalo. *Monumenti Antichi* **41**, 1–101.

Puglisi, S. M., 1959. *La civiltà appenninica. Origine delle comunità pastorali in Italia*. Florence.

QF 1963—various authors. Veio—scavi in una necropoli villanoviana in località 'Quattro Fontanili'. *Not. Scav.*, 77–279.

QF 1965. *Idem. Not. Scav.*, 49–236.

QF 1967. *Idem. Not. Scav.*, 87–286.

QF 1970. *Idem. Not. Scav.*, 178–329.

QF 1972. *Idem. Not. Scav.*, 195–384.

QF 1975. *Idem. Not. Scav.*, 63–184.

Quilici, L., 1974. *Forma Italiae, Regio I, Vol. X, Collatia*. Rome.

Quilici, S. Gigli, 1970. *Tuscania. Forma Italiae*. Rome.

Radmilli, A. M., 1963. *La preistoria d'Italia alla luce dell' ultime scoperte*. Istituto Geografico Militare, Florence.

Radmilli, A. M., 1954 (with Patrizi, S. and Mangili, G.). Sepoltura ad inumazione con cranio trapanato nelle Grotta Patrizi, Sasso Furbara. *Rivista di Antropologia* **31**, 33ff.

Ramage, N. H., 1970. Studies in early Etruscan bucchero. *PBSR* **38**, 1–61.

Raspi Serra J., 1971. *Tuscania: cultura ed espressione di un centro medioevale*. Milan.

Rellini, U., 1920. Cavernette e ripari preistorici nell'Agro Falisco. *Monumenti Antichi* **26**, 5–174.

Renfrew, C. and Whitehouse, R., 1974. The Copper Age of Peninsular Italy and the Aegean. *Annual of the British School at Athens* **69**, 343–90.

Ridgway, D., 1968. Coppe Cicladiche da Veio. *Studi Etruschi* **35**, 311–21.

Ridgway, D., 1973. The First Western Greeks: Campanian coasts and southern Etruria. *In* Hawkes, C. F. C. and Hawkes, S. (Eds.), *Greeks, Celts and Romans*. London.

Ridgway, D., 1978. Composition and provenance of western Greek pottery: a prospectus. *In* Blake, Potter and Whitehouse, (Eds.), 1978.

Schmiedt, G., 1970. *Atlante aerofotografico delle sedi umani in Italia*. Florence.

Silvestrelli, G., 1970. *Città, castelli e terre della regione romana*. 3rd edition. Rome.

Small, A. M. (Ed.), 1977. *Monte Irsi, Southern Italy. BAR* Supplementary Series 20.

Solari, A., 1915–20. *Topografia storica dell'Etruria*. Pisa.

Stefani, E., 1913. Trevignano Romano—antichi sepolchri scoperte in 'Via della Macchia'. *Not. Scav.*, 37–43.

Stefani, E., 1922. Veio—esplorazioni dentro l'area dell'antica città. *Not. Scav.*, 379–404.

Stefani, E., 1944. Scavi archeologici a Veio, in Contrada Piazza d'Armi. *Monumenti Antichi* **40**, 178–293.

Stefani, E., 1953. Veio—Tempio detto dell'Apollo. Esplorazione e sistemazione del santuario. *Not. Scav.*, 29–112.

Stefani, E., 1958. Capena—Ricerche archeologiche nella contrada 'Le Saliere'. *Monumenti Antichi* **44**, 1–203.

Stiesdal, H., 1962. Three deserted medieval villages in the Roman Campagna. *Analecta Romana Instituti Danici* **2**, 63–100.

Sturdy, D. A., 1972. The exploitation pattern of a modern reindeer economy in west Greenland. *In* Higgs, E. S., (Ed.), *Papers in Economic Prehistory*, 161–5. Cambridge.

Taylor, D. M., 1957. Cosa: Black-glaze pottery. *MAAR* **25**, 65–193.

Taylour, Lord William, 1958. *Mycenaean pottery in Italy*. Cambridge.

Tomassetti, G., 1882. Della Campagna Romana nel medio evo. *ASR* **5**, 67–156.

Tomassetti, G., 1897. Del sale e focatico del comune di Roma nel medio evo. *ASR* **20**, 313–68.

Tomassetti, G., 1910. *La Campagna Romana, antica, medioevale e moderna*, Vol. 2, Rome.

Tomassetti, G., 1913. *La Campagna Romana, antica, medioevale e moderna*, Vol. 3. Rome.

Torelli, M., 1961. Rivista di epigrafia etrusca: Veii (loc. Casale Pian Roseto). *Studi Etruschi* **37**, 323–30.

Torelli, M., 1971. Gravisca (Tarquinia). Scavi nella città etrusca e romana. Campagne 1969 e 1970. *Not. Scav.*, 195–299.

Torelli, M., 1976. *In* Potter, 1976a, 263–7.

Torelli, M. and Pohl, I., 1973. Veio—scoperta di un piccolo santuario etrusco in località Campetti. *Not. Scav.*, 40–258.

Toubert, P., 1973. *Les Structures du Latium médiéval: le Latium méridional et la Sabine du IX siècle à la fin du XII siècle*. Bibliothèque des Ecoles françaises d'Athènes et de Rome, 221.

Trump, D. H., 1958. The Apennine culture of Italy. *PPS* **24**, 165–200.

Trump, D. H., 1966. *Central and Southern Italy before Rome*. London.

Vallet, G., 1962. L'introduction de l'olivier en Italie centrale. *In* Renard, M., (Ed.), *Hommages à Albert Grenier*. Collection Latomus 58, 1554–63.

Vianello Córdova, A. P., 1968. Una tomba 'protovillanoviana' a Veio. *Studi Etruschi* **35**, 295–306.

Vighi, R. 1935. Veii—Scavi nella necropoli. *Not. Scav.*, 39–68.

Vita-Finzi, C., 1969. *The Mediterranean Valleys*. Cambridge.

Volpaia, della Eufrosino, 1547. *Mappa della Campagna Romana. Riprodotto dall'unico esemplare esistente nella Biblioteca Vaticana, con introduzione di Thomas Ashby*. Rome, 1914.

Vonwiller, F. R., 1967. Una zona di grande concentrazione protostorica, la vallata del Fiora. *Atti del I simposio internazionale di protostoria italiana*, 67–74. Orvieto.

Vonwiller, F. R., 1975. La cultura Protovillanoviana. *In Popoli e civiltà dell'Italia antica* **4**, 11-60.

Ward-Perkins, Bryan, 1978. Luni: the decline and abandonment of a Roman town. *In* Blake, Potter and Whitehouse, (Eds), 1978.

Ward Perkins, J. B., 1955. Notes on southern Etruria and the Ager Veientanus. *PBSR* **23**, 44-72.

Ward Perkins, J. B., 1957. Etruscan and Roman roads in southern Etruria. *JRS* **47**, 139-43.

Ward Perkins, J. B., 1959a. Excavations beside the North-West Gate of Veii, 1957-8. *PBSR* **27**, 38-79.

Ward Perkins, J. B., 1959b. The problems of Etruscan origins. *Harvard Studies in Classical Philology* **64**, 1-26.

Ward Perkins, J. B., 1961. Veii. The historical topography of the ancient city. *PBSR* **29**, 1-123.

Ward Perkins, J. B., 1962a. Etruscan towns, Roman roads and medieval villages: the historical geography of southern Etruria. *Geog. Journal* **128**, 389-405.

Ward Perkins, J. B., 1962b. Etruscan engineering: road-building, water-supply and drainage. *In* Renard, M., (Ed.), *Hommages à Albert Grenier.* Collection Latomus **58**, 1636-43.

Ward Perkins, J. B., 1964. *Landscape and History in Central Italy.* Second J. L. Myres Memorial Lecture, Oxford.

Ward Perkins, J. B., 1968 (with Kahane, A. and Murray-Threipland, L.). The Ager Veientanus north and east of Veii. *PBSR* **36**, 1-218.

Ward Perkins, J. B., 1970a. Monterosi in the Etruscan and Roman periods. *In* Hutchinson (Ed.), 1970, 10-12.

Ward Perkins, J. B., 1970b. Città e Pagus. Considerazione sull'organizzazione primitiva della città nell'Italia centrale. *Atti del Convegno di Studi sulla città Etrusca e Italica preromana*, 293-7. Bologna.

Ward Perkins, J. B., 1972. Central authority and patterns of rural settlement. *In* Ucko, P. J., Tringham, R. and Dimbleby, G. W., (Eds.), *Man, Settlement and Urbanism*, 867-82. London.

Ward Perkins, J. B., 1974. *Cities of Ancient Greece and Italy: planning in classical antiquity.* New York.

Ward Perkins, J. B. and Kahane, A., 1972. The Via Gabina. *PBSR* **40**, 91-126.

Ward Perkins, J. B. *et al.*, 1972. Excavation and survey at Tuscania, 1972: a preliminary report. *PBSR* **40**, 196-238.

Ward Perkins, J. B. *et al.*, 1973. Excavations at Tuscania 1973: report on the finds from six selected pits. *PBSR* **41**, 45-154.

Wetter, E., 1962. Studies and Strolls in Southern Etruria. *In* Boëthius *et al.*, 1962.

White, R. D., 1970. *Roman Farming.* London.

Whitehouse, D. B., 1965. Forum Ware: a distinctive type of early medieval glazed pottery from the Roman Campagna. *Med. Arch.* **9**, 55-63.

Whitehouse, D. B., 1967. Medieval glazed ware of Lazio. *PBSR* **34**, 40-86.

Whitehouse, D. B., 1969. In Hurst, J. G. (Ed.) Red painted and glazed pottery in Western Europe from the eighth to the twelfth century. *Med. Arch.* **13**, 137-42.

Whitehouse, D. B., 1973. Sedi medievali nella Campagna romana: la *Domusculta* e il villaggio fortificato. *Archeologia e geografia del popolamento, Quaderni Storici* **24**, 861-76.

Whitehouse, R., 1973. The earliest towns in peninsular Italy. *In* Renfrew, C., (Ed.), *Explanations of Cultural Change*, 617–24. London.

Whitehouse, R., 1978. Italian prehistory, carbon 14 and tree-ring calibration. *In* Blake, Potter and Whitehouse, (Eds.), 1978.

Wickham, C., 1978. Historical aspects of medieval south Etruria. *In* Blake, Potter and Whitehouse, (Eds.), 1978.

Wieselgren, T., 1969. *Luni sul Mignone. The Iron Age settlement on the acropolis.* Skrifter utgivna av Svenska Institutet i Rom, 4th series, 27 (2, part 1).

Wiseman, T. P., 1970. Roman Republican road-building. *PBSR* **38**, 122–52.

Zucchetti, G., 1920. *Chronicon di Benedetto, Monaco di Andrea del Soratte*. Rome.

Index